Student Interactive

myView
LITERACY
2

SAVVAS
LEARNING COMPANY

UNIT 4

CONTENTS

Making a Difference

Our Incredible Earth

9

Our Traditions

Essential Question

What makes a tradition?

▶ **Watch**

"Our Traditions" to learn about foods and stories from different family traditions.

TURN and TALK What do you notice about these traditions?

SAVVAS
realize™
Go ONLINE for
all lessons.

▶ VIDEO

🔊 AUDIO

🎮 GAME

✏ ANNOTATE

📖 BOOK

🔍 RESEARCH

Spotlight on Traditional Tales

Reading Workshop

Reading-Writing Bridge

- Academic Vocabulary
- Read Like a Writer, Write for a Reader
- Spelling • Language and Conventions

Writing Workshop

Poetry

- Introduce and Immerse
- Develop Elements • Develop Structure
- Writer's Craft • Publish, Celebrate, and Assess

Project-Based Inquiry

- Inquire • Research • Collaborate

Independent Reading

Follow these steps to help you figure out a word you don't know as you read independently.

1. Sound out the word using what you know about letters and their sounds.

2. See if there is a base word that you know with an ending added to it.

3. Look at the words and sentences around the word for clues to its meaning. For example, see how clues in this sentence help you understand the word **moral**:

   The **moral**, or lesson, of the story is "Be kind to others."

4. When you think you know the word, reread the sentence with its meaning in mind. Does it make sense?

My Reading Log

Date	Book	Pages Read	Minutes Read	My Ratings
				😊 😐 😣
				😊 😐 😣
				😊 😐 😣
				😊 😐 😣
				😊 😐 😣

Unit Goals

In this unit, you will

- read traditional tales

- write a poem

- learn about traditions

 **MY TURN** **Color** the pictures to answer.

I know about different types of traditional tales and understand their elements.	👍	👎
I can use language to make connections between reading and writing.	👍	👎
I can use figurative language and sound devices to write poetry.	👍	👎
I can talk with others about what traditions are.	👍	👎

Academic Vocabulary

| communication | culture | purpose | belief | maintain |

In this unit, you will read traditional stories from different cultures. You'll learn how a **culture** is created by people who share a common **purpose** and a **belief** system. People from the same culture often use the same language for **communication**. They may also enjoy traditional foods and wear traditional clothing and listen to traditional music. Why is it important to **maintain** traditions like these?

TURN and TALK Use the Academic Vocabulary words to talk with your partner about traditions. The picture will help you.

Traditional Tales

People have told stories for a very long time. These traditional tales were told to children, who told them to their children, who told them to their children, and so on.

A **fable** is a short story with a moral, or lesson. It usually has animal characters. In "The Tortoise and the Hare," a speedy hare loses a race to a slow turtle.

Folktales and **fairy tales** usually have good characters and bad characters. Often at the end, the good characters live "happily ever after." In "Sleeping Beauty," a princess is woken from a spell by the kiss of a handsome prince.

A **legend** is an old story about a hero or an important event. Often the story is based on a real person or event. For example, Robin Hood really existed, but people created the story that he robbed from the rich to give to the poor.

Weekly Question

What lessons can we learn from traditional tales?

TURN and TALK

Talk about the stories described here. Tell what you already know about these children's stories. What lesson can you learn from one of the traditional tales described on these pages?

Long i: i, ie, i_e, igh, y

Long **i** can be spelled **i**, **ie**, **i_e**, **igh**, and **y**. Decode, or read, each word below and listen for the long **i** vowel sound.

Long i spelled i:	w<u>i</u>ld	k<u>i</u>nd	sp<u>i</u>der
Long i spelled ie:	l<u>ie</u>	d<u>ie</u>	tr<u>ie</u>s
Long i spelled i_e:	l<u>i</u>f<u>e</u>	wh<u>i</u>t<u>e</u>	dr<u>i</u>v<u>e</u>
Long i spelled igh:	f<u>igh</u>t	ton<u>igh</u>t	br<u>igh</u>t
Long i spelled y:	tr<u>y</u>	wh<u>y</u>	b<u>y</u>

TURN *and* **TALK** Read these sentences with a partner. Find the words with long **i**. Discuss the spellings for long **i**.

1. Why did the pilot fly so high across the night sky?
2. A spider tried to drop out of the light to sit beside Mike.

Both **ie** and **y** can spell long **i** or long **e**.

Long i: i, ie, i_e, igh, y

MY TURN <u>Underline</u> the word that names the picture. Then read and write the word.

ever	back	light
open	bake	late
iron	bike	lot

fleas	dim	cry
flies	dime	crow
flows	dome	crawl

MY TURN Write a sentence that contains two of the words you wrote above.

My Words to Know

Some words are used often in texts. These words are called high-frequency words. You will have to remember these words. Often, you can't sound them out.

MY TURN Read the high-frequency words in the box. Write the correct words on the lines. Form the letters correctly as you write each word. Use connecting strokes to connect the letters.

eyes	earth	thought

1. The _____ here is soft and brown.

2. I have green _____ .

3. I _____ about the answer to your question.

TURN and TALK

Work with a partner. Use the clues to identify the words.

They help you see.

You stand on it.

It's what your brain did yesterday.

Rabbit's Kite

Rabbit's kite was stuck in a tree. Cat walked by. "Can I help, Rabbit?"

"I was flying my kite, and it got stuck," cried Rabbit.

"It's very high up," Cat thought. "But I think I can get it."

Cat went up the tree. He pulled the kite off the branch. The kite fell back to earth.

"Thank you!" said Rabbit. "The next time **you** need help, I will be there to help **you**!"

1. How does Cat help Rabbit?

_____

_____

2. What does Rabbit say he will do? _____

_____

3. Find and write three or more words that have the long **i** sound spelled **i, i_e, ie, igh,** or **y.**

_____

_____

My Learning Goal

I can read fables and identify their themes.

Spotlight on Genre

Traditional Tales: Fables

Traditional tales have been told over and over for years. A **fable** is a traditional tale. It is short, often has animal characters, and ends with a **moral,** or lesson. The moral is the theme.

Sour Grapes

Fox spotted some grapes hanging over a branch. He jumped again and again but could not reach them. Then he said, "Those grapes are probably sour anyway."

Moral: It is easy to say you don't want something when you cannot have it.

TURN and TALK Tell what happens in a fable you know. What is its moral? What makes it a fable?

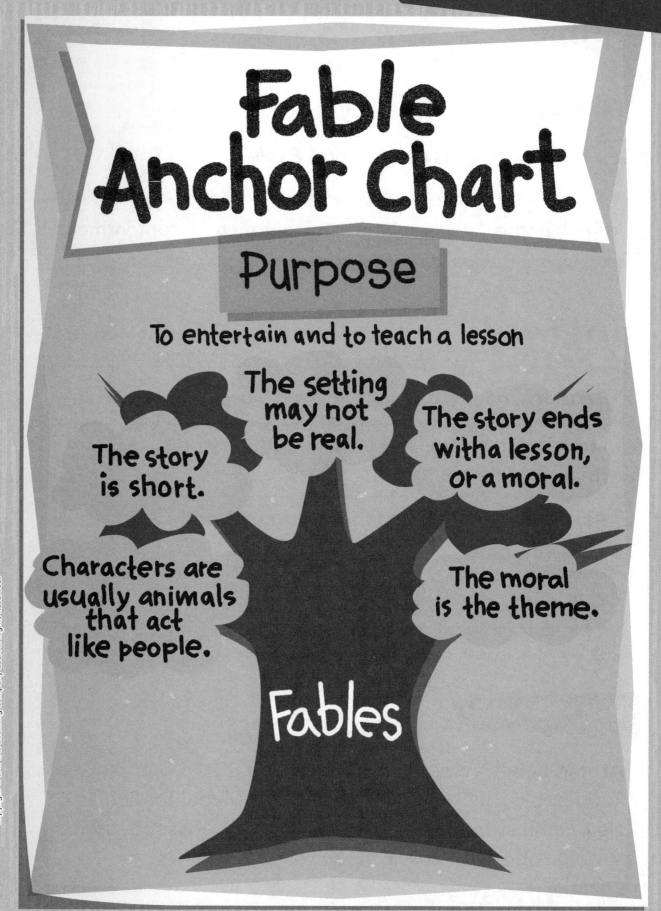

Fables

Preview Vocabulary

Look for these words as you read *Fables*.

| rage | hopes | disappointments | alarmed | contentment |

First Read

Read to understand each fable.

Look at illustrations to help you understand the fables.

Ask such questions as **what** or **why** about confusing parts.

Talk about the fables with a partner.

Meet *the* Author

Arnold Lobel is best known for writing the Frog and Toad books, but he won the Caldecott Medal for *Fables*. He and his wife Anita Lobel wrote some books together. Arnold Lobel wrote almost 100 children's books!

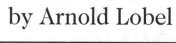

from
FABLES
by Arnold Lobel

THE HEN AND THE APPLE TREE

THE FROGS AT THE
RAINBOW'S END

THE MOUSE AT THE SEASHORE

🔊 **AUDIO**

Audio with
Highlighting

✏️ **ANNOTATE**

THE HEN AND
THE APPLE TREE

**Determine
Key Ideas**
Highlight a detail
that helps you
understand a key
idea about how
the tree looks.

1 One October day, a Hen looked out her window. She saw an apple tree growing in her backyard.

2 "Now that is odd," said the Hen. "I am certain that there was no tree standing in that spot yesterday."

3 "There are some of us that grow fast," said the tree.

4 The Hen looked at the bottom of the tree.

5 "I have never seen a tree," she said, "that has ten furry toes."

6 "There are some of us that do," said the tree. "Hen, come outside and enjoy the cool shade of my leafy branches."

Vocabulary in Context

Underline the word near **quiver** that has almost the same meaning.

7   The Hen looked at the top of the tree.

8   "I have never seen a tree," she said, "that has two long, pointed ears."

9   "There are some of us that have," said the tree. "Hen, come outside and eat one of my delicious apples."

10   "Come to think of it," said the Hen, "I have never heard a tree speak from a mouth that is full of sharp teeth."

11   "There are some of us that can," said the tree. "Hen, come outside and rest your back against the bark of my trunk."

12   "I have heard," said the Hen, "that some of you trees lose all of your leaves at this time of the year."

13   "Oh, yes," said the tree, "there are some of us that will." The tree began to quiver and shake. All of its leaves quickly dropped off.

14   The Hen was not surprised to see a large Wolf in the place where an apple tree had been standing just a moment before. She locked her shutters and slammed her window closed.

15   The Wolf knew that he had been outsmarted. He stormed away in a hungry rage.

16   *It is always difficult to pose as something that one is not.*

Identify Theme

Underline the sentence that tells the theme, or lesson, of this fable. Then underline the sentence on this page that supports the theme.

rage strong anger

THE FROGS AT THE RAINBOW'S END

17 A Frog was swimming in a pond after a rainstorm. He saw a brilliant rainbow stretching across the sky.

18 "I have heard," said the Frog, "there is a cave filled with gold at the place where the rainbow ends. I will find that cave and be the richest frog in the world!"

19 The Frog swam to the edge of the pond as fast as he could go. There he met another Frog.

20 "Where are you rushing to?" asked the second Frog.

21 "I am rushing to the place where the rainbow ends," said the first Frog.

22 "There is a rumor," said the second Frog, "that there is a cave filled with gold and diamonds at that place."

23 "Then come with me," said the first Frog. "We will be the two richest frogs in the world!"

Determine Key Ideas

Highlight the sentence that tells the key idea about what Frog plans to do.

Identify Theme

Underline the theme of this fable. Then underline a sentence that tells the Frogs' highest hopes. Underline another sentence that tells why they were disappointed.

24 The two Frogs jumped out of the pond and ran through the meadow. There they met another Frog.

25 "What is the hurry?" asked the third Frog.

26 "We are running to the place where the rainbow ends," said the two Frogs.

27 "I have been told," said the third Frog, "there is a cave filled with gold and diamonds and pearls at that place."

28 "Then come with us," said the two Frogs. "We will be the three richest frogs in the world!"

29 The three Frogs ran for miles. Finally they came to the rainbow's end. There they saw a dark cave in the side of a hill.

30 "Gold! Diamonds! Pearls!" cried the Frogs, as they leaped into the cave.

31 A Snake lived inside. He was hungry and had been thinking about his supper. He swallowed the three Frogs in one quick gulp.

32 *The highest hopes may lead to the greatest disappointments.*

hopes things wanted in the future

disappointments feelings of not getting what you wanted

THE MOUSE AT THE SEASHORE

Determine Key Ideas

Highlight a key idea that explains why the parents are fearful.

33 A Mouse told his mother and father that he was going on a trip to the seashore.

34 "We are very alarmed!" they cried. "The world is full of terrors. You must not go!"

alarmed felt fearful of danger

35 "I have made my decision," said the Mouse firmly. "I have never seen the ocean, and it is high time that I did. Nothing can make me change my mind."

36 "Then we cannot stop you," said Mother and Father Mouse, "but do be careful!"

37 The next day, in the first light of dawn, the Mouse began his journey. Even before the morning had ended, the Mouse came to know trouble and fear.

38 A Cat jumped out from behind a tree.

39 "I will eat you for lunch," he said.

40 It was a narrow escape for the Mouse. He ran for his life, but he left a part of his tail in the mouth of the Cat.

41 By afternoon the Mouse had been attacked by birds and dogs. He had lost his way several times. He was bruised and bloodied. He was tired and frightened.

42 At evening the Mouse slowly climbed the last hill and saw the seashore spreading out before him. He watched the waves rolling onto the beach, one after another. All the colors of the sunset filled the sky.

43 "How beautiful!" cried the Mouse. "I wish that Mother and Father were here to see this with me."

44 The moon and the stars began to appear over the ocean. The Mouse sat silently on the top of the hill. He was overwhelmed by a feeling of deep peace and contentment.

45 *All the miles of a hard road are worth a moment of true happiness.*

CLOSE READ

Identify Theme
Underline this fable's theme. Then underline a sentence that supports the theme.

contentment feeling of happiness

Develop Vocabulary

MY TURN In the chart, write a vocabulary word from the box that is related to a word in the first column.

rage   hopes   disappointments   alarmed   contentment

Word	Related Word
anger	rage
wishes	
happiness	
surprised	
mistakes	

Check for Understanding

MY TURN Look back at the texts to answer the questions. Write the answers.

1. What makes these stories fables?

_____

_____

_____

2. Why did the author include the sentence in italics at the end of each fable?

_____

_____

_____

_____

3. How are the Frogs in "The Frogs at the Rainbow's End" and the Mouse in "The Mouse at the Seashore" alike? How are they different?

_____

_____

_____

_____

Identify Theme

The **theme** is the message or meaning of a story. In a fable, the lesson or moral is the theme.

👁‍MY TURN Go to the Close Read notes with your teacher and determine the theme using text evidence. Follow the directions to <u>underline</u> the texts. Use the text you underlined to complete the chart.

Fable	Text I Underlined that Supports the Theme	How It Helps Identify the Theme
"The Hen and the Apple Tree"	"The Wolf knew that he had been outsmarted."	The Wolf knows he is not able to pose as something he is not: a tree.
"The Frogs at the Rainbow's End"		
"The Mouse at the Seashore"		

Determine Key Ideas

Key ideas are the important ideas in a text. When you work to understand how key ideas are related and how well they explain a topic, you evaluate a text.

MY TURN Go back to the Close Read notes. Highlight details that help you determine key ideas. Determine how the ideas are related and how they explain the topic. Complete the chart.

Details I Highlighted	Key Idea
"I have never seen a tree that has ten furry toes."	The tree looks like an animal that is pretending to be a tree.

Reflect and Share

Talk About It

Discuss the moral, or lesson, you learned from each of the fables. Which lesson do you think is the most important? Why? Use examples from the texts to support your response.

A fable always has a moral at the end.

Follow Agreed-upon Rules for Discussions

When having a discussion, everyone should have a chance to talk about the topic.

- Take turns speaking. Say what you want to say and then let someone else speak.

- Listen actively to others.

Use these sentence starters to help you take your turn respectfully.

I'd like to say . . .
That's a good point.
I'd like to add that . . .

Weekly Question

What lessons can we learn from traditional tales?

I can use language to make connections between reading and writing.

My Learning Goal

Academic Vocabulary

Related words are words that are connected. They can look like words in other languages. They can share word parts. They can have the same or opposite meanings.

MY TURN For each vocabulary word, write a word that is related to it. Share your words with the class or add them to the Word Wall.

Word	Related Word	How It Is Related
communication	communicate	It shares a word part.
culture		
purpose		
belief		
maintain		

Read Like a Writer, Write for a Reader

Authors have a purpose. They include details that help them meet their purpose.

Author's Purpose in "The Mouse at the Seashore"	Details That Support That Purpose
To teach this moral: "All the miles of a hard road are worth a moment of true happiness."	Hard road: "He had lost his way several times. He was bruised and bloodied. He was tired and frightened." True happiness: "He was overwhelmed by a feeling of deep peace and contentment."

MY TURN Imagine you are writing a story. Your purpose is to teach this moral: **Good things come to those who wait.**

Write two details that support your purpose.

Waiting: _____

_____

A good thing: _____

_____

Spell Words with Long i: i, ie, i_e, igh, y

MY TURN Write words from the list that have the same long **i** spelling as each word below.

child

_____

_____

pie

_____

_____

five

_____

_____

right

_____

_____

my

_____

_____

Spelling Words
try
tried
spy
spied
tonight
dimes
strike
spider
pirate
delight

My Words to Know
earth
thought

Write a My Words to Know word to complete each sentence.

1. We dug a hole in the _____.

2. We _____ it would be fun to play a game.

Verbs: Present Tense

Verbs can tell when actions happen. **Present tense verbs** tell what happens now. Present tense verbs with singular nouns and **he, she,** and **it** usually end in **s.** Present tense verbs with plural nouns and **I, you, we,** and **they** do not end in **s.**

> Leo runs. I walk. Leo and Alice jump.

Some present tense verbs, such as **am, is,** and **are,** do not show action.

> I am ready.

> Ana is ready.

> Mai and I are ready.

MY TURN Edit this draft by crossing out each incorrect verb and writing the correct word above.

Blue are my favorite color. Dad paint my bedroom blue.

Three walls is done. It look great so far! Mom and I

helps by staying out of the way. I is glad it will be

finished soon!

I can use figurative language and sound devices to write poetry.

My Learning Goal

Poetry

In a poem, the poet carefully chooses words to express thoughts and feelings. The words are arranged in lines. Sometimes the words at the ends of lines rhyme.

The poet wants to create pictures in the reader's mind. Sometimes the poet compares different things.

A Red Apple

A ruby red apple
hung high from a tree.
So I shook a branch
and loosened it free.

Compares the color red to a ruby

Words that rhyme

Then I took a bite
and heard a sharp crunch.
That juicy red apple
made me a sweet lunch.

Words that describe sound and taste

Generate Ideas

A poet chooses a topic to write about. Before beginning to write, the poet generates, or thinks of, ideas and feelings about the topic. Drawing is one way to generate ideas and feelings.

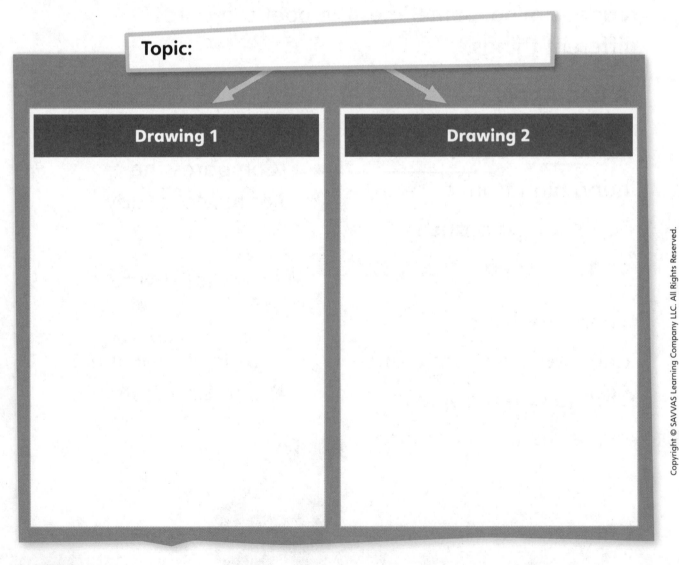

MY TURN Think of a topic for your poem. Draw two pictures that show what you might write about the topic.

Topic:

Drawing 1	Drawing 2

Plan Your Poem

Poets plan what they will compose, or write, in their poems. Brainstorming is one way they generate ideas for writing. Poets develop their ideas by choosing words that give specific and relevant details.

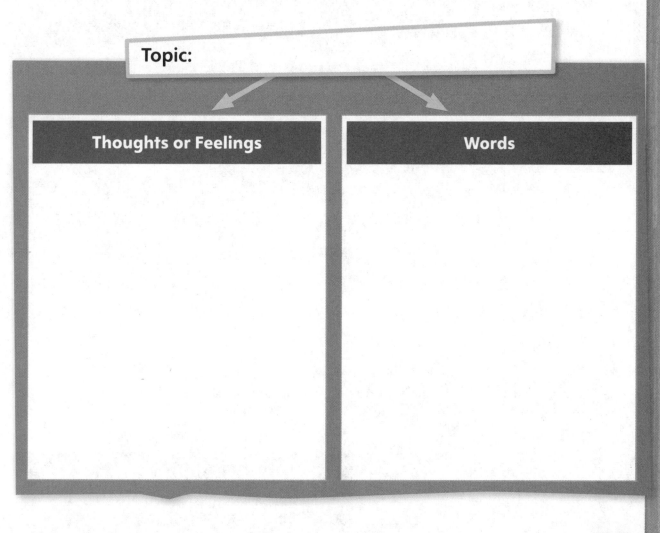 **MY TURN** Generate and develop ideas for your poem. Write the topic. List thoughts or feelings you want to write about. List any words you might want to use, including rhyming words.

Topic:

Thoughts or Feelings	Words

The World of the Storyteller

The Ojibwes (oh JIB wayz) are a large group of Native Americans. Storytelling is important to the Ojibwes. Long ago, the Ojibwes lived near Lake Superior and Lake Huron in North America. They still live in the same area today.

From the shores of Lake Superior, the Ojibwes could see this land they called the Sleeping Giant.

Lake Superior

Canada

Lake Michigan

Lake Huron

Lake Erie

Lake Ontario

United States of America

Winters are cold and snowy where the Ojibwes live.

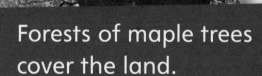

Forests of maple trees cover the land.

In the forests, lovely flowers called lady slippers grow.

Weekly Question

What stories do people tell to understand the world around them?

MY TURN Look at the map and the photos of the land where the Ojibwes live. What do you wonder about the land? Think how the Ojibwes wondered about it. What kinds of stories do you think they might tell? Write your ideas.

Comparative Endings

The endings **-er** or **-est** are used to compare things.

When two things are compared, you'll see the ending -er.	When more than two things are compared, you'll see the ending -est.
Nora is faster than Eli.	Juan is the fastest runner in the school.

Some base words change when **-er** or **-est** is added to them.

When a word ends in y, the y changes to i.	When a word has the CVC pattern, the last consonant is doubled.	When a word has the CVCe pattern, the final e is dropped.
dry, drier, driest	hot, hotter, hottest	late, later, latest

MY TURN Decode, or read, these words. <u>Underline</u> the base word in each. Tell what each word means.

greener   largest   redder   safer

bluest   slower   maddest   flatter

TURN and TALK Take turns with your partner. Make up sentences using these words: sillier, silliest, cuter, cutest.

Comparative Endings

Words that end in **-er** compare two things: **Em is shorter than Ryan.** Words that end in **-est** compare more than two things: **Aria is the shortest girl in the class.**

MY TURN Read each sentence. Write the correct form of the word on the line.

1. That oak tree is the (taller, tallest) in the woods.

   _____

2. My cat is (fuzzier, fuzziest) than your cat. _____

3. Whales are the (bigger, biggest) animal of all.

   _____

4. Ken's band was the (louder, loudest) band in the parade.

   _____

5. The workers are making the sidewalk (wider, widest).

   _____

6. Sue's joke was (funnier, funniest) than Mark's joke.

   _____

My Words to Know

MY TURN Read the high-frequency words in the box. Write a sentence using each word.

along	few	head

_____

_____

_____

_____

TURN and TALK Trade sentences with a partner. Identify the high-frequency words in each other's work. Talk about any corrections.

You can read faster and better when you know high-frequency words.

No Help at All!

Ron asked, "Why is this hill taller than that one?"

"Because," said Hank.

"Why is this the biggest tree on the hill?"
asked Ron.

"Because," said Hank.

"Why do you keep saying because?" asked Ron.

"Come along. Let's go home," said Hank.

"At least you didn't say because!" said Ron.

1. Why is Ron asking questions?

_____

_____

_____

2. Why do you think Hank keeps saying "because"?

_____

_____

_____

3. Find a word in the story that ends with **-er** or **-est**.
   Use it in a new sentence.

_____

_____

My Learning Goal

I can read a traditional tale and understand its plot.

Spotlight on Genre

Traditional Tale: Legend

A legend is an old story that tells about the great deeds of a hero or about an important event. It has special meaning in a culture. Long ago, legends were passed along by word of mouth.

- Some legends are based on a real person or event.

- They have a **plot** that tells the events.

- The plot has a **beginning**, a **middle**, and an **end**.

Be a Fluent Reader Fluent readers read aloud with prosody, or expression. Legends often include exciting events. This makes them a good place to practice reading with expression.

- To read with expression, pay attention to punctuation. Read with excitement when you see an exclamation point.

- When you read dialogue, speak in a different voice for each character.

Legend Anchor Chart

Purpose

To tell a story about a hero or an event

A legend

★ is a well-known story that may be partly true and partly fiction

★ has special meaning in a culture

★ may have been told many times before it was written down

The Legend of the Lady Slipper

Preview Vocabulary

Look for these words as you read *The Legend of the Lady Slipper.*

messenger	moccasins	admiration	medicines	exhausted

First Read

Read to understand the author's purpose.

Look at the pictures.

Ask questions about the sequence of events.

Talk about how this text answers the weekly question.

Meet *the* Authors

Lise Lunge-Larsen

Margi Preus

Lise Lunge-Larsen moved to the United States from Norway. She is a teacher, storyteller, author, and expert on trolls. **Margi Preus** has won many awards for her books for young readers. She also writes plays. Both authors live in Duluth, Minnesota.

THE LEGEND OF THE LADY SLIPPER

By Lise Lunge-Larsen and Margi Preus

Illustrated by Andrea Arroyo

AUDIO

Audio with Highlighting

ANNOTATE

CLOSE READ

Discuss Author's Purpose

<u>Underline</u> the word that the author uses to show the story takes place at an unknown time in the past.

1 Once there was a young girl who lived with her mother and father, sister and brother, aunts and uncles, her many cousins, her grandfathers and grandmothers, and all of her people in a village among the whispering pines. Of all her family, her older brother was her favorite.

2 He was as strong as a bear, as fast as a rabbit, and as smart as a fox. Because of these traits, he was the messenger for the village. When he went on his journeys the little girl begged to go along with him, but all he would say was, "Maybe tomorrow."

messenger someone who carries news or a message to someone else

3   Then one day a terrible disease struck. The little girl watched as, one by one, her people became ill. Her grandparents, her aunts and uncles, her sister, her mother. Even her father fell ill.

4   A neighboring village had the *mash-ki-ki*, the healing herbs, they needed, but the journey was too dangerous to make in winter. It was too cold, the snow was too heavy, and between the villages lay a deep, dark lake covered with groaning ice. Such journeys were not made in *Gichi Manidoo Giizis*, the Great Spirit Moon.

5   Still, her brother said, yes, he would make the trip.

Discuss Author's Purpose
Underline words the author uses to show that the people in the story speak a language other than English.

CLOSE READ

Make Connections

Highlight words that show how the girl feels about her village.

6   But then even he became ill.

7   Now the little girl thought surely there was no one else to go, unless she herself were to make the journey. Maybe tomorrow, she thought. But looking at her brother, his face bright with fever, she knew she had to leave right away.

8   She found her *ma-ki-sins*, the beautifully beaded moccasins her mother had made out of deerskin, and tucked warm rabbit fur inside them. Then she slipped them on and stepped out into a raging storm.

CLOSE READ

moccasins soft leather shoes

CLOSE READ

Vocabulary in Context

You can sometimes figure out the meanings of unfamiliar words by reading words nearby. <u>Underline</u> words in the text that help you understand the meaning of **plunging**.

9 Trees lashed about in the wind, rattling their branches. Falling snow stung her face. "*Mash-ka-wi-zin*," it hissed, "Be strong."

10 The girl bent her head and stalked like a bear into the storm. The snow tugged at her, but she charged through it, plunging into the wind.

11   All day she walked until, at dusk, she stood before the windswept lake. The slick ice lay as if asleep, silent. On the far shore the wigwams of the other village glowed warmly.

12   The little girl stepped out onto the frozen lake and the ice shuddered and woke. *"Da-daa-ta-biin,"* it rumbled, "Go quickly!"

13   So the girl ran like a rabbit, skittering and slipping.

CLOSE READ

Discuss Author's Purpose

<u>Underline</u> the words the author uses to show the girl is a hero to the people in the village.

admiration a feeling of great respect and approval

14   When she reached the other side, all the people rushed out to meet her. She told them her story, and when she finished, she saw their faces glowing with admiration.

15 Then an old woman swept her up and carried her into a lodge. She fed the little girl roasted venison and warm tea. She tucked her in with soft robes. The girl was almost asleep when she remembered the medicines.

16 "The *mash-ki-ki*," she murmured.

medicines things used to make a sick person well

CLOSE READ

Make Connections

Highlight words that show the people in the girl's village are more important to her than her own safety.

17 "We will bring you and the *mash-ki-ki* to your people," the old woman whispered. "Tomorrow. It is too dark and too cold to travel tonight."

18 But when the little girl closed her eyes she saw the sad, pale faces of her family, her friends, and her brother, and she knew she must leave right away. She rose quietly, gathered up the medicine bundle, and crept out.

19 The storm had stopped. Now all was deep cold and silence, except the popping and cracking of the trees. Her eyes stung; she felt the frost gather on her cheeks. She pulled her robe tight and hurried across the lake.

CLOSE READ

Make Connections

Highlight the text that tells you what the lights are called in English. Have you heard of this before?

20   Blue and green lights flickered in the sky. She knew the lights were the spirits of the dead, gaily dressed, rising and falling in the steps of a dance. *Jii-ba-yag-nii-mi-wag*, her people called them, the northern lights.

21   What if someone from her family or one of her people were to join them because she had been so slow? She left the lake and quickened her pace, keeping her eyes on the lights in the sky.

22   Suddenly, the snow collapsed around her and she was buried up to her arms. She kicked and punched at the snow. That was no use. She churned her little legs as fast as she could, as if to run out of the snow. That only dug her in deeper.

23   Above her the dancing spirits leapt and spun. Maybe she would be the next one among them, she thought. She fell back, exhausted.

exhausted very tired

24 *"Nib-waa-kaan!"* the snow around her whispered, "Be wise!" Yes, she must be smart like the fox who *thinks* his way around the trap.

25 She lay back to think and felt the snow relax its grip. She lay further back and it let go a little more. Slowly, she wriggled and turned, paddled and swam her way out of the snow.

26 "Ho-whah!" she sang out. Her feet were free!

CLOSE READ

Discuss Author's Purpose

Underline the text that shows who gives the girl advice.

27 But then, "*Gaa-wiin*! Oh, no!" she cried. Her feet were bare and cold. Her moccasins were gone, buried deep in the drift. She dug in the snow, but it was too soft and loose. She wiped her nose on her sleeve and continued on barefoot.

28   With the very first step, icy crystals cut into her flesh and her feet began to bleed. In every footprint bright red drops of blood mingled with the white snow. Still, she stumbled ahead until dawn, when she reached the edge of her village. There she called out before sinking into the snow.

CLOSE READ

Make Connections

Highlight the text that shows what the girl does to get the medicine to the people in her village. What does that help you understand about the girl?

CLOSE READ

Make Connections

Highlight the text that shows how the people from the village feel about the girl.

29 The people from her village—even some of the sick ones—ran out when they heard her cry. They carried her back to her lodge and wrapped her swollen and bleeding feet in thick, warm deerskins.

78

30   Because of the *mash-ki-ki*, the people were healed. The little girl remained weak for a long, long time, but soon after the snow melted, she too recovered.

CLOSE READ

Discuss Author's Purpose

<u>Underline</u> the text that shows what the girl and her brother find when they search for her moccasins.

31   When the forest turned green, she and her brother went to search for her lost moccasins. What they found there filled them with wonder.

32   On the very spot where she had lost her moccasins and wherever she had stepped with her bleeding feet, beautiful new flowers grew. They were pink and white and shaped just like the little moccasins the girl had worn on her journey.

33　The Ojibwe people named the new flower *ma-ki-sin waa-big-waan*, which means the moccasin flower. Today it is also called the lady slipper. The people gave the little girl her name, too, "*Wah-Oh-Nay*," or "Little Flower," because although she was as strong as a bear, fast as a rabbit, and smart as a fox, she was also as lovely and rare as a wild spring flower.

CLOSE READ

Fluency
Practice reading with fluency. Read aloud paragraphs 14–19 several times with a partner. Read the dialogue with feeling, or prosody. Read in a different voice for the old woman and the little girl to show their points of view.

Develop Vocabulary

MY TURN Write the word from the box that belongs in each word group.

| admiration   exhausted   medicines   messenger   moccasins |

1. _____ boots   slippers

2. tired   weary _____

3. mail carrier _____ delivery person

4. respect   approval _____

5. cures   remedies _____

Check for Understanding

MY TURN Look back at the text to answer the questions. Write the answers.

1. What are some clues that this story is a legend?

_____

_____

2. Find an example of a word or phrase from a language other than English in this story and tell what it means. How does the author help you understand the meaning of these words?

_____

_____

3. What evidence from the text supports the idea that the girl puts the needs of her village above her own needs? Is that a good way to live? Why or why not?

_____

_____

Discuss Author's Purpose

Authors write for different reasons, or purposes. They may write to entertain readers or to give information. Authors use the structure of a text to make it fun to read. For example, an author may start with a problem and wait to the end to tell how it turned out.

MY TURN Go to the Close Read notes. Underline details that help you discuss the author's purpose. Then complete the chart.

Paragraph	What did you underline?	What was the author's purpose?
1		
24		
32		

Make Connections

You make all kinds of connections when you read. Some of the connections you can make include:

Connections to personal experiences

Connections to other texts

Connections to society

MY TURN Go back to the Close Read notes and highlight text evidence. Then complete the chart. For each example, tell if you made a connection to your own experience, other texts, or society.

When I read ...,	I made connections to ...
how close the girl feels to her village,	
about the northern lights,	
how the people from the village take care of the girl,	

Reflect and Share

Write to Sources

The Legend of the Lady Slipper is a story that explains why a flower grows. Think about other stories you have read in the unit. On a piece of paper, write a paragraph to tell why you think people make up stories to explain things.

Focus on One Main Idea

Your opinion paragraph should focus on one main, or central, idea.

- All sentences should relate to the main idea.

- Develop your idea with specific details.

Begin your paragraph with a sentence that states your main idea. Use details from the texts to support it. Use linking words, such as *because* and *also*, to connect ideas.

Weekly Question

What stories do people tell to understand the world around them?

I can use language to make connections between reading and writing.

Academic Vocabulary

Synonyms mean the same thing. **Big** and **large** are synonyms. **Antonyms** have opposite meanings. **Dark** and **light** are antonyms. Sometimes you can figure out a word by looking for a synonym or an antonym near it.

MY TURN Find a synonym or antonym for each highlighted word. Then explain what the word means.

The girl communicates with her brother. They tell each other everything.

Underline a synonym. **Communicates** means _____.

Finding a cure is the purpose for the journey. It is a good reason to go.

Underline a synonym. **Purpose** means _____.

The girl maintains hope. She does not lose it.

Underline an antonym. **Maintains** means _____.

The brother believes in the girl. He does not doubt her.

Underline an antonym. **Believes** means _____.

Read Like a Writer, Write for a Reader

Authors organize their stories with a structure. They include a beginning to start the action and an ending to finish it.

Structure of *The Legend of the Lady Slipper*	What This Tells Me
Beginning: "Once there was a young girl . . . "Then one day a terrible disease struck."	I learn who the story is about and what happens to start the action.
End: "Because of the *mash-ki-ki*, the people were healed."	I learn how the action ends.

MY TURN Write a sentence that could begin a story you might write. Then write a sentence that ends the story.

Spell Words with Comparative Endings

To spell words with endings, spell the base word and then the ending. A base word sometimes changes when an ending is added. Notice the spelling changes in **busy** and **hot** when you add endings.

MY TURN Write the Spelling Words in the blanks.

1. Be nice, not _____.

Add **-er** and **-est** to that word:

_____ _____

2. He is poor, not _____.

Add **-er** and **-est** to that word:

_____ _____

3. She is resting, not _____.

Add **-er** and **-est** to that word:

_____ _____

4. It is the _____ day of the year!

5. Ouch! I bumped my _____.

6. Come _____ with us!

Spelling Words

mean

meaner

meanest

rich

richer

richest

busy

busier

busiest

hottest

My Words to Know

head

along

Verbs: Past Tense and Future Tense

Verbs can tell when actions happen. **Past tense verbs** tell what happened in the past. Many past tense verbs end with **-ed**. **Future tense verbs** tell what will happen in the future. They use **will** before the verb.

Verb	Past Tense	Future Tense
learn	Last week we **learned** about whales.	Next week we **will learn** about sharks.
cook	Jo **cooked** dinner last night.	She **will cook** again tonight.
visit	Last fall we **visited** Ohio.	Next fall we **will visit** Maine.

MY TURN Edit this draft by crossing out the incorrect verbs and writing the correct verbs above.

I will finish my book a week ago. Last night I will call my cousin to tell her about it. My cousin said she went to the library tomorrow. She borrowed the book to read next week.

My Learning Goal

I can use figurative language and sound devices to write poetry.

Imagery

A poet often uses words that help the reader imagine what something looks like. The words paint a picture in the reader's mind. These "word pictures" are called imagery.

> A ruby red apple
> hung high from a tree

Can you picture an apple that is as red as a jewel? Is it dangling from a high tree branch? That is imagery.

MY TURN Fill in the chart below using two poems from your classroom library.

Title of Poem	Example of Imagery	What I Picture

Sensory Details

A poet uses **sensory details.** Sensory details describe what you see, hear, taste, smell, and touch.

See: A ruby red apple

Hear: and heard a sharp crunch

Taste: That juicy red apple / Made me a sweet lunch.

Smell: sweet cinnamon bread baking

Touch: tossing and turning on the lumpy pillow

MY TURN Plan sensory details to use in your poem. Some senses may have more details.

Topic:
See:
Hear:
Taste:
Smell:
Touch:

Word Choice

Poets carefully choose their words. They choose interesting, colorful words that sound good together. They choose words that help the reader see their ideas.

The cat
The little black cat

Slept on a mat
Snoozed peacefully on a mat.

MY TURN Add or change words to improve this sentence. Choose words that are more interesting to help readers see the idea better.
A flower grew in a lot.

_____

_____

MY TURN Use interesting words as you compose your poem.

Telling a Story

The story of Cinderella is hundreds of years old. It has been told in different countries around the world. But the story is not always the same.

In some stories, a fairy godmother helps Cinderella. In other stories, a white bird in a wishing tree helps her.

In some stories, Cinderella wears glass slippers. In other stories, she wears gold slippers.

In some stories, a pumpkin turns into a coach and mice turn into coachmen to take Cinderella to a ball. But many stories don't explain how Cinderella gets to the ball at all.

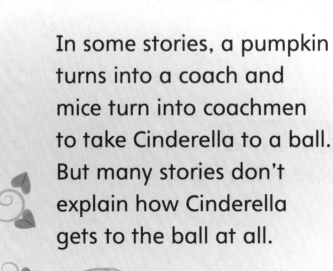

In some stories, Cinderella must leave the ball by midnight. In other stories, she leaves just because she is tired!

Weekly Question

How can a traditional story be told in different ways?

 TURN and TALK

Tell the Cinderella story to a partner. First, draw your story. Draw the beginning, two important middle events, and the end. Next, use your pictures to tell your Cinderella stories to each other. Tell your story with descriptive details such as how Cinderella looked and how she got to the ball. Speak clearly in complete sentences. Then talk about how your stories are alike and different.

r-Controlled Vowels: er, ir, ur

When a vowel is followed by **r**, the vowel has a different sound. The vowel is called **r-controlled**. The letter pairs **er**, **ir**, and **ur** make the same sound.

MY TURN Read, or decode, the words with r-controlled words. Listen for the **r**-controlled sound.

er	ir	ur
her	stir	fur
jerk	girl	turn
perfect	dirty	hurry

TURN and TALK Reread the words in the chart with a partner. Underline the **r**-controlled vowel pattern in each word.

Then choose one word from each column and use the words in sentences. Share your sentences with your partner.

When I say **her**, **stir**, and **fur**, I hear words that rhyme.

r-Controlled Vowels: er, ir, ur

MY TURN Practice decoding the words in the box. Then use the words to complete the sentences.

bird	burn	curly
serve	thirsty	perfect

1. The cake may _____ if the oven is too hot.

2. On this hot day, we are _____ .

3. That _____ has bright yellow feathers.

4. Will's black hair is very _____ .

5. What food should we _____ for lunch?

6. The sunny weather was _____ for our hike.

My Words to Know

MY TURN Read the high-frequency words in the box. Then read the sentences. Write the missing words. Form the letters correctly as you write each word. Use connecting strokes to connect the letters.

something	example	paper

Wait! I think I forgot _____.

An apple is an _____ of a fruit.

Write your name on the _____.

TURN and TALK Read these sentences aloud with a partner. Identify the high-frequency words. Then write your own sentences. Identify and read the words in each other's writing.

Ron drew a picture on white paper.

The teacher asked for an example of a noun.

You look happy. Did something good happen?

Perfect!

Bird sits in his cage. "I want something else. I want a nest," he says.

He finds a nest made of ferns. "Too little," says Bird. He finds a nest on the earth. "Too dirty," says Bird. The third nest is not little or dirty. "I like this nest!" says Bird. "I think I'll stay."

Bird sees Hawk. "Oh no!" Bird says. He hurries back. "My cage is a perfect home!"

1. Why does Bird like the third nest?

   _____

2. What fairy tale does this remind you of?

   _____

3. Write three words from the story with **r**-controlled vowels: one with **er**, one with **ir**, and one with **ur**.

   _____

   _____

My Learning Goal

I can read folktales and compare versions of the same tale.

Spotlight on Genre

Traditional Tales: Folktales

Folktales are traditional tales, or well-known stories, that people have told again and again. A folktale:

- may have been told for years before it was written.

- has a problem to solve.

- has characters that are either all good or all bad.

- may be told in different ways, or **versions**.

Establish a Purpose for Reading When you read different versions of the same story, you might read to compare them.

TURN and TALK The story of Cinderella is a folktale. It is also called a fairy tale because it has magic in it. Share what you know about this tale. Look at the pictures in *Interstellar Cinderella* and *Cendrillon*. How might these Cinderella stories be the same as the traditional Cinderella story? How might they be different?

Folktale Anchor Chart

These stories

- were first told out loud and were later written down
- have problems to solve
- have good characters and bad characters

Folktales

told by different people

developed over time into different versions of the same folktale

retold in different places

Interstellar Cinderella

Preview Vocabulary

Look for these words as you read *Interstellar Cinderella*.

stranded	mechanic

First Read

Read for the purpose you set.

Look at the illustrations to help you understand the text.

Ask questions about any confusing parts.

Talk about the text with a partner.

Meet the Author

Deborah Underwood wanted to be an astronomer when she was growing up. She ended up being a singer and an author. She has worked hard to write better stories than the first story she wrote. She also writes informational texts and sings in a choir.

INTERSTELLAR CINDERELLA

By Deborah Underwood
Illustrated by Meg Hunt

Visualize Details

Highlight words that help you picture in your mind the place where Cinderella lives.

1 Once upon a planetoid,
amid her tools and sprockets,
a girl named Cinderella dreamed
of fixing fancy rockets.

2 She fixed the robot dishwashers
and zoombrooms in her care,
but late each night she snuck away
to study ship repair.

3   One day her wicked stepsisters
    came dashing in, excited.
    "The Prince's Royal Space Parade!
    Our family's invited!"

4   "I wish that you could come, my dear.
    Alas, no room! Although . . .
    why don't you fix that broken ship
    and fly it to the show?"

CLOSE READ

stranded not able
to leave because
there is no way to
get anywhere else

5 "My toolbox!" Cinderella cried,
"we're stranded here, I guess."
But Murgatroyd the mouse sent out
a cosmic SOS.

106

6   "I'm here—your fairy godrobot!
I'll make you brand-new tools.
You'll need a space suit, too, of
course: Atomic blue! With jewels!

7   This power gem will speed your ship
across the starry sky.
It only lasts till midnight—
after that, your ship won't fly."

8   "Oh, thank you!" Cinderella said.
She quickly fixed the rocket,
then tucked the sonic socket wrench
inside her space-suit pocket.

Visualize Details

Highlight the words that help you picture how Cinderella's ship will move.

9   She zoomed past stars and nebulae,
    and parked beside a moon.
    The space parade was glorious!
    Each starship made her swoon.

10 At last the royal ship approached.
    Her heart was filled with yearning.
    The ship of Cinderella's dreams!
    But heavens! What was burning?

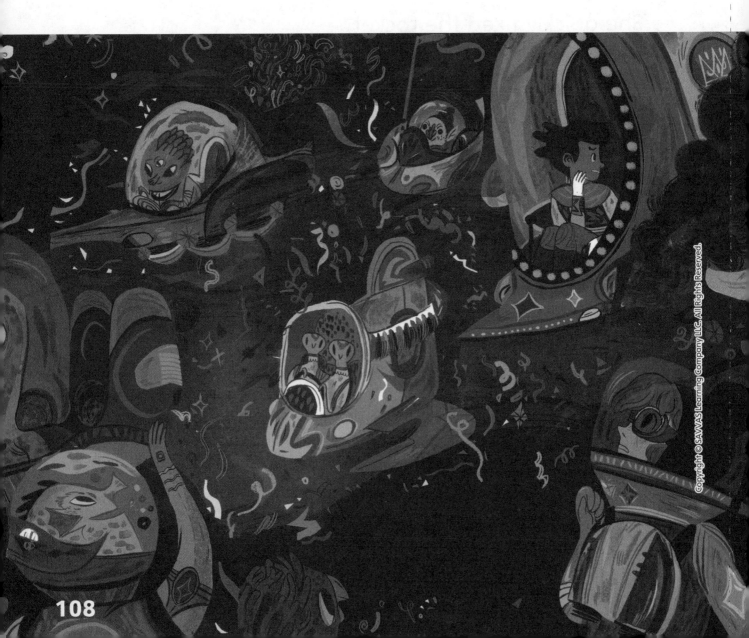

11 The prince's spaceship jerked and
    hissed
    and spewed a cloud of grit.
    The prince hopped out. "Oh blast!
    What now?
    My chief mechanic quit!"

12 But Interstellar Cinderella
    knew just what to do.
    She zipzapped with her socket
    wrench—
    the ship was good as new!

13 The prince invited her aboard.
    Last stop? Galactic Hall!
    He said, "I hope you'll join me
    for the Gravity-Free Ball."

CLOSE READ

Compare and Contrast Stories

Underline two details that are the same as in the Cinderella story that most people know.

mechanic someone whose job is fixing machines

Vocabulary in Context

Underline words near **cosmos** that can help you figure out its meaning.

14 They talked for hours of rocket ships.
The time went whizzing by.
Then Cinderella saw the clock
and said, "I have to fly!"

15 "But wait!" the prince called after her.
"Please tell me how to find—"
The girl was gone—but she had left
her socket wrench behind.

16 The prince sent a transmission
to the farthest edge of space.
"I'll search the cosmos for her.
How I wish I'd seen her face!"

17 "The prince's ship!" Grisilla screeched.
    Her sister squealed in fear.
    "The prince won't marry one of us
    if Cinderella's here!"

18 Their mother said, "Don't worry.
    He won't find her in this house!
    I've trapped her in the attic
    with that useless robot mouse."

CLOSE READ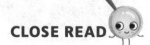

Vocabulary in Context

The word **craft** is short for **spacecraft**. Underline a word near it that has nearly the same meaning. What is another meaning of **craft?**

19 The prince's cargo door revealed a broken craft within. "The girl I seek can fix a ship. So—who'd like to begin?"

20 He gave the sonic socket wrench to one, then to the other. Alas, they couldn't fix the ship (and neither could their mother).

21 Cinderella struggled,
but the space rope held her tight,
till Murgatroyd's robotic teeth
cut through it with one bite.

Compare and Contrast Stories

Underline a detail that is the same as in the more well-known Cinderella story. Then underline a detail after it that is different.

22 "The ship! It's leaving!
Wait—what's this?"
She made a fast repair,
then strapped the rusty jet pack on
and blasted through the air.

23 She landed right beside the prince.
"That wrench is mine!" she cried.
She quickly fixed the ailing ship.
The prince said, "Be my bride!"

24 She thought this over carefully.
Her family watched in panic.
"I'm far too young for marriage,
but I'll be your chief mechanic!"

25 Amid her fleet of sparkling ships,
and friends both old and new,
a joyful Cinderella cried,
"My stars! Dreams do come true!"

Cendrillon: An Island Cinderella

Preview Vocabulary

Look for these words as you read *Cendrillon*.

blossoms	expensive	forgave

Read and Compare

Read to compare and contrast this version of a Cinderella story to *Interstellar Cinderella*.

Look at illustrations to help you understand the text.

Ask such questions as **who** or **where** about the characters.

Talk to restate or summarize the text.

Meet the Author

Tracey Baptiste grew up on the Caribbean island of Trinidad. She collects Cendrillon stories. Her novel *The Jumbies* is based on a folktale from Haiti. In that story, a brave girl named Corrine saves her island home from creepy creatures called jumbies.

Cendrillon: An Island Cinderella

By Tracey Baptiste
Illustrated by Sophie Diao

AUDIO

Audio with Highlighting

ANNOTATE

CLOSE READ

Visualize Details

Highlight words that help you picture the place where Cendrillon lives.

blossoms flowers of a plant that produces fruit

1   A gentle breeze blew over the little island. It curved around palm trees and swept over rice fields. Then it landed softly against a girl watering her orange tree. The orange blossoms made the air smell sweet. The girl was named Cendrillon. Her mama had planted the tree before she became sick. Now her mama was gone.

2   Cendrillon was lonely without her mother.

3   "I must find a new mother for my girl," thought her father. Later that day, he sailed to another island.

4   A few weeks later, Papa returned with a beautiful lady and her two daughters.

5   "This is your new family," he told Cendrillon.

6   At first, Cendrillon's new family was kind
to her. Then Cendrillon's life changed. There
was a shipwreck, and Papa did not return.
Cendrillon's stepmother turned cold and
cruel. She sent Cendrillon to the kitchens.
She made her scrub pots and sweep the floor.
Cendrillon scrubbed and swept until her
fingers were raw.

7　　One day, a fancy letter arrived. Cendrillon picked it up, but her stepmother snatched it from her and read it.

8　　"The mayor's son will choose a wife! All young ladies have been invited to a ball!"

9　　For days, Cendrillon's stepmother and stepsisters shopped for expensive clothes to wear to the ball. Cendrillon had to scrub, wash, sew, and sweep.

Compare and Contrast Stories

Compare and contrast this story and *Interstellar Cinderella*. <u>Underline</u> a detail that is different in the two stories. Then <u>underline</u> a detail that is nearly the same.

expensive costing a lot of money

Visualize Details

Highlight the words that help you picture in your mind how Cendrillon's stepsisters treat her.

10   On the night of the ball, Cendrillon wanted to go, but the stepsisters tore her simple dress and left without her. Cendrillon sat crying under the orange tree.

11   Then the gentle breeze blew orange blossoms into her hair and covered her in leaves, making a beautiful new dress!

12   "Go to the ball!" the breeze whispered.

13   When Cendrillon arrived at the ball, the mayor's son looked only at her. All night, they danced to the music of guitars and drums. At midnight, though, her leaves and flowers began to dry up and fall. Cendrillon ran home.

14 Cendrillon's stepmother saw the leafy trail.

15 "You were at the ball!" she screamed.

16 A knock at the front door stopped her. It was the mayor's son! A stepsister pushed Cendrillon out the back door and locked her outside.

17 "I am looking for the girl in the leaf dress," said the mayor's son. Then he saw the trail of leaves. He followed it through the door.

18　There was Cendrillon. The mayor's son recognized her at once.

19　He took Cendrillon's hand. "Will you marry me?" he asked.

20　Before long, there was a great wedding. Cendrillon moved into a grand house with her new husband. She forgave her stepmother and stepsisters because she was a kind and gentle person.

21　And they all lived happily ever after, soothed by a sweet, gentle breeze that always smelled of orange blossoms.

CLOSE READ

Compare and Contrast Stories

Underline a key detail that is nearly the same in *Interstellar Cinderella* and this story. Then underline a key detail that is different.

forgave stopped being angry toward someone for something the person did

Develop Vocabulary

 MY TURN Fill in each blank. Circle the context clues that helped you decide which word to use.

| stranded mechanic blossoms expensive forgave |

1. The cherry trees are covered with pink

_____, or flowers.

2. When their car broke down, the family was

_____ with no way to get home.

3. I can't buy that _____ shirt.
It costs more money than I have right now.

4. Our car lost a lot of oil, so we asked

a _____ to fix it.

5. She hurt my feelings, but I _____ her and
tried to forget about it.

Check for Understanding

MY TURN Look back at the texts to answer the questions. Write the answers.

1. What parts, or characteristics, of the Cinderella fairy tale make it a typical folktale?

_____

_____

_____

2. Why do you think the authors wanted to retell the Cinderella story in different settings?

_____

_____

_____

3. In what ways are the main characters the same in these stories and other Cinderella stories you know?

_____

_____

_____

Compare and Contrast Stories

When you **compare** things, you tell how they are alike.
When you **contrast** things, you tell how they are different.

MY TURN Go to the Close Read notes. <u>Underline</u> the details that help you compare and contrast stories. Use what you have underlined to complete the chart.

Story	How It's Like Another Cinderella Story	How It's Different from Another Cinderella Story
Interstellar Cinderella	Like the traditional *Cinderella* story:	Unlike the traditional *Cinderella* story:
Cendrillon: An Island Cinderella	Like *Interstellar Cinderella:*	Unlike *Interstellar Cinderella:*

Visualize Details

When you visualize details in a story, you create mental images. This means that you picture the story's characters, places, and events in your mind. Visualizing details helps you have a deeper understanding of the text.

TURN and TALK Go back to the Close Read notes. Highlight details that help you create mental images in *Interstellar Cinderella* and *Cendrillon: An Island Cinderella*. Choose one detail that you highlighted. Close your eyes and form a picture in your mind. Then draw the picture.

The detail I visualized is _____

_____

Reflect and Share

Talk About It

This week you read two versions of the well-known story *Cinderella*. You've probably read, heard, or seen other versions of this tale. Talk as a class about the theme of Cinderella and the version you liked best. Use text evidence to support your view.

Stay on Topic

It is important to share information and ideas that focus on the topic under discussion.

- Make comments about the topic only.
- If the discussion gets off track, find a way to come back to the topic.

I would like for us to keep talking about . . .
That's really interesting, but let's get back to . . .

Use these sentence starters to help others stay on topic.

Weekly Question

How can a traditional story be told in different ways?

I can use language to make connections between reading and writing traditional tales.

My Learning Goal

Academic Vocabulary

Context clues are words that give hints about a word's meaning. You can determine the meaning of an unfamiliar word by looking for clues in nearby words and sentences.

MY TURN Circle the context clues that help you understand each **bold** word or phrase. Then determine the meaning of the word and fill in the blank.

1. The girl meant to break the toy. She did it **on purpose**.

   In this sentence, **on purpose** means _____

   _____ .

2. Taking care of an old house isn't easy. Home **maintenance** is expensive.

   In this sentence **maintenance** means _____

   _____ .

3. Mario looked at Leo in **disbelief.** He did not believe him.

   In this sentence, **disbelief** is the opposite of _____ .

Read Like a Writer, Write for a Reader

Authors choose words carefully to help them tell the events of their stories.

Text from *Cendrillon: An Island Cinderella*	What This Word Choice Says
"At first, Cendrillon's new family was kind to her. Then Cendrillon's life changed. There was a shipwreck, and Papa did not return. Cendrillon's stepmother turned cold and cruel."	Cendrillon's stepmother began to treat her differently. These words lead to story events that follow.

MY TURN Imagine you are writing the story of Cinderella. Start with this sentence and write two more sentences. Choose words to help develop story events.

Cinderella's stepsisters are getting ready for the ball.

Spell Words with r-Controlled Vowels er, ir, ur

MY TURN Sort the spelling words by their **r**-controlled vowel pattern.

ir

_____

_____

_____

ur

_____

_____

er

_____

_____

_____

_____

Spelling Words
fern
term
chirp
first
curb
burn
perky
birthday
alert
perfect

My Words to Know

something
paper

Write a My Words to Know word to answer these clues.

What word is the opposite of nothing? _____

What are you writing on now? _____

Irregular Verbs

You add **-ed** to most verbs to show action in the past. **Irregular verbs** do not follow this rule. Instead, these verbs change spelling for the past tense.

Present	Past
sit	sat
tell	told
see	saw
take	took
hide	hid

MY TURN Edit this draft by crossing out the incorrect verbs and writing the correct verb above.

We played hide-and-seek yesterday. I hided in my closet. I sitted on one side and pulled a coat over my head. It taked the others a long time to find me. My sister seed me last. She telled me it was a great place to hide.

My
Learning
Goal

I can use figurative language and
sound devices to write poetry.

Simile

A poet can use **similes** to create imagery. A **simile**
compares two things using the word **like** or **as**.

She eats like a bird.

I'm as hungry as a bear.

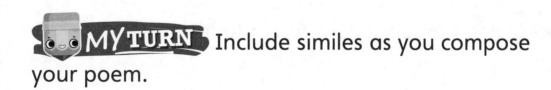 **MY TURN** Replace the underlined word or
words in each sentence with a simile. Write the
new sentence.

1. My book bag weighs <u>a lot</u>.

_____

_____

2. I slept <u>well</u>.

_____

_____

MY TURN Include similes as you compose
your poem.

Alliteration

Poets sometimes choose words that have the same beginning sound. This sound pattern is called **alliteration**. Poets use alliteration to make their poems sound pleasing. An example is this Mother Goose rhyme:

Three gray geese in a green field grazing,

Gray were the geese and green was the grazing.

MY TURN Think of ways to use alliteration in your poem. Write three phrases you might use.

Topic of Poem	
Phrase	
Phrase	
Phrase	

MY TURN Compose your poem to include alliteration.

Audio Recording

The sound of a poem is as important as its meaning. Poets make sure their poems sound good when read aloud.

MY TURN Make an audio recording of your poem. Then play it back. Listen to the sound of your poem. Look for ways to make the poem better.

1. When I listened to my poem,

_____

_____

_____

2. To make my poem sound better, I can

_____

_____

_____

The Wabanaki

The Wabanaki (wah-buh-NAH-kee) are made up of five Native American groups in the northeastern United States and southeastern Canada. The Abanaki, who you will read about later this week, are members of the Wabanaki.

Long ago, the Wabanaki peoples lived in wigwams.

Long ago, the Wabanaki traveled in birch bark canoes.

Long ago, the Wabanaki peoples made baskets to carry things.

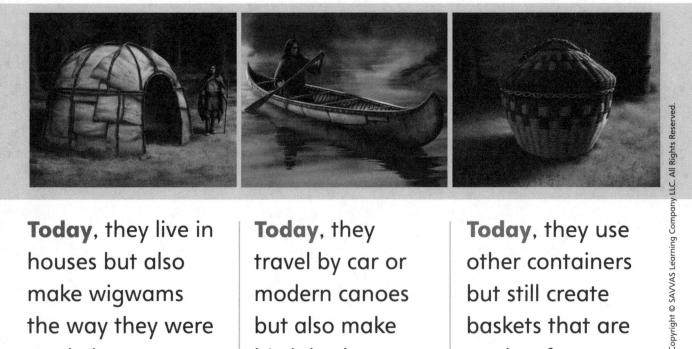

Today, they live in houses but also make wigwams the way they were made long ago.

Today, they travel by car or modern canoes but also make birch bark canoes.

Today, they use other containers but still create baskets that are works of art.

Today, the Wabanaki peoples live much like other people. But they sometimes do things in traditional ways to keep their culture alive.

Long ago, the Wabanaki celebrated with dancing and drumming.

Today, they still celebrate this way.

Weekly Question

What makes a Native American tradition?

Quick Write Circle the names of four traditions that Wabanaki peoples sometimes follow today. What makes these things traditions? How do they compare to traditions your family follows?

Diphthongs ou, ow, oi, oy

The words **house** and **crown** have the same vowel sound. This sound is called a diphthong and can be spelled **ou** or **ow**.

 house

 crown

The words **coin** and **boy** have the same vowel sound. It is also a diphthong. It can be spelled **oi** or **oy**.

 coin

 boy

Read, or decode, these words and listen for the vowel sounds that are alike.

ou	ow	oi	oy
loud	plow	boil	toy
count	clown	point	enjoy
about	power	poison	royal

TURN and TALK Read these sentences. Find words with vowel sounds like the ones in **mouse** and **joy**.

The thirsty soil enjoys a shower that soaks the ground.

A crowd of people made a joyful noise as the player ran around the bases.

Diphthongs ou, ow, oi, oy

MY TURN Write a word from the box to finish each sentence. Then read the words.

| towel | pointed | mountain | oily | royal |

1. The cowboy rode his horse up a _____ .

2. The _____ palace has a tall tower.

3. I used a brown _____ to clean

   up the _____ mess.

4. The treetops were not round but _____ .

MY TURN Underline other words in the sentences that have the same vowel diphthong sounds as **house, now, boil,** and **joy**. Read the words.

My Words to Know

MY TURN Read the high-frequency words in the box. Then identify and <u>underline</u> the words in the sentences.

often	important	took

Lin went to the library often. She loved to read. Books were very important to her. She always took her library card.

TURN and TALK Work with a partner. Read the sentences. Answer the questions.

1. Yesterday, what were some things you **took** home from school?

2. What are two things that are very **important** to you?

3. What games do you **often** play?

Reading the high-frequency words with your partner will help you learn them.

The Story

A boy asked the storyteller, "Why is that flower so red?"

"Ah, that is important to know. I will tell you a story. Find the other boys and girls. Have them join us," she said.

The storyteller sat on a stump. The boys and girls sat down around her on the ground.

The storyteller began her story. The boys and girls learned how the flower came to be so red.

1. Why does the storyteller tell a story?

_____

2. What do the children learn?

_____

3. Write four words from the story. Write one with each vowel team: **ou, ow, oi, oy.**

_____

_____

My Learning Goal

I can learn more about traditions by reading about Native American life.

Informational Text

Informational text tells facts about real people, things, or events. Informational text is different from other kinds of text.

- Headings organize the information.
- Photos show what you are reading about.
- The text is usually in the present tense.

TURN and TALK Work with a partner. Think about the traditional tales you have read so far in this unit. Compare them to informational text. How are the two genres alike? How are they different? Write your thoughts on the lines below.

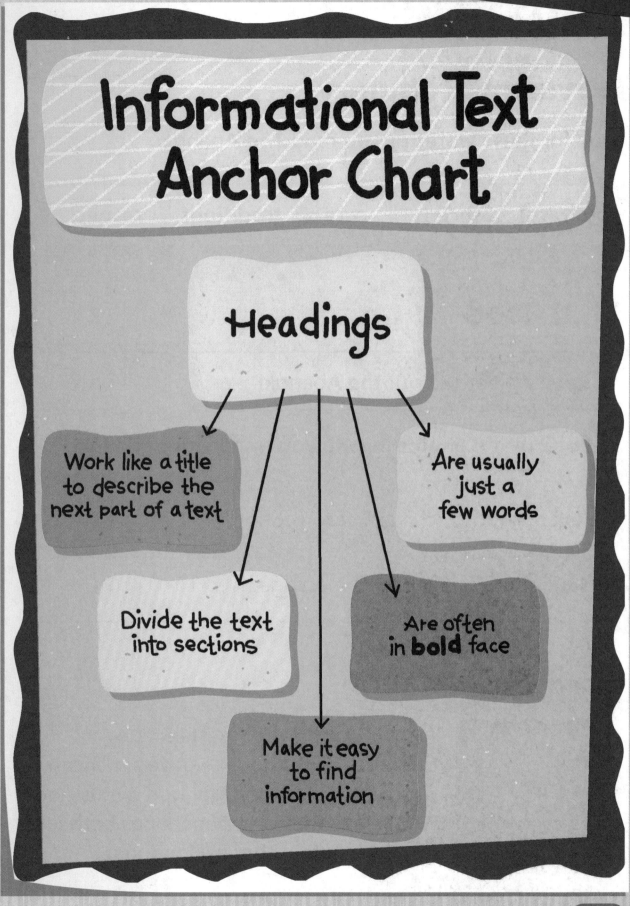

Informational Text Anchor Chart

Headings

- Work like a title to describe the next part of a text
- Are usually just a few words
- Divide the text into sections
- Are often in **bold** face
- Make it easy to find information

The Abenaki

Preview Vocabulary

Look for these words as you read *The Abenaki*.

| natural | society | cure | traditions | respect |

First Read

Read to learn about the Abenaki.

Look at the photos to help you understand the text.

Ask questions to clarify information.

Talk about the author's message.

Meet the Author

Joseph Bruchac has written many children's books about Native American people. He is a storyteller and a musician who tells stories and sings songs both in English and the Abenaki language.

Genre Informational Text

The Abenaki

By Joseph Bruchac

Illustrations by Len Ebert

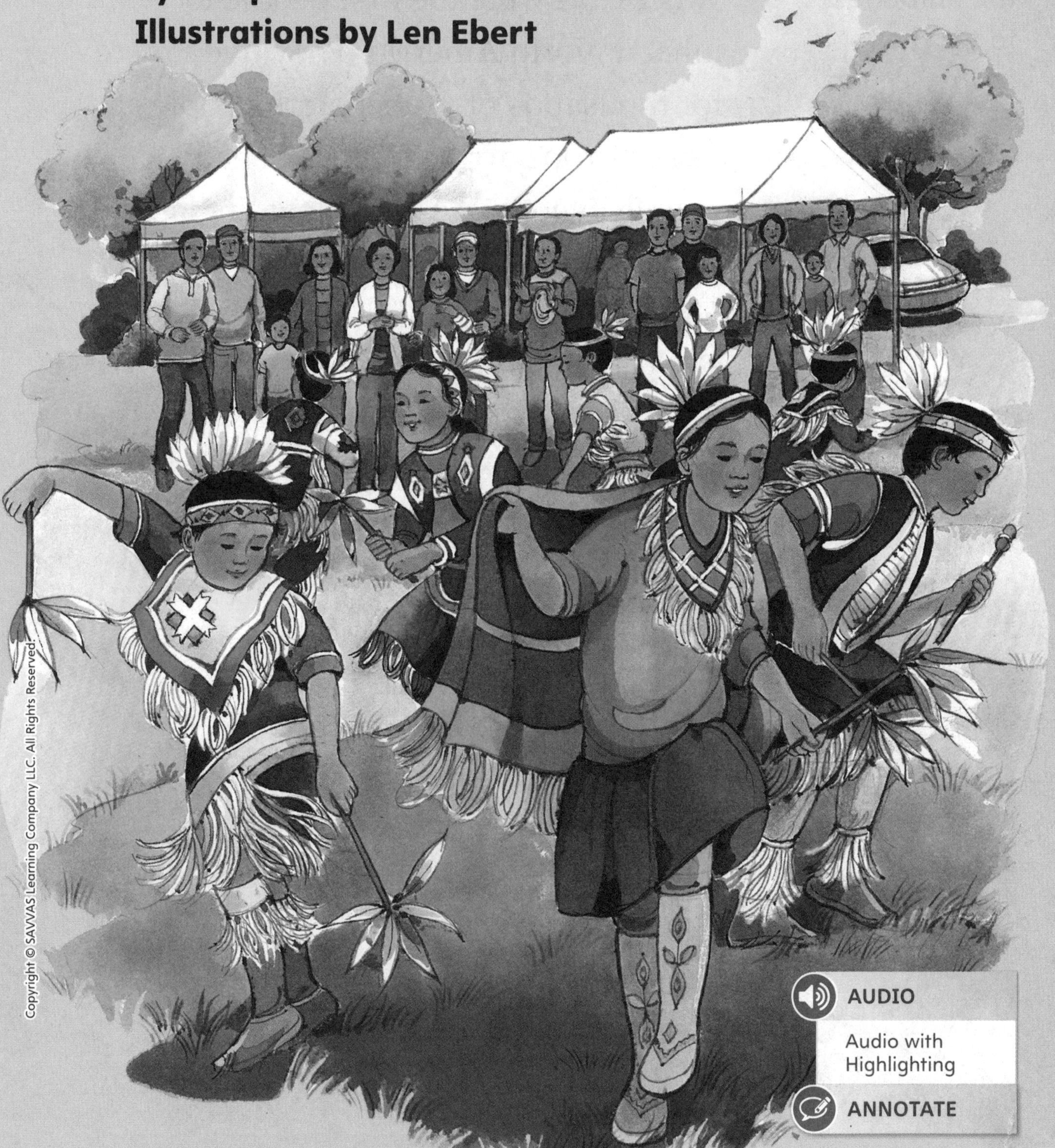

AUDIO

Audio with Highlighting

ANNOTATE

Discuss Author's Purpose

<u>Underline</u> words the author uses to tell the topic of this section.

Who are the Abenaki people?

1   The Abenaki (ah'-buh-nah-kee) are a group of Native Americans. Their homeland is the northeast. Native Americans were the first people to inhabit North America. They lived there for thousands of years before people from Europe arrived. The Abenaki people lived in Western New England. Many Abenaki still live there today. Some Abenaki also live in parts of Quebec, Canada.

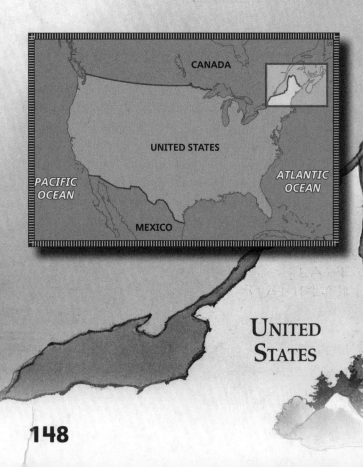

CANADA

CANADA

UNITED STATES

PACIFIC OCEAN

ATLANTIC OCEAN

MEXICO

ABENAKI HOMELANDS

UNITED STATES

2　Abenaki means "Dawn Land Place."
Dawn is the time of day when the sun rises.
The sun comes up in the east. The Abenaki
homelands are in the east. Their name means
that they live in the east, where the sun rises.
The Abenaki speak their own language.
Their language is called Algonquin.

ATLANTIC OCEAN

What was life like long ago for the Abenaki?

3   Long ago, Abenaki people lived in small communities. They called their houses wigwams. *Wigwam* means "house." A wigwam was made of thin bent wooden poles. The Abenaki covered the skinny poles with the bark of birch trees. Birch bark was a strong covering. It was effective in keeping out the wind and the rain. There were many wigwams in an Abenaki village. Their doors opened to the east, toward the dawn.

4   The Abenaki were hunters, fishers, and farmers. They survived by using the natural resources around their homes. They fished in the ocean, rivers, and lakes. They hunted in the thick forests. They grew crops such as corn, beans, and squash. They also used deerskins and the skins of other animals for clothing.

CLOSE READ

Vocabulary in Context

Sometimes you can figure out an unfamiliar word by looking for examples in the words around it. <u>Underline</u> examples of **crops** that help you understand what a crop is.

natural produced by nature, not people

151

society a group of people living together

traditions beliefs, stories, and ways of living passed down from parents to children

What is life like for the Abenaki today?

5   Today, Abenaki people are part of American society. They dress and work like other Americans. They no longer live in wigwams. They choose to live in modern homes. They live in towns and cities mostly in New England and Canada. Although the Abenaki live like many other Americans today, they keep their culture and traditions alive.

What customs from long ago are still important to the Abenaki?

6   The Abenaki still follow many of the same ways of life from long ago. They wear traditional clothing at festivals and big celebrations called powwows. Three traditional customs continue to be important to the Abenaki.

7   Storytelling—to teach children

8   Plants—to aid healing

9   Traditional songs—to give thanks

Make Connections

Highlight words that show traditional customs that are important to the Abenaki today. Connect to another text. Which of these customs helps the villagers in *The Legend of the Lady Slipper*?

Make Connections

Highlight words that tell how the first corn plant comes about.

What are Abenaki stories about?

10   Many Abenaki stories are about nature. These stories tell how the natural world came to be. One story tells how corn came to the Abenaki. In the story, a beautiful golden-haired woman helps the people. She becomes the first corn plant. Other stories tell about children. They show young people the importance of being respectful and polite.

How do Abenaki people use storytelling?

11   Abenaki storytellers teach important lessons to children. Stories make the lessons fun. They are easy to remember. For example, the story about corn also teaches a lesson about farming. It tells how to know when corn is ready to be picked. Other stories teach children lessons such as being kind to old people.

How do the Abenaki use medicine plants?

12   Long ago, the Abenaki learned to use plants as medicine. Some forest plants, such as the pine tree, helped heal sickness. Today, the Abenaki still make tea from pine needles. The tea helps cure sore throats and colds. Abenaki people use medicine plants as well as modern medicines. In fact, many modern medicines, such as aspirin, come from plants.

cure get rid of sickness

How do the Abenaki give thanks through song?

13   Nature has given the people many gifts. These gifts include food, water, and medicine plants. The Abenaki are grateful for these gifts. So, the people sing to thank nature. One song is called the "Green Corn Song." Every year when corn is ready to be harvested, or picked, the Abenaki sing this song. It gives thanks for the gift of corn.

CLOSE READ

Discuss Author's Purpose
Underline words the author used to explain how the Abenaki show they are grateful.

Why are the traditional ways of the Abenaki important to them today?

14   The Abenaki feel it is important to preserve their culture. That is why they still tell stories. It is why they use medicine plants and sing songs of thanks. These customs and traditions connect the Abenaki to the past. The Abenaki feel that knowing about the past helps them know about themselves today.

15 The Abenaki do not want to lose their traditions. Their culture teaches them how to behave. It teaches that it is good to be thankful. It teaches that it is good to respect nature and one's elders. Knowing their ways from long ago is a source of pride. These traditions help the Abenaki stay proud of their culture and their history.

respect show honor to

Develop Vocabulary

MY TURN Use the definitions on the selection pages to write what each word means.

Word	Meaning
natural	
society	
cure	
traditions	
respect	

Check for Understanding

MY TURN Look back at the text to answer the questions. Write the answers.

1. What makes this text an informational text?

_____

_____

_____

2. Why did the author include the questions in bold in this text?

_____

_____

_____

3. How is life for the Abenaki today the same as it was long ago?

_____

_____

_____

Discuss Author's Purpose

Author's purpose is the reason the author wrote a text. An author might write a text to entertain, to explain, or to give information. The words and text structure an author chooses support the author's purpose.

MY TURN Go to the Close Read notes. Underline words that show the author's purpose and use of text structure. Use what you underlined to complete the chart and discuss the author's purpose.

What did you underline?	Why do you think the author made that choice?

Make Connections

Sometimes ideas from one text will remind you of another text. That's one way of making connections. Making connections as you read can help you understand a text and remember what you read.

MY TURN Go back to the Close Read questions. Highlight connections in the text you can make. Use what you highlighted to complete the chart.

When I read . . .,	it reminded me . . .
that the Abenaki use plants to aid healing,	
about the story that tells how a woman helps people and becomes the first corn plant,	

Reflect and Share

Write to Sources

This week, you read about Native American traditions. What purpose do traditions have in a society? On another piece of paper, compose a report to tell why traditions are important.

> Traditions are beliefs, stories, and ways of living passed down from parents to children.

Use Facts and Definitions

Facts and definitions help readers understand your topic.

- Use facts about the Abenaki and the Wabanaki from the texts you read.

- Define words such as **Abenaki, traditions**, and **society**.

- Use your own words when you retell facts from texts.

In your report, write one sentence that tells why traditions are important. Use facts and definitions from this week's texts to support and explain your topic.

Weekly Question

What makes a Native American tradition?

I can use language to make connections between reading and writing.

Academic Vocabulary

Adding a suffix can change the meaning of a word. For example, a word may change from a verb to a noun. If you know the meaning of the base word, you may be able to figure out the meaning of the word with a suffix.

The word **communication** is made up of two parts:

communicate + tion = communication
(base word)   (suffix)   (new word)

Adding the suffix **-tion** to the verb **communicate** and dropping the **e** makes the noun **communication**.

MY TURN Add the suffix **-tion** to each word to build a new word. Then use each noun in a sentence.

Verb		Noun
participate		
inflate	**+ tion**	
pollute		
introduce		

Read Like a Writer, Write for a Reader

Authors organize information so it makes sense to their readers. In nonfiction, information is often organized in sections with headings.

Text from *The Abenaki*	What This Organization Tells Me
What are Abenaki stories about? Many Abenaki stories are about nature. These stories tell how the natural world came to be. One story tells how corn came to the Abenaki. . . .	The heading tells me a main idea that I will read about. The sentences under the heading give information about that main idea. Their order makes sense.

MY TURN Read the paragraph below. Write a heading for the paragraph that tells the main idea.

_____

There are many ways to enjoy nature. Start by going outdoors. Look for living things all around you. Then close your eyes and focus on what you hear and smell.

Spell Words with ou, ow, oi, oy

MY TURN Write the missing vowels to make a
spelling word from the list. Then write the word.

1. c _____ nt   _____

2. sp _____ l   _____

3. f _____ nd   _____

4. j _____ n   _____

5. ab _____ t   _____

6. l _____ al   _____

7. am _____ nt   _____

8. n _____ se   _____

9. cl _____ n   _____

10. fl _____ er   _____

Spelling Words
about
amount
count
clown
join
spoil
noise
flower
loyal
found

My Words to Know
often
took

Write a My Words to Know word to complete each sentence.

11. She _____ her lunch out of the bag.

12. We _____ visit our cousins on Sundays.

Subject-Verb Agreement

The subject and the verb in a sentence must work together. When the subject and verb work together, they agree. Add **-s** to most present tense verbs to agree with a singular subject. A **singular** subject is about **one** person or thing. If the subject is a plural noun or pronoun, do not add **-s**. A **plural** noun or pronoun is about **more than one** person or thing.

Verb	Singular Subject	Plural Subject
fall	The leaf **falls**.	The leaves **fall**.
eat	Max **eats** breakfast.	The boys **eat** breakfast.

MY TURN Edit the sentences by crossing out each incorrect verb and writing the correct word above so the subject and verb agree.

My cousins lives next door. They have two dogs.

The dogs plays in the yard. One dog bark a lot.

We hears him at my house. My sister like the dog even

though he make a lot of noise.

I can use figurative language and sound devices to write poetry.

My Learning Goal

Revise Drafts by Rearranging Words

Authors may rearrange words, or move them around, to make their writing clearer or more interesting. For example:

> for lunch
> The sandwiches∧are in the refrigerator ~~for lunch~~.
> Revised: The sandwiches for lunch are in the refrigerator.

> thirsty
> The∧boy drank a glass of water. ~~He was thirsty~~.
> Revised: The thirsty boy drank a glass of water.

MY TURN Revise the following sentence. Rearrange words to make the sentence clearer.

My friends on the playground met for a game of kickball.

_____

_____

MY TURN Revise your poem by rearranging words to make it more interesting.

Edit Adjectives

An **adjective** describes people, places, or things.
An adjective can tell how many, what size, what color,
or what shape.

three dogs   **tall** tree   **green** apple   **round** hole

The words **a, an,** and **the** are special adjectives called
articles. The refers to a specific person, place, or thing.
A does not. Use **an** before a noun that begins with a vowel.

the boy   **a** boy   **an** egg

Authors edit their writing to make sure they have used
adjectives well and articles correctly. For example:

     tiny   tall green   an
I saw a ∧ frog hop in the ∧ grass and land on ~~a~~ ant.

MY TURN Edit the sentences. Use at least one
adjective in the first sentence. Make sure the correct article
is used in the second sentence.

A lion roars.

An children are singing.

MY TURN Edit your poem for adjectives and articles.

Edit for Past, Present, and Future Verb Tenses

Verb tenses tell what happened in the past, what happens in the present, and what will happen in the future. Authors edit their writing to make sure they have used verb tenses correctly. For example:

love
I ~~loved~~ to read.
                    got
Yesterday Dad ~~gets~~ a book for me.
                    will
Tomorrow we ∧read it together.

MY TURN Edit the sentences. Change each verb to the correct tense.

I visit my grandparents next Sunday.

We walk on the river trail last week.

MY TURN Edit your poem for correct verb tenses.

Traditional Foods

These traditional foods come from different areas of the world. People have made (and eaten!) them for hundreds of years.

Since the days of the Mayans, Mexicans have eaten enchiladas. They are tortillas wrapped around meat or fish.

MOROCCO

MEXICO

In Morocco, the pasta called couscous is served with meat or vegetables.

Weekly Question

How does food help make a tradition?

MY TURN Look at the pictures of food from different parts of the world. On a sticky note, draw a picture of a traditional food you like to eat. Place it on the map and draw a line to the country it comes from.

In China, families eat dumplings for Chinese New Year.

CHINA

INDIA

In India, people enjoy a flat wheat bread called chapati.

173

Vowel Teams oo, ue, ew, ui

The vowel teams **oo**, **ue**, **ew**, and **ui** can make the vowel sound in **moon**. These vowel teams are called digraphs.

MY TURN Read, or decode, the words in the chart and listen for the vowel sound in each word.

oo	ue	ew	ui
zoo	blue	crew	suit
boot	true	jewel	juice

TURN and TALK Reread the words in the chart with a partner. Underline the vowel team in each word. Then pick a word. Have your partner use it in a sentence. Take turns until you have used two words each.

Vowel Teams oo, ue, ew, ui

MY TURN <u>Underline</u> the words in the sentences with the vowel teams **oo**, **ue**, **ew**, and **ui**. There are two vowel team words in each sentence. Then write the words in the correct column in the chart.

1. Glue the pictures of fruit to the poster.

2. Charlie lost his front tooth, but he will grow a new one.

3. We found a clue to tell us what animal likes to chew on the plants.

4. Tina fell at the pool and got a bruise.

oo	ue	ew	ui

My Words to Know

MY TURN Read the high-frequency words in the box. Then identify and <u>underline</u> them in the sentence.

hear	idea	enough

Do you have enough time to hear my idea?

Write a sentence that uses each word.

_____

_____

_____

TURN and TALK Read each sentence aloud with a partner. Have your partner find and name the high-frequency word in your sentence. Take turns.

Sue's New School

Sue stopped outside the classroom. Sue's family had just moved, and it was her first day at a new school. "Moving was not my idea!" she thought. "I liked my old school."

Sue sighed and went into the room. She saw fruit and other food on the desks. A girl gave her a big card. It said, "Yay for Sue! We hope you'll like it here!"

Sue smiled. She knew she would.

1. Why does Sue stop outside the classroom?

_____

2. Why is there food on the desks?

_____

3. Write one word from the story with each vowel team: **oo**, **ue**, **ew** and **ui**.

_____

_____

My Learning Goal I can learn more about traditions by reading a story about traditional foods.

Procedural Text

My Food, Your Food is a realistic fiction story that ends with a recipe. A recipe is an example of **procedural text**. A procedural text has **instructions**, or orders to follow, for completing a task. It often includes:

- **numbered steps,** or a related sequence of actions that tell you what to do first, next, and last.

- **headings** and **pictures** to help you understand the steps.

TURN and TALK Preview the recipe in *My Food, Your Food*. Name two types of text features in the text. Tell a partner how you think the text features will help you follow what the recipe says to do.

Procedural Text Anchor Chart

Purpose: to tell how to do something

Text Features in Procedural Text

- Headings
- Labels for pictures
- Numbered steps

How to eat yogurt

1. Open the container of yogurt.

2. Use a spoon to put some yogurt in a bowl.

3. Enjoy eating the yogurt!

1.
yogurt

2.
spoon

3.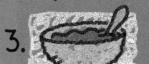

My Food, Your Food

Preview Vocabulary

Look for these words as you read *My Food, Your Food.*

| sauce | plain | products | spicy | ingredients |

First Read

Read to learn about foods from different cultures.

Look at illustrations to help you understand the text.

Ask questions to clarify information.

Talk about what you found interesting.

Meet *the* Author

Lisa Bullard writes everything from informational books to mysteries. She also teaches children and adults how to write their own books. She has written books about people around the world, including *My Clothes, Your Clothes* and *My Language, Your Language.*

Genre Realistic Fiction/Procedural Text

My Food, Your Food

By Lisa Bullard
Illustrated by Christine M. Schneider

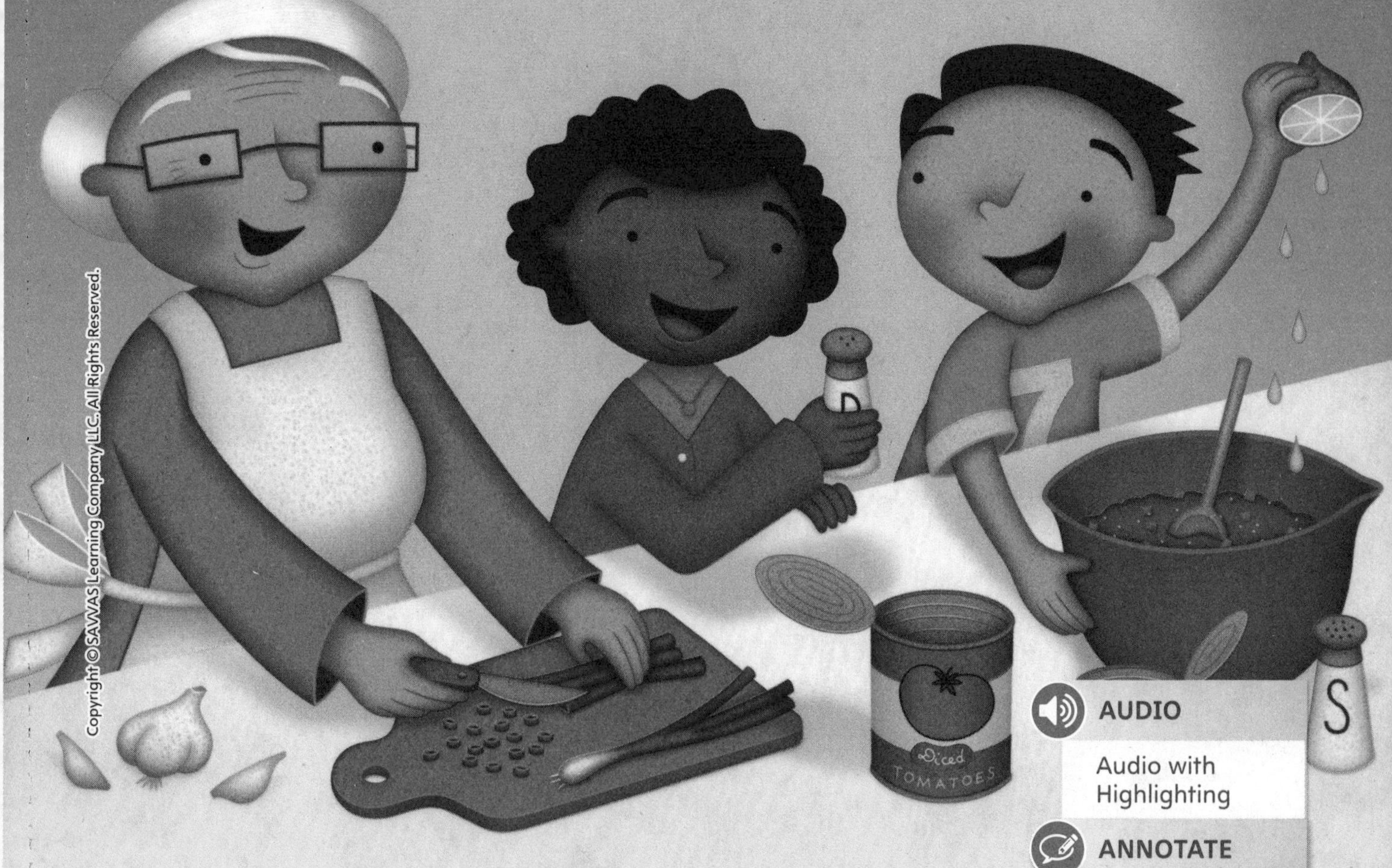

AUDIO
Audio with Highlighting
ANNOTATE

Chapter One
It's Food Week!

1 Hi, I'm Manuel. My teacher, Ms. Chen, says we're learning about food this week. We each get to tell about **something special that our family eats.**

egg rolls

2 I whisper to Ms. Chen what I want to talk about. **I'm going to surprise our class!**

Understand Text Features

<u>Underline</u> the label for a kind of soup that is one of the foods the students are learning about.

This week:
Foods of
the World

borscht   kimchee

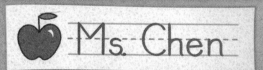

Ms. Chen

183

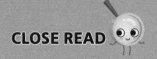
Make Inferences

Highlight the words that help you infer, or figure out, what foods Manuel may be thinking of when he says the words in bold print.

3 Tonight, Abuela is making a **tasty dinner**. Abuela means "Grandmother." She cooks the kind of food she grew up eating, first in Mexico and then in California.

4   Her burritos and salsa make my stomach happy! Now I can't wait for my turn to talk on Friday.

Does your family have a favorite dinner?

185

sauce a liquid served with food to make the food taste better

Chapter Two
Noodles from Different Places

spaghetti

Italy

5   At school on Tuesday, it's Tony's turn to talk. "My great-grandparents came here from Italy," he says. "My family loves **spaghetti with marinara sauce.** That's a kind of tomato sauce."

6   Ms. Chen tells us that people have moved to the United States from all over the world. They still make many of the foods from their home countries. **Spaghetti and marinara sauce are Italian foods.**

What parts of the world does your family come from? Do they like to eat any special foods from those places?

CLOSE READ

Understand Text Features

Look for the feature in a box that asks you questions. Underline the first question in the box.

7   Ms. Chen shows us another kind of noodle dish. It's called yi mein. "Many cultures eat noodles," she says. "My parents moved here from China. They use **chopsticks** to eat their noodles."

8 A cafeteria worker brings in plain noodles so we can try using chopsticks. Ms. Chen shows us how.

9 **Noodles sure are sneaky!**

Make Inferences
Highlight the sentence that helps you know how Manuel feels about using chopsticks.

plain simple; nothing on it

Chopsticks are very common in parts of Asia. Do you know how to use them?

Chapter Three

Flat Bread, Puffy Bread

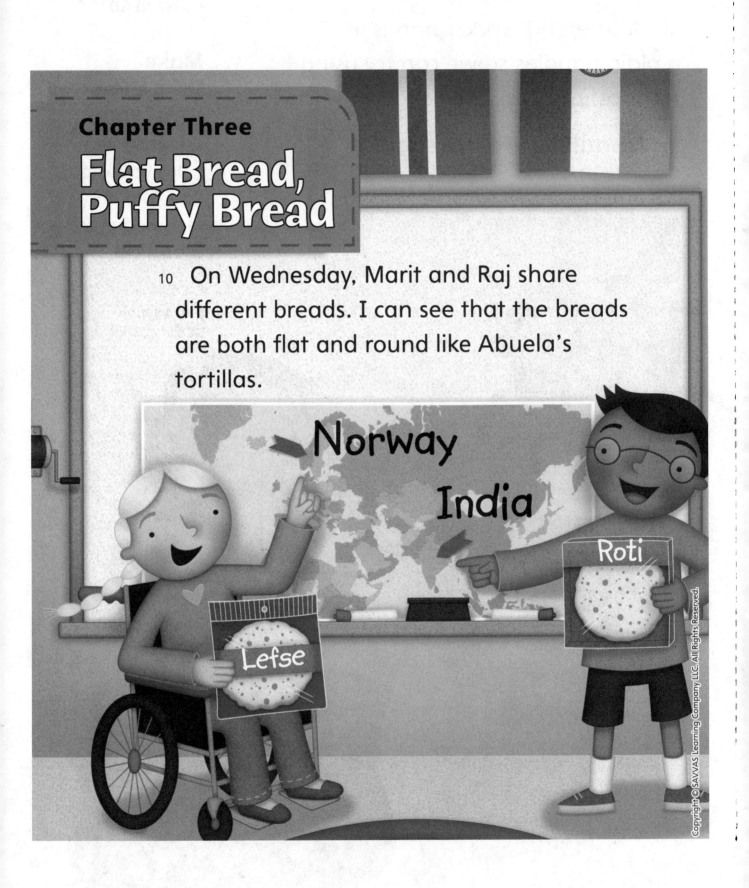

10   On Wednesday, Marit and Raj share different breads. I can see that the breads are both flat and round like Abuela's tortillas.

Norway

India

Lefse

Roti

11 Raj's bread is called roti. His dad ate it growing up in India. It's chewy and good.

12 Marit's bread is called lefse. It's from Norway. That's where her family comes from.

13 **It melts in my mouth.**

Make Inferences

In the sentence shaped like a hill, highlight the words that help you know if Manuel likes lefse.

CLOSE READ

Vocabulary in Context

Underline words that help you understand what **Shabbat** means.

14   Then Lara shows us a braided bread called challah. It's puffy instead of flat.

15   Lara's family is Jewish. They eat challah every Friday night. It's part of their religious tradition called **Shabbat.**

16 Ms. Chen tells us that many religions have traditions with food. For example, some people don't eat pork because of their religion.

Understand Text Features

Underline the heading that tells you the topic of this chapter.

Chapter Four
Families Make Different Choices

17 On Thursday, Jayla shows us her fishing pole. She tells us about fishing with her dad. They **cook** and **eat** the fish they catch.

18 "People have hunted and fished for food for thousands of years," Ms. Chen says.

19 She also says some families choose not to eat meat or fish. Others don't eat anything from animals.

20 **That means no meat, eggs, or dairy products.**

products things people use or eat

21 Thursday after school, Abuela and I get busy in the kitchen. **We're making the food I'm going to talk about in school.**

Do you help your family cook meals? What food would you like to learn how to make?

CLOSE READ

Vocabulary in Context

<u>Underline</u> the words that help you know what **salsa** means.

spicy having a strong, sharp flavor

Chapter Five
Finally, Friday

22 It's finally Friday. Have you guessed my food? "**Salsa** is a Mexican sauce," I say. "Abuela and I make ours with tomatoes. I like it spicy."

Mexico

salsa

198

23 Ms. Chen brought salsa for everyone. "There are tomatoes in lots of foods," she says. "Remember, they're in Tony's Italian marinara sauce too."

24 Here's what I learned this week: **even when food is different, it still can be alike!**

25 Make Your Own Salsa

Ingredients

1 can (28 ounces,
   or 794 grams) diced
   tomatoes

1 can (4 ounces,
   or 113 g)
   diced green chiles

2 green onions, thinly sliced

1 clove minced garlic

1 tablespoon lemon or lime juice

1/8 teaspoon salt

1/8 teaspoon pepper

Directions

You can make salsa just like Manuel
did! You'll need an adult to help you
with some tasks, such as opening
cans, chopping, and using a blender.

1) Wash your hands.

2) Drain the tomatoes. Set aside 1/4
   cup of the tomato juice.

3) In a large bowl, mix together 1/4 cup tomato juice, drained tomatoes, and the other ingredients. You can leave out the green chiles if you don't like spicy food.

4) For chunky salsa, stir together and enjoy!

5) For smoother salsa, put everything into a blender. Blend on the slowest setting for just a few seconds. Continue blending a few seconds at a time until the salsa is as smooth as you like.

6) Serve the salsa with tortilla chips or with Mexican dishes like tacos or burritos.

Vocabulary in Context

Antonyms are words with opposite meanings. <u>Underline</u> a word that is the opposite of **chunky**.

Develop Vocabulary

MY TURN Answer the questions in the chart.
Use the vocabulary words in your responses.

Word	Questions
products	What dairy products have you tried?
sauce	What kind of sauce do you like on spaghetti?
plain, spicy	Which foods do you like better, plain or spicy? Why?
ingredient	What is your favorite ingredient on a pizza? Why?

Check for Understanding

MY TURN Look back at the text to answer the questions. Write the answers.

1. What part of the text is realistic fiction? What part of the text is procedural, or has instructions that tell how to do something?

_____

_____

_____

2. Why do you think the author included a salsa recipe? What is the recipe's first step?

_____

_____

_____

3. How do the children feel about sharing their special foods with the class? How do you know?

_____

_____

_____

Understand Text Features

Authors use **text features** to help readers locate and understand information.

- **Headings** tell what parts of the text will be about.

- **Illustrations,** or pictures, give extra information.

- **Labels** give more information about a picture.

- **Texts in boxes** ask questions or tell facts.

- **Numbered steps** tell how to do parts of a task in order.

MY TURN Go to the Close Read notes. Underline text features. Complete the chart.

Text Features the Author Used	Information It Helped Me Understand

Make Inferences

When you make inferences, you use evidence and what you already know to support your understanding of a text.

MY TURN Go back to the Close Read notes. Highlight words that help you figure out what Manuel is thinking. Use what you highlighted to complete the chart.

What I Highlighted	What I Know	My Inference

Reflect and Share

Talk About It

You read about some traditional foods. Talk about your own traditions. What traditional foods does your family enjoy? Choose one, and tell how it is prepared.

Give and Follow Oral Instructions

Here are some tips for giving clear instructions.

- Tell what to do in order.

- Use words like **first, then,** and **last**.

When your partner tells you a recipe, repeat it back.

First, put 2 cups of water in a pot. Then add 1 cup of rice.

- Restate the instructions. That way you will know if you understood.

Weekly Question

How does food help make a tradition?

I can use language to make connections between reading and writing.

Academic Vocabulary

You have learned many different words in this unit. One word you have learned is **culture**. Complete the word web with words that have something to do with the word **culture**.

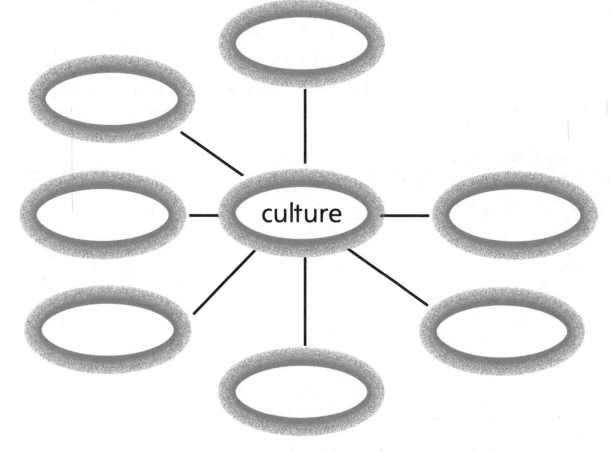

TURN and **TALK** Tell your partner about your word web. Explain why you chose the words you did.

culture

Read Like a Writer, Write for a Reader

Authors organize the information in their writing to make it clear to their readers. Look back at the recipe in the text.

Text from "Make Your Own Salsa"	What This Structure Tells Me
Ingredients	This part lists what you need to make salsa. It is important because you need to make sure you have everything before you begin.
Directions	This part gives the steps, in order, for making salsa. It is important because you need to follow the steps in order so that the salsa is made correctly.

MY TURN Write a recipe that tells how to make your favorite sandwich.

_____

_____

_____

_____

Spell Words with Vowel Teams oo, ue, ew, ui

MY TURN The vowel sound in **moon** can be spelled **oo**, **ue**, **ew**, or **ui**. Write a Spelling Word or a My Words to Know word to complete each sentence.

1. A _____ is a kind of bird.

2. The opposite of false is _____ .

3. The _____ is my favorite time of day.

4. They _____ about which show to watch.

5. I fell and got a _____ on my arm.

6. There is _____ room for you.

7. I _____ a picture to go with my story.

8. Five is _____ than six.

9. There is your _____ to go on stage.

10. A _____ covers a growing butterfly.

11. Speak louder so I can _____ you.

12. A _____ on a boat is fun.

Spelling Words
fewer
true
cue
goose
drew
cocoon
afternoon
argue
bruise
cruise

My Words to Know
hear
enough

Adverbs

Adverbs tell about things that happen.

An adverb can tell	Example
how something happens.	We walk **quickly**.
about **time**, or **when** something happens.	We walk **early**.
about **place**, or **where** something happens.	We walk **outside**.

MY TURN Edit this draft by adding adverbs to the sentences. You may use adverbs from the Word Bank.

Word Bank

down   carefully   sometime   tonight   outside

I helped make dinner. I filled the big pot with

water and got the pasta from the shelf. I stirred

the sauce. We ate on the patio. I want to cook again!

I can use figurative language and
sound devices to write poetry.

My Learning Goal

Edit for Nouns

A singular noun names a person, place, or thing.
Plural nouns name more than one of these. Common
nouns are general names. Proper nouns name
something specific and are capitalized.

MY TURN Edit this draft. Read once to look for
mistakes with singular and plural nouns. Read it again
to look for mistakes with common and proper nouns.

Last saturday I helped mr. Chin make a

fruit salad. He cut up a melon, two bananaes,

three peachs, and an orange. We

mixed all the fruites together in one big bowls.

Then I added some grapes. We served the salad in

small dishs to everyone at the summer picnic.

MY TURN Edit your poem to make sure you
used nouns correctly.

Edit for Prepositions and Prepositional Phrases

Prepositions are words like **in, on, by,** and **under**. Prepositional phrases begin with prepositions.

Authors edit their writing to make sure they have used prepositions and prepositional phrases correctly.

MY TURN Edit this draft. Check that prepositions have been used correctly.

My family wanted to have pizza by dinner. We got

on our car and drove above town to our favorite

restaurant. We sat in a table over the door. We

ordered a pizza by mushrooms. When the waiter put

the pizza at the table, I couldn't wait to eat!

MY TURN Edit your poem to make sure you used prepositions and prepositional phrases correctly.

Publish and Celebrate

Read your poem to classmates.
When you read, follow these tips:

Poems are meant to be read aloud so listeners can hear the sounds of the words.

1. Speak clearly and loudly enough so that everyone can understand you and hear you.
2. Read with expression.
3. Don't pause at the end of a line unless you've placed a comma or period there.
4. Look up at your audience every now and then.

Reflect

MY TURN Complete the sentences.

The sensory details that best created imagery in my poem are

_____

_____

The words or phrases I think are most interesting are

_____

_____

UNIT THEME

Our Traditions

TURN and TALK

Share It With your partner, write something you learned from each text about stories people tell or other things they share. Use this information to help you answer the Essential Question.

WEEK 3

Interstellar Cinderella and Cendrillon: An Island Cinderella

_____

_____

Gendrillon: An Island Cinderella
By Tracey Baptiste
Illustrated by Sophie Diao

INTERSTELLAR CINDERELLA
By Deborah Underwood
Illustrated by Meg Hunt

★ BOOK CLUB

WEEK 2

The Legend of the Lady Slipper

_____

_____

THE LEGEND OF THE LADY SLIPPER
By Lise Lunge-Larsen and Margi Preus
Illustrated by Andrea Arroyo

★ BOOK CLUB

WEEK 1

Fables

_____

_____

from FABLES
by Arnold Lobel

THE HEN AND THE APPLE TREE
THE FROGS AT THE RAINBOW'S END
THE MOUSE AT THE SEASHORE

WEEK **6**

The Abenaki

THE ABENAKI
By Joseph Bruchac
Illustrations by Len Ebert

WEEK **4**

BOOK CLUB

BOOK CLUB

WEEK **5**

My Food, Your Food

My Food, Your Food
By Lisa Bullard
Illustrated by Christine M. Schneider

Essential Question

MY TURN

In your notebook, answer the Essential Question: What makes a tradition?

BOOK CLUB

Project

WEEK **6**

Now it is time to apply what you learned about traditions in your **WEEK 6 PROJECT:** Celebrate at School!

s Sound Spelled c; j Sound Spelled g or dge

The letter **c** can make the **s** sound you hear in **see**. A **c** makes the **s** sound when it comes before the letter **e**, **i**, or **y**. Read these words.

cent   pencil   icy

The letter **g** can make the **j** sound you hear in **just**. A **g** sometimes makes the **j** sound when it comes before the letter **e**, **i**, or **y**. The letter group **dge** also stands for the **j** sound. Read these words.

page   giraffe   gym   badge

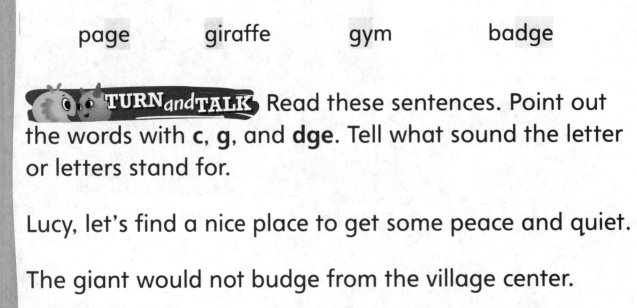 **TURN** and **TALK** Read these sentences. Point out the words with **c**, **g**, and **dge**. Tell what sound the letter or letters stand for.

Lucy, let's find a nice place to get some peace and quiet.

The giant would not budge from the village center.

Twice, George and Bruce sat on the ledge by the flag.

s Sound Spelled c; j Sound Spelled g or dge

 **MY TURN** Practice reading the words in the box. Then use the words to complete the sentences.

circus	dodge	bridge
strange	fancy	germs

1. We looked down from the _____ at the river.

2. The clowns at the _____ squeezed into the tiny car.

3. I have never seen that _____ bug before.

4. Wash your hands so _____ don't spread.

5. Dora had to be quick to _____ the ball.

6. The gift had a _____ bow on it.

My Words to Know

 MY TURN Read the high-frequency words in the box. Identify and <u>underline</u> them in the sentence below.

group	book	almost

Our teacher said, "Our group is almost finished reading this book!"

TURN *and* **TALK** Read the clues below to a partner. Your partner should guess which word goes with each meaning. Take turns.

 **Clues Set 1**

something you read

nearly

a bunch

 **Clues Set 2**

just about

many together

words on pages

Spell Words with s Sound Spelled c and j Sound Spelled g or dge

MY TURN Guide words tell the first and last word on a dictionary page. Write the list word you would find between each pair of guide words.

mew-middle   **gift-glad**

mice   _____

Write the rest of the Spelling Words and the My Words to Know in alphabetical order. To alphabetize words, say the alphabet to yourself. Write the words in ABC order. If two words start with the same letter, look at the second letter for which comes first.

_____   _____

_____   _____

_____   _____

Spelling Words
badge
edge
judge
pace
mice
peace
huge
giraffe
gems
price

My Words to Know
group
almost

CELEBRATE AT SCHOOL!

RESEARCH

Activity

School traditions are important. Write an opinion letter to your principal. Tell about a tradition you think your school should begin. Give reasons the school should have the tradition.

Let's Read!

This week you will read three articles about traditions. Today's article explains what makes a tradition.

① **A Tradition to Remember**

② **Blanket Toss!**

③ **Birthdays Around the World**

Generate Questions

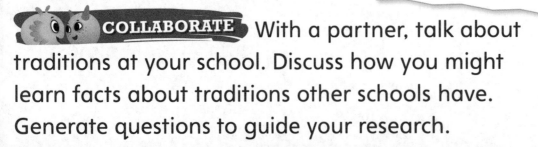 **COLLABORATE** With a partner, talk about traditions at your school. Discuss how you might learn facts about traditions other schools have. Generate questions to guide your research.

Use Academic Words

 COLLABORATE Choose a school tradition you want to celebrate. Talk about it with your partner. Use the academic vocabulary you have learned. Use these words when you write your letter to the principal.

Academic Vocabulary

belief	purpose
culture	maintain
communication	

School Traditions Research Plan

A research plan is a guide you will follow as you work on your project. Complete this plan with help from your teacher. Every day you will do a step to follow the plan.

Day 1 List questions and key words to guide research.

Day 2 _____

Day 3 Write an opinion letter to your principal.

Day 4 _____

Day 5 Present your letter to your classmates.

Here's What I Think

In an opinion paragraph, an author introduces the topic and states her opinion about it. An **opinion** is what someone thinks. It cannot be proven true or false.

Next, the author gives reasons that support her opinion. A reason may include facts. A **fact** is a statement you can prove to be true. An author also uses linking words to connect her opinion and reasons. Finally, she restates her opinion in a concluding statement.

Opinion Phrases: I believe, the best, my favorite

Linking Words: because, also, finally

COLLABORATE Read "Blanket Toss!" with a partner. Then complete the chart.

Author's topic	
Author's opinion	
Words the author uses to connect ideas	
Reasons and facts the author gives	

Search Online

Your letter to the principal will be stronger if you include facts to support your opinions. Keywords can help you find facts on the Internet. Choose the best keywords to search for information about school traditions.

1. _____

2. _____

Use the keywords to identify and gather relevant sources and information to answer your questions about school traditions. It is a relevant source if it answers your question. If you don't understand a source, ask an adult or find another source you do understand.

COLLABORATE What information did you learn from the keyword search? Was it relevant? Did you understand it? Did it answer your questions? Discuss with your partner. Are there other keywords you should try?

_____

_____

_____

_____

Opinion Letter

Authors use opinion phrases and linking words to tell and support their opinions. In a letter, the author uses a capital letter in the greeting and the closing.

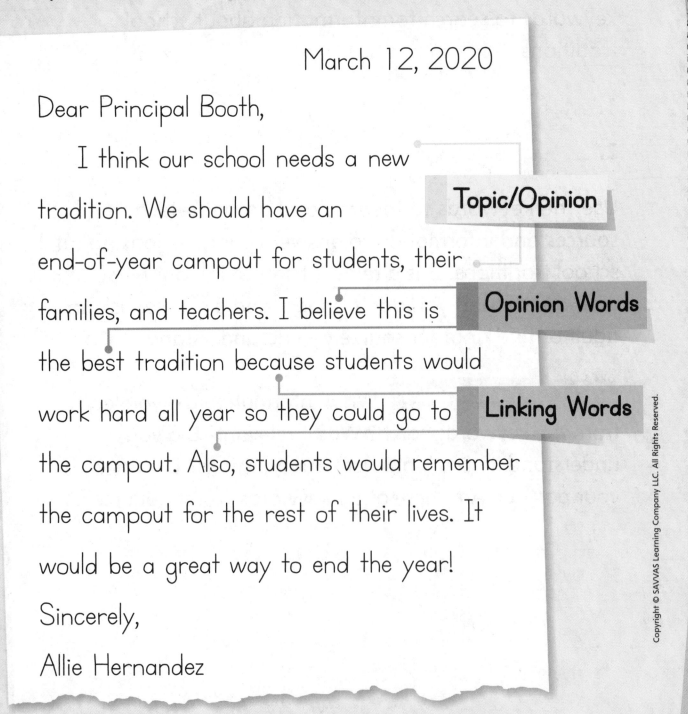

March 12, 2020

Dear Principal Booth,

    I think our school needs a new tradition. We should have an end-of-year campout for students, their families, and teachers. I believe this is the best tradition because students would work hard all year so they could go to the campout. Also, students would remember the campout for the rest of their lives. It would be a great way to end the year!

Sincerely,

Allie Hernandez

Topic/Opinion

Opinion Words

Linking Words

Cite Sources

A primary source comes from someone who saw an event. A secondary source comes from someone who learned about the event from other sources. When you use primary and secondary sources, you need to cite, or name, them. This tells readers where you got your information.

This is the information you need to cite an online article:

1. Name of author (last name, first name)
2. Title of the article (in quotations)
3. Title of the home page (in italics)
4. Web
5. Date you read the information

Example: Wallis, Camden. "Another Great Campout." *School News*. Web. March 16, 2020.

COLLABORATE Cite an online source you used. Tell if it is a primary or a secondary source.

Write a Thank You Note

After you send an opinion letter to your principal, you may want to write the principal a thank you note. Thank your principal for reading your letter and thinking about your idea. A thank you note often has five parts. The body is usually shorter than a friendly letter.

March 30, 2020 — **Heading**

Dear Principal Booth, — **Greeting**

    Thank you for reading my letter about the end-of-year campout. You are a great principal who cares about the students. — **Body**

Sincerely, — **Closing**

Allie Hernandez, Nick Bell, Jana McCoy — **Signature**

COLLABORATE With a partner, plan and write a thank you note to your principal. Thank him or her for thinking about your idea for a new school tradition.

Revise

COLLABORATE When you revise, it helps to read your writing out loud. You may need to add, delete, or rearrange words, phrases, or even sentences. Reread your opinion letter with your partner. How does it sound?

Did you...

☐ clearly state your opinion?

☐ give reasons that support your opinion?

☐ use opinion words?

☐ use linking words to connect your reasons to your opinion?

Edit

COLLABORATE As you work with your partner to edit your opinion letter, think about conventions you learned this week.

Did you...

☐ use a capital letter in your greeting and closing?

☐ capitalize the month in your heading?

Share

COLLABORATE With your partner, read your opinion letter to another pair of classmates. Ask them to pretend they are the principal and to ask any questions they may have about your opinion. Remember to follow these rules for speaking and listening.

- Speak clearly at a pace that is not too fast or too slow.

- As you share ideas, use the conventions of language. Use complete sentences and correct subject-verb agreement.

- Allow listeners to ask questions.

- Listen carefully to questions.

- Ask questions after your partner reads his or her letter.

Reflect

MY TURN Complete the sentences.

I'm most proud of _____

in my letter because _____

_____

The next time I write an opinion letter I will _____

_____

_____

Reflect on Your Goals

Look back at your unit goals at the beginning of this unit. Use a different color to rate yourself again.

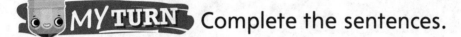 Complete the sentences.

Reflect on Your Reading

I would tell my friend to read _____

_____

_____

from this unit because _____

_____

_____

Reflect on Your Writing

I most enjoyed writing _____

because _____

_____

_____

Making a Difference

Essential Question

Why is it important to connect with other people?

▶ Watch

"Making Connections" to learn ways to connect with other people in a community.

TURN and TALK How does each person in the video make a difference?

SAVVAS realize™

Go ONLINE for all lessons.

- ▶ VIDEO
- 🔊 AUDIO
- 🎮 GAME
- ✏️ ANNOTATE
- 📖 BOOK
- 🔍 RESEARCH

Reading Workshop

Reading-Writing Bridge

- Academic Vocabulary
- Read Like a Writer, Write for a Reader
- Spelling • Language and Conventions

Writing Workshop

Narrative Nonfiction

- Introduce and Immerse
- Develop Elements • Develop Structure
- Writer's Craft • Publish, Celebrate, and Assess

Project-Based Inquiry

- Inquire • Research • Collaborate

Independent Reading

When you read on your own, choose books on the unit theme that you want to read.

As you read, make sure you understand the text. If you do not, you can do one of these things:

1. **Reread.** Go back and read sentences again. See if you missed important information.

2. **Use your background knowledge.** Think of what you know about the topic. That may help you understand new information.

3. **Check for visual cues.** See if there are photos, illustrations, or other graphics that help explain the text.

4. **Ask questions.** Ask others who have read the book if they can explain something you don't understand. Ask your teacher to help too.

My Reading Log

Date	Book	Pages Read	Minutes Read	My Ratings
				☺ 😐 ☹
				☺ 😐 ☹
				☺ 😐 ☹
				☺ 😐 ☹
				☺ 😐 ☹
				☺ 😐 ☹

Unit Goals

In this unit, you will

- read narrative nonfiction
- write a personal narrative
- learn about connections among people

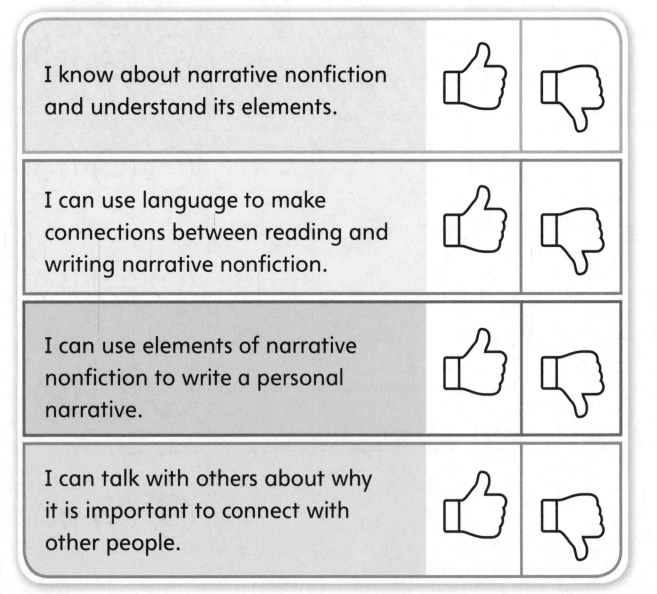

MY TURN **Color** the pictures to answer.

I know about narrative nonfiction and understand its elements.	👍 👎
I can use language to make connections between reading and writing narrative nonfiction.	👍 👎
I can use elements of narrative nonfiction to write a personal narrative.	👍 👎
I can talk with others about why it is important to connect with other people.	👍 👎

Academic Vocabulary

discuss	connect	responsible	equal	improve

In this unit, you will read about real people who make a difference. You will also **discuss** why it's important to **connect** with other people and **improve** your community. Think about who is **responsible** for making the world a better place. Do we all play an **equal** role?

TURN and TALK Use the Academic Vocabulary words to talk with your partner about ways kids can make a difference. The pictures will help you.

People Who Were First

Some people are the first to accomplish something important. They inspire others to follow them.

Astronaut Ellen Ochoa was the first Hispanic American woman to fly in space. She spent about 40 days in space on four different missions.

Dr. Norman Shumway was the first doctor in the United States to transplant a human heart. His work helped many people live longer.

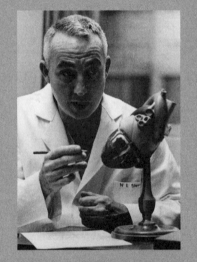

Pilot Bessie Coleman was the first African American woman to become a pilot. She also had Native American ancestors. Coleman put on one-woman air shows.

Baseball legend Jackie Robinson was the first African American to play Major League Baseball. Before Robinson, African Americans were not allowed in the league. Robinson became an All-Star.

Weekly Question

How can others inspire us to reach a goal?

MY TURN Do you feel inspired when you read about these people? Who else might inspire you? Write your thoughts here.

Closed Syllables VC/V

A syllable is a word part that has just one vowel sound. When a syllable ends with a consonant, it is called a closed syllable. The vowel usually has a short sound.

| rap | The **a** has a short **a** sound. |

Many words have more than one syllable. A two-syllable word may have a vowel-consonant-vowel (VCV) pattern. When you divide the word into syllables after the consonant (VC/V), the vowel in the first syllable is usually short.

| rapid | rap/id | The **a** has a short **a** sound. |

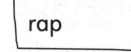 **MY TURN** Read, or decode, the VC/V words in the box. Divide the words into two syllables.

| pedal | limit | robin | punish |

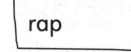 **TURN and TALK** Take turns with a partner. For each word in the box, read each syllable separately. Then blend the syllables to read the word.

Closed Syllables VC/V

MY TURN Divide each VC/V word. Write the syllables in the boxes next to the word. Blend the syllables and read each word.

1. wagon

2. finish

3. salad

4. habit

5. closet

6. lemon

7. model

8. visit

My Words to Know

MY TURN Some words are used often. These words are called high-frequency words. You will have to remember these words. Often, you can't sound them out. Read the words in the box. Identify and <u>underline</u> the words in the paragraph.

sometimes	mountains	young

When Rick was young, he lived near mountains. Sometimes he climbed to the top of the highest peak. The view was amazing!

TURN and TALK Work with a partner. Decide which word from the box goes with each clue. Form the letters correctly as you write each word. Use connecting strokes to connect the letters.

1. the opposite of old _____

2. very tall, steep hills _____

3. not all the time _____

Helen's Story

Helen was never good at sports. Then her dad took her to the pool in the park. "They can teach you to swim here," he told Helen.

Now she's a star on the swim team! She wins medals!

Sometimes Helen hears a young child say, "I'm not good at sports."

Helen says, "Try swimming!"

1. How did Helen's dad help her?

_____

_____

2. How does Helen try to help others?

_____

_____

3. Draw a line between the syllables in these words. Read the words. Then underline them in the story.

never   medals

My Learning Goal

I know about narrative nonfiction and understand its elements.

Biography

A **biography** is the true story of a real person's life written by someone else. It can be about a person's whole life or just a part of it. In a biography, the author

- tells about events in chronological order, or the order in which they happened.

- uses words such as **once, at first,** and **finally** to talk about when events happened.

- often tells about the person's achievements.

TURN and TALK Tell a partner about a text you have read. Look back at the features of a biography. Discuss with your partner why the text you read was or was not a biography. Take notes on your discussion.

Biography Anchor Chart

Who Says Women Can't Be Doctors?

Preview Vocabulary

Look for these words as you read *Who Says Women Can't Be Doctors? The Story of Elizabeth Blackwell.*

allowed	challenge	determined	refused	accept

First Read

Look at the title and the illustrations.

Ask questions about the text before you read it

Read to learn about Elizabeth Blackwell.

Talk about what you found most interesting.

Meet the Author

Tanya Lee Stone is an award-winning author of many books for children and teens. She likes to write books that tell the stories of unknown or not well-known women and people of color.

Genre Narrative Nonfiction

Who Says Women Can't Be Doctors?
The Story of Elizabeth Blackwell

by Tanya Lee Stone
illustrated by Marjorie Priceman

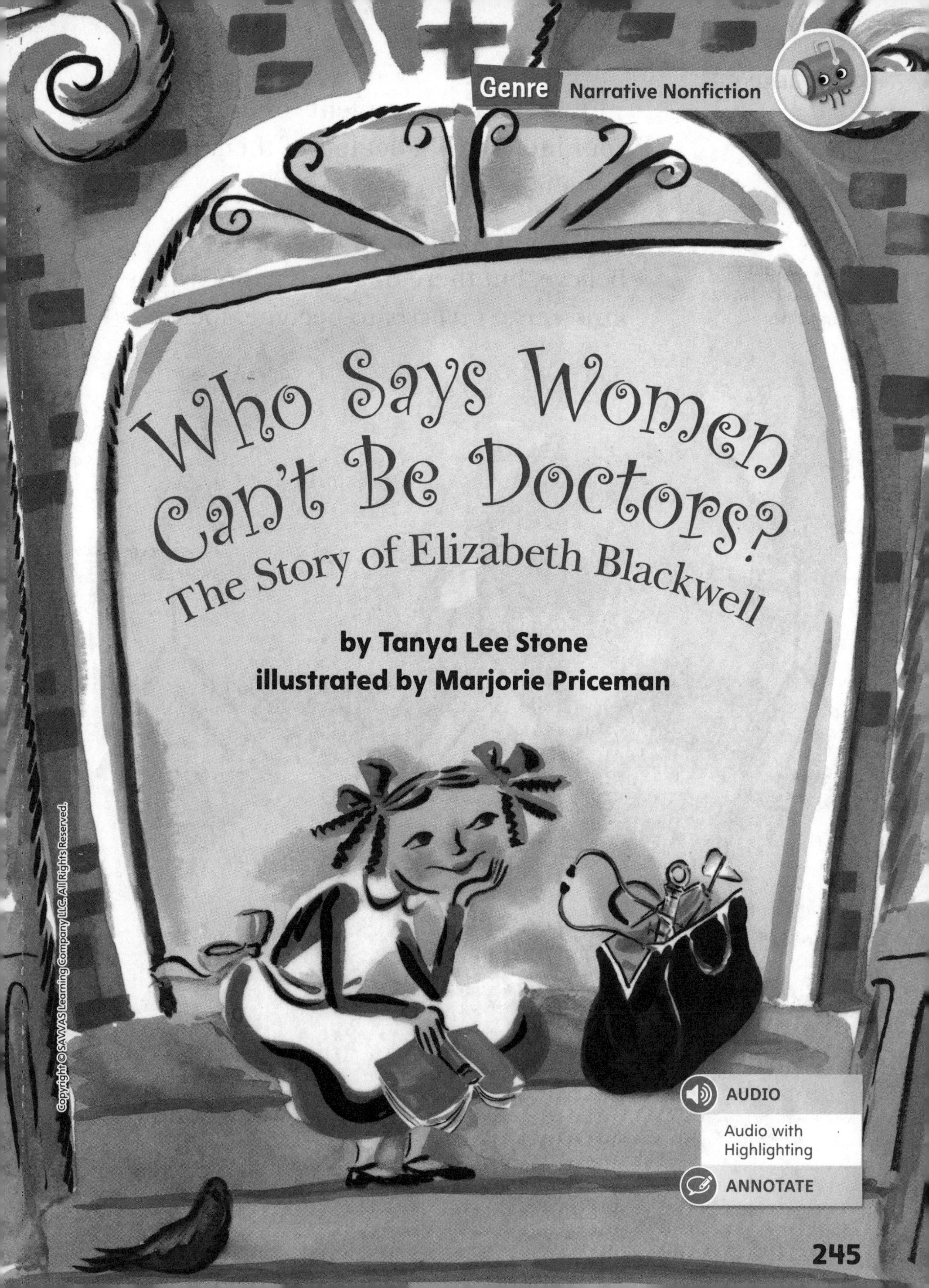

AUDIO
Audio with Highlighting
ANNOTATE

allowed told you
could do or have
something

1   I'll bet you've met plenty of doctors in
your life. And I'll bet lots of them were
women.

2   Well, you might find this hard to
believe, but there once was a time when
girls weren't *allowed* to become doctors.

3   Back in the 1830s, there were lots of things girls couldn't be. Girls were only supposed to become wives and mothers. Or maybe teachers, or seamstresses.

4   Being a doctor was definitely not an option.

5   What do you think changed all that? Or should I say … WHO?

CLOSE READ

Identify Text Structure

A biography is written in time, or chronological, order. The author starts when the person is young. <u>Underline</u> the words that tell when this biography begins.

challenge
something difficult that requires extra work

6   Elizabeth Blackwell, that's who. A tiny wisp of a girl who wanted to explore around every corner and who never walked away from a challenge.

Ask and Answer Questions

Highlight any text that you can ask questions about. What is one question you might ask about the text you highlighted?

7   This was a girl who had once carried her brother over her head until he backed down from their fight.

8   A girl who tried sleeping on the hard floor with no covers, just to toughen herself up.

9   A girl who climbed up to her roof and stretched out as far as possible with a spyglass to see what was happening on the other side of town.

10 But she hadn't always wanted to be a doctor. Actually, blood made her queasy. One time, her teacher used a bull's eyeball to show students how eyes work. Elizabeth was repulsed.

11 And she hadn't always wanted to help the sick. She had no patience for being sick herself. Whenever she felt ill, she simply went outside for a walk. Once, when she was little, she hid in a closet until she felt better. She hated anyone fussing over her.

12 So why did she become the first woman doctor? Because one person believed she could and told Elizabeth she was just the kind of smart, determined girl who would change the world.

13 That person was Mary Donaldson. When Elizabeth was twenty-four, she went to visit her friend who was very ill. Mary told Elizabeth that she would have much preferred being examined by a woman. She urged Elizabeth to consider becoming a doctor.

Identify Text Structure

<u>Underline</u> the words that tell why Elizabeth Blackwell decided to become a doctor.

determined showing strong purpose; unwilling to quit

14 At first, Elizabeth could not believe her ears. Even if a girl *could* be a doctor, why would *she* want to be one?

15 But Mary's idea gnawed at Elizabeth.

16 A female doctor.

Vocabulary in Context
<u>Underline</u> the words on this page that help you know what **gnawed at** means.

17 Elizabeth thought about it the second she got up in the morning.

18 She thought about it during sewing circles.

19 She thought about it over tea.

20 She even dreamed about it at night.

21 Finally, Elizabeth asked doctors and friends. Some thought it was a good idea, but didn't think there was any way it could be done. Others said it wasn't right.

Ask and Answer Questions

Highlight any text on this page that you can ask a question about.

22 "Women are too weak for such hard work."

23 "Women aren't smart enough."

Identify Text Structure

Underline the words that tell the reason why Elizabeth became a teacher.

24   Some people actually laughed at her. They thought she was joking! Elizabeth didn't see *anything* funny about a woman becoming a doctor.

25   Elizabeth thought it was a fine idea, and her family supported her. She worked as a teacher to earn money and applied to a handful of medical schools. But they all sent back the same answer:

26 No women allowed. She tried other schools. More letters arrived at her door. One by one, the answer was always the same.

27 Twenty-eight NOs in all.

28 In different ways, the letters all said the same thing:

Women *cannot* be doctors.

They *should* not be doctors.

Identify Text Structure

<u>Underline</u> the words that tell the effect, or result, of Elizabeth not giving up.

refused did not do something

29   But Elizabeth didn't believe in *couldn't* or *shouldn't*. She refused to give up. She was as stubborn as a mule. Quite rightly!

30   One day, an envelope arrived from a college. She opened it and everything changed. The answer was …

YES!

31   Elizabeth packed her bags for Geneva Medical School in upstate New York.

32   The townspeople were expecting her.

33   As she walked down the street, some pointed and stared. They whispered to themselves that she must be wicked—or crazy.

34   Elizabeth thought that at least the students wanted her there.

35   Except they didn't.

Ask and Answer Questions

Highlight any details that you have questions about.

accept to take something that is offered; to see something as right or correct

36   The teachers had let the students vote on whether or not to allow Elizabeth to come. And the boys, figuring the school would never really accept a girl, said yes. They planned to turn the whole thing into a big joke.

37   But the joke was on them!

38 Their raucous laughter turned to silence as the ladylike Elizabeth took her seat.

39 They wondered what kind of girl she was.

40 The kind of girl who wouldn't take the bait.

41 Some thought a girl wouldn't be able to keep up.

42 Except Elizabeth did keep up, often studying past midnight.

43 Elizabeth proved she was as smart as any boy.

44 And soon the boys wanted to know what Elizabeth thought about this or that.

45 It took the townspeople longer to accept her. Some people are afraid of anything new or different.

46 Not Elizabeth.

CLOSE READ

Ask and Answer Questions

Highlight any detail you can ask a question about to deepen your understanding.

CLOSE READ

Identify Text Structure

<u>Underline</u> the part of the text that tells when Elizabeth became a doctor.

47 On January 23, 1849, Elizabeth graduated … with the highest grades in the whole class!

48 She had become the first woman doctor in America.

49 Although many people were proud, others were angry. One doctor even wrote, "I hope, for the honor of humanity, that [she] will be the last."

50 But as you know, she certainly was

NOT.

Develop Vocabulary

 TURN *and* **TALK** Words can have shades of meaning. **Walk** and **run** both tell ways to move, but they mean slightly different things. Work with a partner. Look back in the Close Read notes to find a vocabulary word that has a similar meaning to each word in the chart. Then work with your class to write the definition of each vocabulary word.

allowed	challenge	determined	refused	accept

Word	Vocabulary Word	Meaning
stopped		
steady		
welcome		
let		
test		

Check for Understanding

MY TURN Look back at the text to answer the questions. Write the answers.

1. What makes this text a biography?

_____

_____

_____

2. How do the illustrations help you understand the text?

_____

_____

_____

3. Someone who **inspires** you makes you work harder. Who inspired Elizabeth Blackwell to reach her goal of becoming a doctor?

_____

_____

_____

Identify Text Structure

Information in a text can be organized in many ways. In a cause-and-effect structure, a writer shows how one thing (a cause) leads to another (an effect).

You can recognize an effect by asking "What happens?" You can recognize a cause by asking "Why does it happen?"

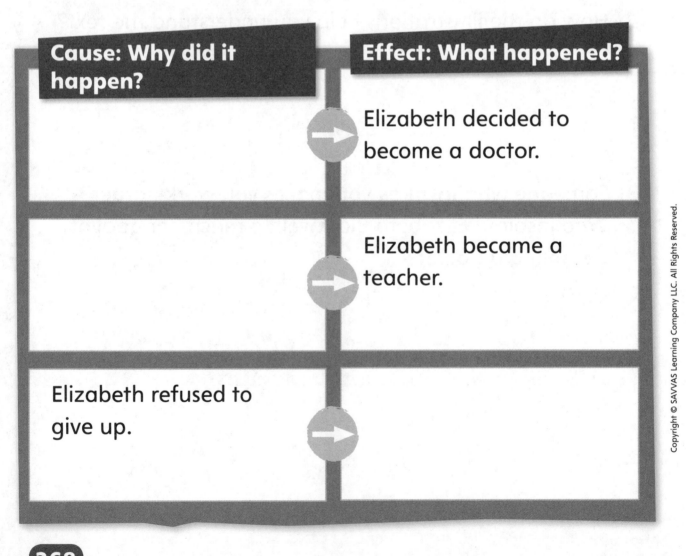 **MY TURN** Go to the Close Read notes on Text Structure. Underline evidence related to cause and effect. Use what you underline to complete the chart.

Cause: Why did it happen?		Effect: What happened?
	→	Elizabeth decided to become a doctor.
	→	Elizabeth became a teacher.
Elizabeth refused to give up.	→	

Ask and Answer Questions

When you generate, or ask, questions before, during, and after reading, you deepen your understanding.

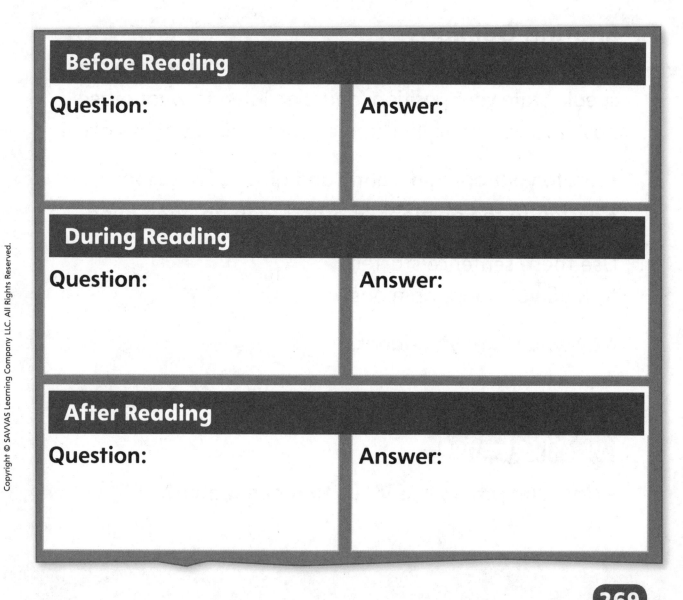 **MY TURN** Write a question you had before reading. Go back to the Close Read notes and highlight text. Write a question about a detail you highlighted. Then write a question you still have after reading.

Before Reading	
Question:	**Answer:**

During Reading	
Question:	**Answer:**

After Reading	
Question:	**Answer:**

Reflect and Share

Talk About It

Do you think people are motivated by someone saying that they **can** do something or that they **cannot**? Use examples from the texts to support your response.

Sharing Opinions

When sharing your opinion, ask politely whether you may speak. State your position, and then listen to what others have to say. You might change your mind, and that's okay!

- State your opinion clearly and give your reasons.
- Listen to the opinions of others with an open mind.

Use these sentence starters to help you share opinions.

Now you share your ideas.

I think that . . .
because . . .
You made a very
good point about . . .

Weekly Question

How can others inspire us to reach a goal?

I can use language to make connections between reading and writing narrative nonfiction.

My Learning Goal

Academic Vocabulary

When you add a suffix to a base word, the base word and the word with a suffix are related. Learning related words can help you grow your vocabulary.

The word **discuss** is a verb. When you add the suffix **-ion** to **discuss**, the new, related word is **discussion**. The suffixes **-ion**, **-tion**, and **-sion** all mean "the act of," so **discussion** means "the act of discussing."

MY TURN Read each verb and the related word with a suffix. Write what the new word means. Then use each word with a suffix in a sentence.

Verb	Related Word with Suffix	What the New Word Means
connect	connection	
complete	completion	
divide	division	

Read Like a Writer, Write for a Reader

Often authors use words to mean exactly what they say, or **literal** language. But sometimes they use words that do not have their regular meaning, or **figurative** language. One kind of very common figurative language is called an **idiom**.

Author's Words	What the Words Mean
". . . girls weren't allowed to become doctors. Mary's idea gnawed at Elizabeth."	Girls could not be doctors. (literal) Elizabeth kept thinking about the idea. (figurative)

TURN and TALK With your teacher's help, identify whether each sentence uses literal or figurative language. Discuss the difference.

She worked as a teacher to earn money. _____

At first Elizabeth could not believe her ears. _____

Underline the idiom in this sentence. Explain what it means.

She was the kind of girl who wouldn't take the bait.

_____

Write a sentence with figurative language. Write another with the idiom **make up my mind**.

Spell Words with Closed Syllables VC/V

When you divide a word into syllables after the consonant (VC/V), the vowel in the first syllable is usually short.

MYTURN Write the word that belongs in each group.

1. lake, stream _____

2. Earth, Mars _____

3. cold, shake _____

4. fast, quick _____

5. lime, orange _____

6. smart, quick-thinking _____

7. sky, light _____

8. correct, right _____

9. passenger, car _____

10. hot, jungle _____

11. always, never _____

12. baby, child _____

Spelling Words

lemon

shiver

planet

clever

river

rapid

comet

driven

tropic

proper

My Words to Know

sometimes

young

Adjectives and Adverbs

Adjectives describe persons, places, and things. That means they describe nouns. The words **a, an,** and **the** are special adjectives called **articles.** Use **a** before a word with a consonant and **an** before a word with a vowel sound.

A big green bug landed on an empty table.

Adverbs describe actions. That means they describe verbs. They can describe adjectives and other adverbs too. Adverbs tell how, where, or when.

We played happily outside today.

MY TURN Edit this draft. Cross out the incorrect adjectives and adverbs. Write the correct words above.

I was coughing bad, so I went to see my doctor. I had to wait in a office chair for a few minutes. I have a nicely doctor. She checked my throat careful. Then she gave my mother a awful lot of papers. I feel much better now!

I can use elements of narrative
nonfiction to write a personal narrative.

Personal Narrative

In a **personal narrative**, an author tells about a real
event in his or her life. The author, or narrator, is the
person telling about the event and uses words like **I** and
me. Personal narratives have a beginning, middle, and
end and include details that make the events come alive.

My Trip to the Grand Canyon

　　　One hot, sunny day last summer, my
family traveled to the Grand Canyon. At first
I was excited, but as we walked toward the
canyon rim, I stopped. It was so deep! I didn't
want to get any closer. Then my little brother
passed me. I thought, "Okay, I can do this." I
slowly walked up to the canyon rim and
stopped again, but not because I was scared.
The canyon was amazing! The colorful rock
layers and forms stretched for miles. I had
never seen anything so beautiful. By the end
of my day at the Grand Canyon, I knew that
I want to be a geologist when I grow up.

Beginning

Detail

End

Generate Ideas

An author generates, or thinks of ideas, before beginning to write. For a personal narrative, an author considers events from his or her life that might be interesting to tell. Examples include a special time or an experience that was funny, sad, or scary.

 **MY TURN** Think of special times in your life. List three possible topics for your personal narrative.

Topics

_____

_____

_____

_____

_____

Use this checklist to help you decide which topic to use.

☐ This event is a real experience from my life.

☐ It focuses on one event.

☐ It has a clear beginning, middle, and end.

☐ I can include interesting details to make the story come alive.

Plan a Personal Narrative

Authors organize their ideas to plan what they will write.

MY TURN Decide on a topic for a personal narrative. Use the organizer to plan it. Then share your ideas in Writing Club. Listen for feedback.

Topic

When and where it happened

Beginning	Details

Middle	Details

End	Details

Creative Places

Art is not just pictures hanging on a wall.
Buildings are creative works of art as well.

The CN Tower in Toronto, Ontario, Canada, has a round pod for great views and a place to eat. It was mostly designed by John Andrews.

The Guggenheim Art Museum in New York City is a work of art itself. Frank Lloyd Wright was the architect.

The Pritzker Pavilion in Chicago is used for outdoor shows. It was designed by architect Frank Gehry.

Weekly Question

How can our creations affect others?

 **MY TURN** How do buildings affect us as a community? Is there a building that you think helps your community? Draw the building on a sheet of paper. Or illustrate a building that you would like to see built someday.

The Taj Mahal in Agra, India, was built by the emperor Shah Jahan to remember his wife.

Open Syllables V/CV

When a syllable ends with a vowel, it is called an open syllable. The vowel usually has a long vowel sound.

go   The **o** has the long **o** sound.

Some two-syllable words have a vowel-consonant-vowel (VCV) pattern. When you divide the word into syllables after the first vowel (V/CV), the vowel in that open syllable is long.

paper   pa/per   The **a** has the long **a** sound.

MY TURN Read, or decode, the V/CV words in the chart. Divide the words into syllables. Underline the open syllable.

| bonus | spider | hotel | music |

TURN and TALK Reread the words in the chart with a partner. First, say each syllable. Then blend them to read the words.

Open Syllables V/CV

MY TURN Divide each V/CV word. Write each syllable on the lines. Circle the open syllable. Then read the word.

1. robot

_____ _____

2. tiger

_____ _____

3. human

_____ _____

4. label

_____ _____

5. even

_____ _____

My Words to Know

MY TURN Read the words in the box. Complete the sentences using the words.

being	song	talk

1. My dad is sleeping, so please _____ softly.

2. That bird is singing a pretty _____.

3. The puppy is _____ very good.

TURN and TALK Read the sentences aloud with a partner. Then use each word to make up your own sentences. Exchange papers and read each other's sentences.

Spider's Web

It had been a long, hot summer. All the animals were grouchy! Spider began to spin a great web. He strung it over the stream. He stretched it to the treetops. He wove flowers into the threads.

The next day, he could hear the animals talk.

"This is art!" said Tiger.

"Stunning!" said Fox.

All the animals were pleased. Spider was very proud.

1. Why were the animals grouchy?

2. How did the web affect the animals?

3. Divide these words into syllables. Then <u>underline</u> them in the story.

Spider   over   Tiger

My Learning Goal

I can read a biography and use print and graphic features.

Spotlight on Genre

Biography

A **biography** is a type of informational text. It tells the story of a real person's life, but it is written by another person. A biography includes **main ideas** and important **details** about the person.

- It may cover a person's whole life or part of the person's life.

- It may include **graphic features,** such as **photos** and **illustrations,** that make a text easier to understand.

In a biography, I can look at the pictures to learn more about the person.

Be a Fluent Reader When you practice appropriate fluency, read at the same rate you talk, not faster or slower. Also, read in a voice that matches the feeling of the text and the punctuation. For example, raise your voice for question marks. Reading with expression that sounds like speech is called prosody.

Biography Anchor Chart

A biography

is about the life of a real person.
has images like photos or illustrations.
gives facts about the person.
explores what makes him or her special.

Abraham Lincoln
was the president of
the United States
from 1861 to 1865.

Amelia Earhart
was the first
woman pilot to fly
alone across the
Atlantic Ocean.

Building on Nature

Preview Vocabulary

Look for these words as you read *Building on Nature: The Life of Antoni Gaudí.*

observes	architect	monuments	creations	arches

First Read

Read to understand the kind of art Antoni Gaudí made.

Look at the pictures to help you understand the art.

Ask such questions as **who** and **where** to clarify information.

Talk about what you found interesting.

Meet *the* Author

Rachel Rodríguez attended many different schools because her family moved often. Reading books helped her adjust to being "the new kid." She now enjoys living in San Francisco.

Genre Narrative Nonfiction

Building on Nature: The Life of Antoni Gaudí

by Rachel Rodríguez
illustrated by Julie Paschkis

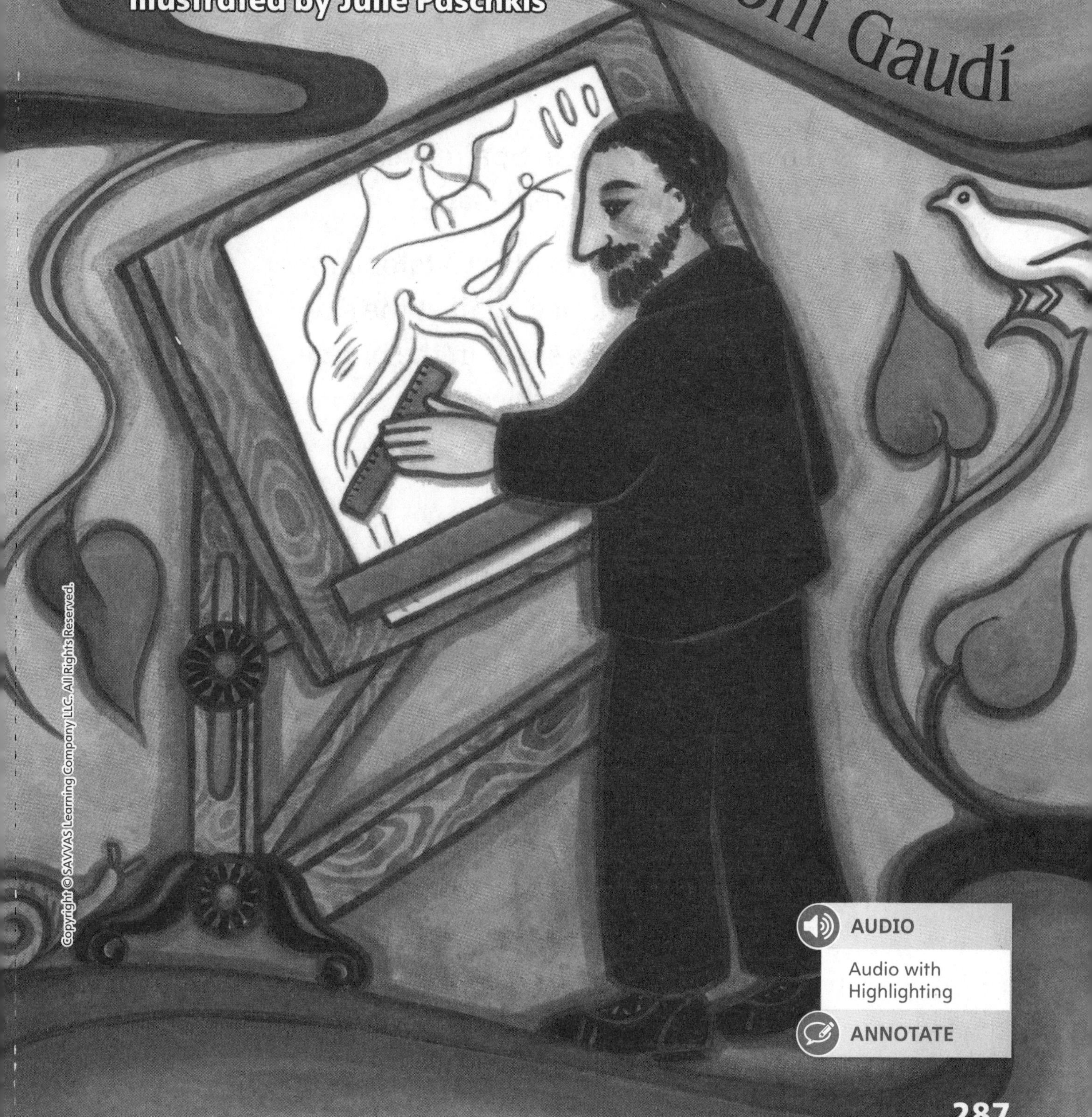

AUDIO

Audio with Highlighting

ANNOTATE

1   In a small village in Spain lives a boy
    named Antoni Gaudí.

2   For him, the world is Catalonia.
    Mountain peaks jag against the sky.
    Silvery olive trees sway in the breeze.
    The sea sparkles blue.

3 Little Gaudí often feels sick.
His bones and joints ache.
He can't always run and play
with his sister and brother.

4 But Gaudí has time to notice.
With wide eyes, he observes the world.
All around him is light, form, and
the Great Book of Nature.
He will read from it all his life.

Use Text Features
<u>Underline</u> the words that give more details about the picture.

observes watches carefully

5   Gaudí's father works with copper and fire.
His mother's family are metalsmiths, too.
Over and over, he watches flat pieces of metal
become shapes with a hollow space inside.

6 Gaudí grows stronger.
He makes friends with two boys.
Together, they explore an ancient monastery.
He dreams of rebuilding the ruins.

CLOSE READ

Vocabulary in Context

Sometimes you can figure out the meaning of an unfamiliar word by looking at words around it. Underline the words that help you understand the meaning of **ruins**.

Make Connections

Highlight details that tell how Antoni Gaudí learns to be an architect. Who helps him learn?

architect a person who designs buildings

monuments buildings, statues, and places that honor a person or an event

7   After high school, Gaudí goes to Barcelona to be an architect.

8   He studies important monuments and reads at the library.
    Other architects teach him.

9   Gaudí wears fine top hats and coats.
    He attends the opera and goes to church, too.

10 He designs his own desk.
    He creates lampposts for the city.

11 Soon others ask Gaudí to build for them.

12   His first big project is the Vicens House.

13   Everywhere, zinnia tiles bloom.
     The house is a checkerboard of color.
     Passersby stop and stare.
     They aren't used to Gaudí's bright colors.

14   Gaudí brings nature inside the
     house, too.

15   Leaves climb up walls.
     Cherries hang overhead.
     Birds wheel around and soar to the sky.

Make Connections

Highlight the words that help you understand that Gaudí creates things that other people will find fun to use.

16   Gaudí works on several projects at once.
He begins to design the Holy Family Church.
For years, he will plan and dream it into life.
His faith inspires his work.

17   For Gaudí, building is serious.
Everything must function.
But he isn't afraid to use his imagination.

18   Each time visitors use a door knocker, they squash a bedbug underneath.

19   A peephole looks like a honeycomb.

20   Gaudí makes people notice his smallest creations.

creations things that are made or produced

21 He designs a gate for his friend Güell's
country home.
A dragon perches atop diamonds and
squares, baring his fangs and slithery tongue.
Gaudí's creations get braver.

22 For Güell's Palace in town, Gaudí builds a
curving ramp to a basement stable.
Horses clomp down to it.
Upstairs, sunlight enters a domed ceiling.
The family enjoys their salon beneath a
starry sky.

Use Text Features

<u>Underline</u> the words that the picture makes easier to understand.

23 How do you build a chapel underground? Gaudí studies this giant problem for ten years.

24 He creates an upside-down model that resembles a colony of bats.

25 Gaudí learns how the arches and columns will work.
He turns it right side up and begins to build the Colonia Crypt.

arches curved structures that often form the tops of doors, windows, and gateways

297

26 At Casa Batlló, a fireplace hides under a
mushroom cap.
Hallways look like underwater caverns.
The house sparkles like the sea.

27 The roof arches in a dragon's spine.
Pillars are giant animal feet, balconies are
bones, and round walls are smooth
serpent skin.

A sword of a tower slays the beast.

CLOSE READ

Vocabulary in Context

<u>Underline</u> the word that helps you figure out the meaning of **slays**.

28 Everyone gapes at Gaudí's grand twists
of imagination.
But not everyone enjoys his strange
buildings.
Gaudí pays no attention to the talk.
He listens to himself.

29 Casa Milà waves and swells.
Rounded rooms cluster into a giant beehive.
Gaudí is turning nature into art.

30 He decorates chimneys on the roof,
a moving wonderland.
The rooftop courtyard looks like a ship.
Visitors feel rolling ocean waves beneath their feet.

Use Text Features

<u>Underline</u> the words for things that the picture helps you understand.

31 Casa Milà causes an uproar.
A few people even hate it.
"What is this?" they ask.
"A mountain," some guess.
"Or a hornet's nest."

32 Maybe it's a sand castle or a giant cake.

33 Some say Gaudí's building is laughing at the others on its street.

Casa Milà fascinates everyone.

34 Park Güell is a fantasyland set on a hillside.
Gatehouses warp and wave hello.
A mosaic lizard stands guard.

35 A long bench snakes around a playground.
Gaudí's workers smash old tiles, glass, and plates to bits.
They decorate the endless curving bench.
Gaudí praises his talented craftsmen.

36 Visitors pour in to celebrate Gaudí's vision of Catalonia.

Use Text Features
<u>Underline</u> three examples of things in the text that the picture shows in a colorful way.

Use Text Features

<u>Underline</u> the words that the picture shows. How does the picture help the author achieve her purpose?

37 Gaudí grows older, and still he works on his Holy Family Church. He uses the lessons from all his other buildings and dedicates his final years to it.

38 Tile and Venetian glass encrust soaring towers.
Inside, light filters through a stone forest.

39 Gaudí's church shimmers like a dream over Barcelona.

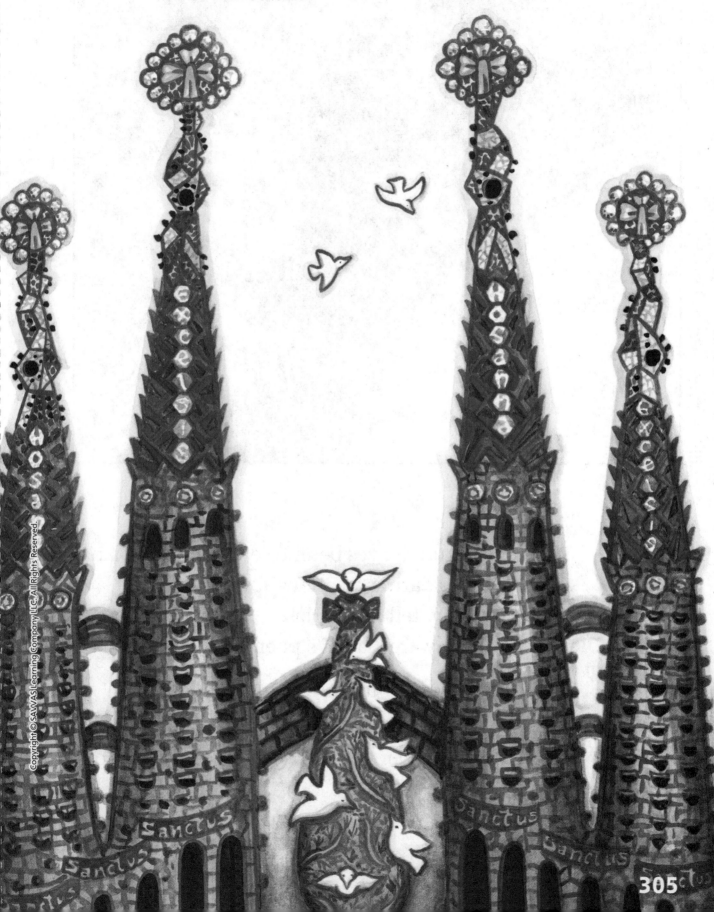

CLOSE READ

Make Connections

Highlight the words that help you understand what Gaudí left behind for society.

40 Gaudí leaves behind few words or plans.
His daring creations speak for him.
They tell his stories.
They are Gaudí's poem to the world.

41 Gaudí's buildings curve and arch.
They sparkle and glitter and whisper with joy.

42 They stand waiting for you to see with your very own eyes.

Fluency

Practice reading fluently. Read aloud paragraphs 28–33 several times with a partner. Read at the rate you talk, and group words as you read with expression.

Develop Vocabulary

MY TURN Write words from the box to complete the newspaper article.

observes	architect	monuments	creations	arches

Meet Jenna Caro

Jenna Caro is a famous _____ in our

town. She _____ how people live and

work. Then she and her partners design buildings,

houses, and other _____. They just

finished working on two _____ over a

sidewalk. Now they are working on three

_____ that will honor teachers.

Check for Understanding

MY TURN Look back at the text to answer the questions. Write the answers.

1. How does the title let you know that this text is a biography?

_____

_____

_____

2. How do the illustrations help you understand what Gaudí's buildings look like?

_____

_____

_____

3. How did Gaudí's illness as a child affect his work as an architect?

_____

_____

_____

Use Text Features

Titles, pictures, captions, headings, and words in darker print are all **text features.** Authors use print and graphic text features for these purposes:

- to give readers extra information

- to make information easier to locate and understand

MY TURN Go to the Close Read notes. Follow the directions to underline text. To complete the chart, choose three illustrations that go with the parts you underlined. Discuss why the author used these pictures.

Illustration	Author's Purpose for the Illustration
Gaudí walking near trees	It shows how Gaudí observes nature as a child.

Make Connections

When you read, you can make connections to

- personal experiences, or things you have done.
- ideas in other texts you have read.
- society, or most people.

MY TURN Go back to the Close Read notes and highlight the text. Complete the chart with connections you made to your own experience, other texts, or society.

When I read . . .,	it reminded me . . .
about Gaudí's life when he was learning to be an architect,	
about things Gaudí created for people to enjoy,	
about what Gaudí left behind for society,	

Reflect and Share

Write to Sources

This week the sources you read told how Gaudí and others created interesting buildings and objects. Some people liked them, but others did not. Describe your personal connection to two of the buildings. On a sheet of paper, write a paragraph with brief comments that give your opinion on the buildings.

Write an Opinion

Your opinion tells how you think or feel.

- State your opinion clearly.

- Give reasons and examples to support your opinion.

- Use opinion words, such as **I think, my favorite,** and **the best** or **the worst.**

Choose two buildings from the texts you read. State your opinion about how the buildings affected you. Use adjectives to describe the buildings. Include details that show your understanding of the texts.

Weekly Question

How can our creations affect others?

I can use language to make connections between reading and writing narrative nonfiction.

My Learning Goal

Academic Vocabulary

Antonyms are words with opposite meanings. You can find antonyms in a thesaurus and use them in your writing.

MY TURN Explain the meaning of each bold word. Then identify an antonym for it. Use a thesaurus if you need to. On a piece of paper, write a sentence that uses a word and its antonym.

Word	Meaning	Antonym
disconnect the wires		
irresponsible person		
destroy a building		
argue with her		

Read Like a Writer, Write for a Reader

Authors include descriptive language to help their readers understand and picture what they are writing about. They use clear, precise words. They include details that appeal to the senses: seeing, hearing, smelling, tasting, and touching.

Author's Details	What the Details Show Me
"A dragon perches atop diamonds and squares, baring his fangs and slithery tongue."	I can picture these buildings very clearly.
"Pillars are giant animal feet, balconies are bones, and round walls are smooth serpent skin."	I can sense how the smooth, round walls feel.

TURN and TALK Discuss the author's use of descriptive details. Why did the author use these words?

MY TURN On a sheet of paper, write two or three sentences that describe your classroom. Include details that appeal to the senses.

Spell Words with Open Syllables V/CV

An open syllable ends with a vowel. The vowel usually has a long sound. Learn this syllable division pattern.

MY TURN Unscramble the letters to make Spelling Words. Write each word.

Spelling Words				
bonus	lazy	tulip	meter	bacon
human	diner	silent	crater	cubic

1. mteer _____

2. slient _____

3. yzal _____

4. riden _____

5. utpil _____

6. hanmu _____

7. ccubi _____

8. buson _____

9. cabno _____

10. crtaer _____

My Words to Know
talk   being

Complete each sentence with a My Words to Know word.

Please _____ louder so I can hear you.

Someone who doesn't share is _____ selfish.

Comparative and Superlative Adjectives

Add **-er** to the end of an adjective to compare two things. Add **-est** to compare three or more things.

If the word ends with . . .	Follow this rule	Examples
a short vowel and consonant	Double the consonant.	hot + -er = hotter hot + -est = hottest
e	Drop the final **e**.	late + -er = later late + -est = latest
a consonant followed by **y**	Change the **y** to **i**.	windy + -er = windier windy + -est = windiest

MY TURN Edit this draft by crossing out the incorrect adjectives and writing the correct words above.

My sister Alix is the younggest one in my family.

I am one year oldest, but she is biggest than I am.

Alix has an easyier time making friends. She has

many friends, but I am her closer friend.

My
Learning
Goal

I can use elements of narrative nonfiction to write a personal narrative.

Compose Setting

The setting is when and where a story takes place. The author of a personal narrative uses sensory details to vividly describe the setting.

MY TURN Fill in the chart to plan the setting for your personal narrative. List at least three details. Compose the setting for your personal narrative in your writer's notebook.

When

Where

Sensory Details

The Narrator: You

The narrator of a personal narrative is the author. In a personal narrative, authors describe an event and tell what they were thinking and feeling at the time.

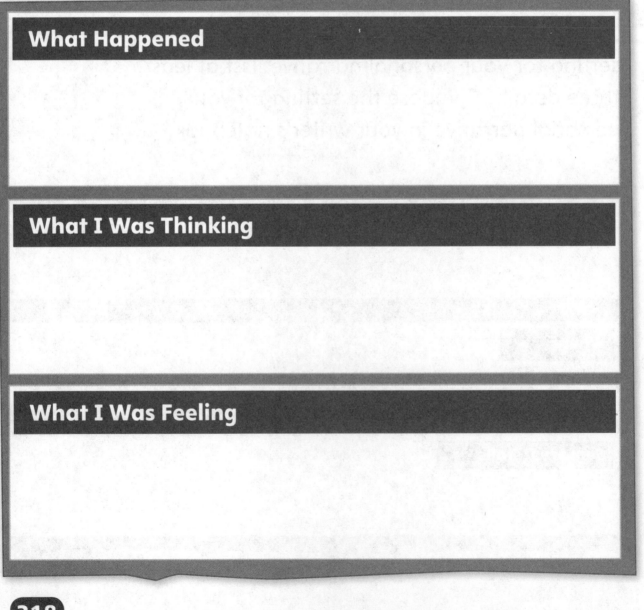 **MY TURN** Fill in the chart to help you plan what you will write. Then compose your personal narrative.

What Happened

What I Was Thinking

What I Was Feeling

Problem and Resolution

A personal narrative has a beginning, middle, and end. In the beginning, the author tells the reader about a **problem** or experience. In the middle, the author tells about trying to solve the problem. The ending, or **resolution**, tells how the problem was solved.

MY TURN Fill in the chart to plan the problem and resolution you will write about. Then compose your personal narrative.

Topic

Problem

Resolution

Community Care

People can work together to pick up litter in parks and along roads.

People can show they care about their communities in many different ways.

People can develop friendships by having a street festival.

People can work together to clean cars at a car wash.

What can people do to make a difference in their communities?

People can work together to build homes for those who do not have them.

People can make their community bright and colorful by painting a mural.

TURN and TALK

How do people in your community show they care about the community? With a partner, discuss ways you have seen or helped people making a difference. Then draw what you have done or seen.

Suffixes -ly, -ful, -er, -less, -or

A suffix is a group of letters that is added to the end of a base word to make a new word. The suffix adds its own meaning to the base word.

-ly	-ful	-er, -or	-less
in a certain way	full of	a person or thing that	without

neat + -ly = neatly = in a neat way

care + -ful = careful = full of care

teach + -er = teacher = person who teaches

edit + -or = editor = person who edits

care + -less = careless = without care

MY TURN Read the words with suffixes below. Find the suffix in each word and (circle) it. Underline the base word.

-ly	-ful	-er	-or	-less
quickly	playful	painter	sailor	useless

TURN and TALK Reread the words above. Choose two of the words and use them in sentences. Share your sentences with your partner.

Suffixes -ly, -ful, -er, -less, -or

MY TURN Read the words in the box. Circle the suffix in each word. Then use the words to complete the sentences.

| loudly | worker | careless | visitor | colorful |

1. Megan's paper had many mistakes because

   she was _____.

2. Tom spoke _____ so everyone
   could hear.

3. Lili is a _____ from England.

4. The red, pink, and yellow flowers are very

   _____.

5. Kyle washed the dishes. He is a great

   _____.

My Words to Know

 MY TURN Read the words in the box. Identify and underline the words in the paragraph. Then use each word to write your own sentences about your family. Form the letters correctly as you write each word. Use connecting strokes to connect the letters.

above	family	music

Henry and his family go on a picnic. They sit under a tree. The branches above make shade. They play music after they eat.

_____

_____

_____

_____

_____

_____

TURN and TALK Read your sentences aloud with a partner. Talk about the sentences, and help each other fix mistakes.

A Place to Play

"My children need a place to play," said Ms. Wood.

"All our kids do," said Mr. Lee.

"Let's make a playground!" said Ms. Chung. She was a leader. She got everyone to work together quickly.

Ms. Wood was speechless. "It's beautiful, isn't it?" said Ms. Chung. Soon people found out, and visitors came from miles around.

1. What do Ms. Wood's children need?

_____

_____

2. How is the playground finished quickly?

_____

_____

3. Find one word with each suffix: **-ly**, **-ful**, **-er**, **-or**, **-less**. Write the words on the line.

_____

_____

My Learning Goal I can learn more about making a difference by reading a story.

Realistic Fiction

Realistic fiction is a made-up story that could really happen. It has characters, a setting, and events that make up the beginning, middle, and end of the story. Realistic fiction often has a **theme**, or big idea about life. To determine the theme:

- as you read, stop at different points and ask yourself what the story is about so far.

- connect events to find out how they are related.

- after reading, ask yourself what message the author wants you to learn.

A story's theme is true for everyone, not just the characters in the story.

Establish Purpose The purpose for reading realistic fiction might be to enjoy a good story and to understand its theme, or message about life.

 TURN and TALK With a partner, establish a purpose for reading *The Garden of Happiness*.

326

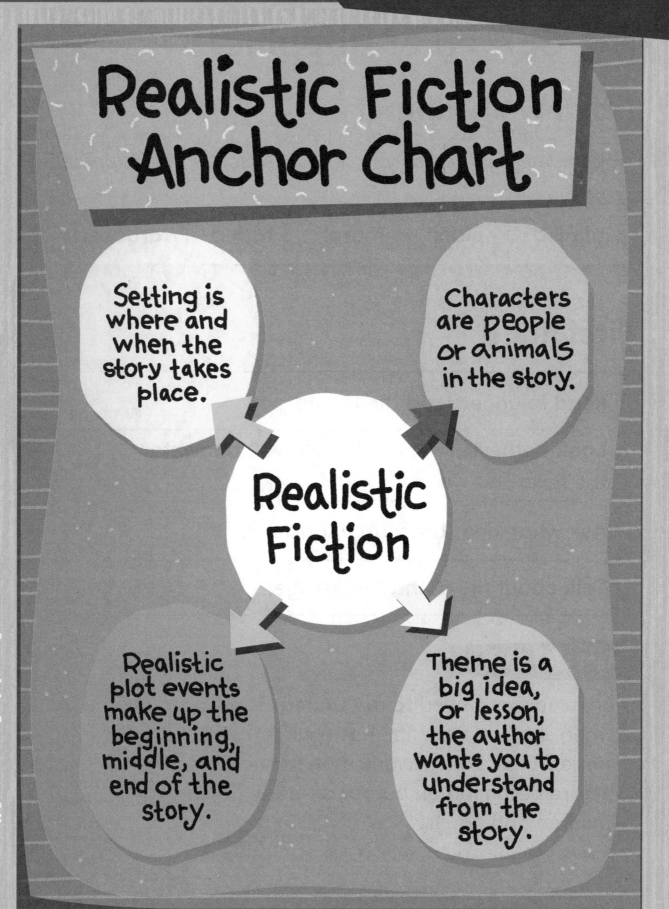

Realistic Fiction Anchor Chart

Setting is where and when the story takes place.

Characters are people or animals in the story.

Realistic Fiction

Realistic plot events make up the beginning, middle, and end of the story.

Theme is a big idea, or lesson, the author wants you to understand from the story.

The Garden of Happiness

Preview Vocabulary

Look for these words as you read *The Garden of Happiness*.

inhaled	plots	mural	faded	drooped

First Read

Read to understand the theme.

Look at the illustrations to help you understand the text.

Ask what ideas are most important.

Talk about the author's message.

Meet *the* Author

Erika Tamar moved to the United States from Austria when she was four. She has always loved telling stories. Erika Tamar worked on movies and TV shows before becoming an author of many books for children and adults.

The Garden of Happiness

by **Erika Tamar**
illustrated by **Barbara Lambase**

AUDIO

Audio with Highlighting

ANNOTATE

1   On Marisol's block near East Houston Street, there was an empty lot that was filled with garbage and broken, tired things. It had a funky smell that made Marisol wrinkle her nose whenever she passed by.

2 One April morning, Marisol was surprised to see many grown-ups busy in the lot. Mr. Ortiz carried a rusty refrigerator door. Mrs. Willie Mae Washington picked up newspapers. Mr. Singh rolled a tire away.

Create New Understandings

Highlight the words in the text that describe what Marisol notices one morning.

3　The next afternoon, Marisol saw people digging up stones. Mr. Ortiz worked with a pickax.

4　"*¿Qué pasa?*" Marisol asked.

5　Mrs. Willie Mae Washington leaned on her shovel and wiped her forehead. "I'm gonna grow me black-eyed peas and greens and sweet potatoes, too," she said. "Like on my daddy's farm in Alabama. No more store-bought collard greens for me."

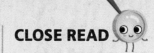

6   "We will call it The Garden of Happiness," Mr. Singh said. "I am planting *valore*—such a beautiful vine of lavender and red. Yes, everyone is happy when they see this bean from Bangladesh."

7   On another day, Marisol watched Mr. Castro preparing the ground. Mrs. Rodriguez rolled a wheelbarrow full of peat moss. Marisol inhaled the fresh-soil smell of spring.

8   "Oh, I want to plant something in The Garden of Happiness!" Marisol said.

9   "Too late, *niña*," Mr. Ortiz said. "All the plots are already taken."

Determine Theme

Underline the names of the grown-ups working on the garden, beginning with paragraph 3. Then underline the words Mr. Singh uses to name the garden.

inhaled breathed in

plots small pieces of land used for a purpose

Create New Understandings

Highlight details that describe Marisol's patch of land.

10 Marisol looked everywhere for a leftover spot, but the ground was crisscrossed by markers of sticks and string. She looked and looked. Just outside the chain-link fence, she found a bit of earth where the sidewalk had cracked.

11 "*¡Mira!* Here's my patch!" Marisol called. It was no bigger than her hand, but it was her very own. She picked out the pebbles and scraped the soil with a stick.

12 Marisol noticed a crowd of teenagers across the street from the lot. They were staring at a brick wall. It was sad and closed up, without windows for eyes. Marisol crossed over to ask what they were doing.

13 "City Arts is giving us paint to make a mural on the wall," a girl told her.

14 "What will it be?" Marisol asked.

15 "Don't know yet," one of the big boys said. "We haven't decided."

16 "I'm making a garden," Marisol said. "I haven't decided, either, about what to plant."

17 In The Garden of Happiness, the ground had become soft and dark. Mr. Castro talked to his seedlings as he placed them in straight rows. "Come on now, little baby things, grow nice and big for me."

mural a large picture painted directly on a wall

Determine Theme

<u>Underline</u> the words that tell what Marisol takes for her patch.

18 Marisol had no seedlings or even small cuttings or roots. *What can I do*, she thought, *where can I find something to plant?*

19 She went to the corner where old Mrs. Garcia was feeding the pigeons.

20 Marisol helped herself to a big flat seed. The birds fluttered about angrily.

21 "Only one," she told them, "for my garden."

22   Marisol skipped back to her patch. She poked a hole with her finger, dropped in the seed, and patted the soil all around. And every single day that spring, Marisol carried a watering can to the lot and gave her seed a cool drink.

Vocabulary in Context

<u>Underline</u> words in the text that help you understand the meaning of **shoot**.

23 Before long, a green shoot broke through in Marisol's patch. Even on rainy days, she hurried to the lot to see. Soon there were two leaves on a strong, straight stalk, and then there were four. It became as high as Marisol's knee!

24   Green things were growing all around in The Garden of Happiness. Mr. Castro's tiny seedlings became big bushy things with ripe tomatoes shining like rubies.

25   "What's my plant?" Marisol asked. Now it reached to her shoulder. "What's it going to be?"

26   "Dunno," Mrs. Willie Mae Washington answered. "But it sure is *somethin'!*"

CLOSE READ

Create New Understandings

Highlight details of the action happening at the wall.

27 Marisol pulled out the weeds in the late afternoons, when it wasn't so summer-hot.

28 Sometimes she watched the teenagers across the street. They measured the wall. They talked and argued about what they would paint.

29 Often Marisol saw Mr. Ortiz in his plot, resting in a chair.

340

30 "I come back from the factory and breathe the fresh air," he said. "And I sit among my *habichuelas*, my little piece of Puerto Rico."

31 "Is my plant from Puerto Rico? Do you know what it is?" Marisol asked.

32 Mr. Ortiz shook his head and laughed. "*¡Muy grande!* Maybe it's Jack's beanstalk from the fairy tale."

33 By the end of July, Marisol's plant had grown way over her head. And then, at the very top, Marisol saw a bud! It became fatter every day. She couldn't wait for it to open.

34 "Now don't be lookin' so hard,"
Mrs. Willie Mae Washington chuckled,
"It's gonna open up behind your
back, just when you're thinkin' about
somethin' else."

35 One morning, Marisol saw an amazing
sight from halfway down the block. She
ran the rest of the way. Standing higher
than all the plants and vines in the
garden was a flower as big as a plate!
Her bud had turned into petals of yellow
and gold.

36 "A sunflower!" Mrs. Anderson
exclaimed as she pushed her shopping
cart by. "Reminds me of when I was a
girl in Kansas."

37 Mrs. Majewska was rushing on her way
to the subway, but she skidded to a stop.
"Ah, *słoneczniki!* So pretty in the fields of
Poland!"

CLOSE READ

Vocabulary in Context

<u>Underline</u>
words in the
text that help
you understand
the meaning of
skidded.

Create New Understanding

Highlight words that the author uses to explain where sunflowers grow.

38   Old Mrs. Garcia shook her head. "No, no, *los girasoles* from Mexico, where they bring joy to the roadside."

39   "I guess sunflowers make themselves right at home in every sun-kissed place on earth," Mrs. Willie Mae Washington said.

40   "Even right here in New York City," Marisol said proudly.

41   The flower was a glowing circle, brighter than a yellow taxi. *A flower of sunshine*, Marisol thought, *the happiest plant in The Garden of Happiness.*

42   All summer long, it made the people on the street stop and smile.

Create New Understanding

Highlight words that describe what happens to Marisol's sunflower before she talks to Mrs. Willie Mae Washington. Why does Marisol think spring is too far away?

faded lost freshness

drooped hung down

43 Marisol watered and watered until a stream ran down the sidewalk. But her flower's leaves began to fall.

44 "Please get well again," Marisol whispered.

45 Every day, more golden petals curled and faded.

46 "My flower of sunshine is sick," Marisol cried. "What should I do?"

47 "Oh, child," Mrs. Willie Mae Washington said. "Its season is over. There's a time to bloom and a time to die."

48 "No! I don't want my flower to die!"

49 "*Mi cariño*, don't cry," Mrs. Rodriguez said. "That's the way of a garden. You must save the seeds and plant again next spring."

50 Marisol's flower drooped to the ground. The Garden of Happiness wasn't happy for her anymore. The vines had tumbled down. The bushy green plants were gone. She collected the seeds and put them in her pocket, but spring was much too far away.

Create New Understanding

Highlight words that describe how Marisol feels after her sunflower dies. Why doesn't she look at the place where the flower once grew?

51 Marisol was too sad to go to the empty lot anymore. For a whole week, she couldn't even look down the block where her beautiful flower used to be.

52 Then one day she heard people calling her name.

53 "Marisol! Come quick!"

54 "Marisol! *¡Apúrate!* Hurry!"

Determine Theme

Underline details that show people in the community are excited about the wall painting. The theme of this story has to do with the community. How have the garden and the mural affected the community?

55   A golden haze shone on the street. There was a big crowd, like on a holiday. Music from the *bodega* was loud and bright. And what she saw made Marisol laugh and dance and clap her hands.

Develop Vocabulary

MY TURN For each word or phrase in the chart, write a vocabulary word from the box that has a similar meaning. Then write a meaning for each word.

| | inhaled | plots | faded | mural | drooped | |

	Vocabulary Word	Meaning
painting	mural	large picture painted on a wall
became dull		
smelled		
sagged		
bits of land		

Check for Understanding

MY TURN Look back at the text. Write brief comments to answer the questions.

1. What about this story makes it realistic fiction?

2. How do the illustrations help you understand the story?

3. What do you think is the best thing about The Garden of Happiness?

Determine Theme

The **theme** is the lesson or main message of a story. To determine, or figure out, the theme of a story, think about what happens in the story and ask yourself, "What big idea is the story about?"

 MY TURN Go to the Close Read notes. Follow the directions to underline the text. Working with your class, use three of the parts you underlined to complete the chart.

Text Evidence That Helps Me Determine the Theme:

Theme or Big Idea:

Create New Understandings

When you synthesize information, you combine what you have learned to understand something new.

| One Bit of Information | + | Another Bit of Information | = | New Understanding! |

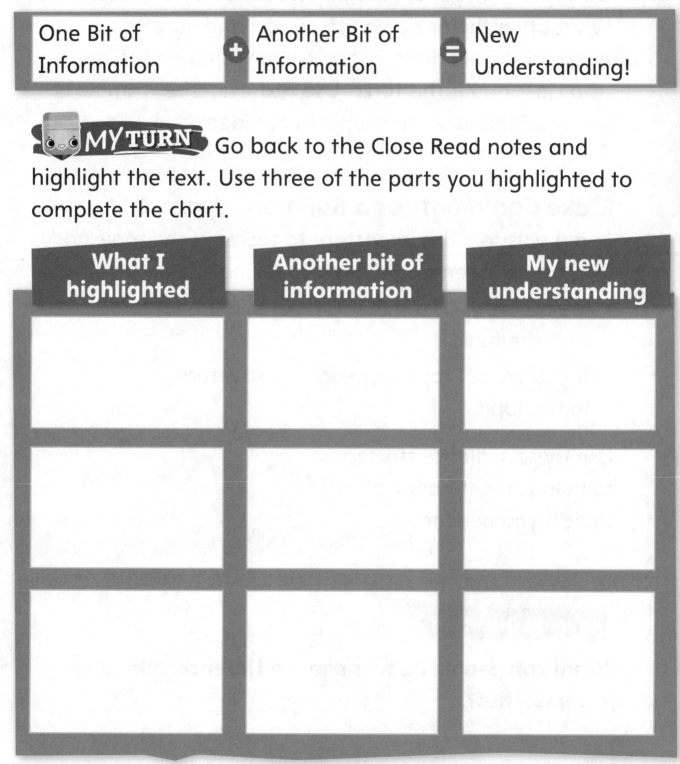

MY TURN Go back to the Close Read notes and highlight the text. Use three of the parts you highlighted to complete the chart.

What I highlighted	Another bit of information	My new understanding

Reflect and Share

Talk About It

Do you think your community would enjoy a garden? What other things do you think you and your neighbors could do to improve your community? Talk as a class about this topic. Use text evidence from texts you read this week to support your ideas.

Make Comments and Build on Ideas

In a discussion, it is important to focus on the topic and use complete sentences when speaking.

- Make sure your comments have something to do with the topic.
- If you get off topic, apologize and return to the topic.

Use these sentence starters to help you get back on topic if you need to.

To get back to the topic, I wanted to say . . .
I'm sorry I got off topic. I think . . .

Weekly Question

What can people do to make a difference in their communities?

I can use language to make connections between reading and writing narrative nonfiction.

My Learning Goal

Academic Vocabulary

You can use **context clues** to figure out the meaning of a new word or phrase. Look for clues in nearby words.

MY TURN Circle the context clues that help you understand each bold word or phrase. Then complete the sentences.

1. The girls want to be treated the same as the boys. They want **equal rights.**
   In this sentence, **equal rights** means _____
   _____.

2. It is your **responsibility** to turn your homework in on time. You have a duty to keep up.
   In this sentence, **responsibility** means _____
   _____.

3. People who don't know their neighbors might feel **disconnected** and alone.
   In this sentence, disconnected means _____
   _____.

Read Like a Writer, Write for a Reader

Authors write stories from a narrator's **point of view.** If the story is told in the **first person**, the narrator is a character in the story and uses the pronouns **I** or **we.** If the story is told in the **third person**, the narrator is not a character in the story and uses the pronouns **he, she,** or **they.**

Author's Words	Point of View
"She couldn't wait for it to open." "Mama was away that night and I couldn't sleep."	Third person; not told by a character in the story First person; told by a character in the story

 MY TURN Underline the pronouns. Tell whether the sentences are in first or third person.

1. I told him how I wanted to count all the stars in the sky.

2. They talked and argued about what they would paint.

3. Write two sentences in the first or third person. Identify which point of view you used.

Spell Words with Suffixes -ly, -ful, -er, -less, -or

 MY TURN Sort the spelling words by suffixes.

-er

_____

_____

-or

_____

-ly

_____

_____

-ful

_____

_____

-less

_____

Spelling Words
fearless
useful
teacher
visitor
weekly
helpful
helper
sailor
cheerful
quickly

My Words to Know
above
family

Write a My Words to Know word to complete each sentence.

There are three children in my

_____ .

She saw the moon in the sky

_____ .

Commas in Dates and Letters

When you write a letter, use a comma in these places.

Between the day and year	After the greeting	After the closing
May 15, 2018	Dear Mom and Dad,	Love, Joshua

MY TURN Edit this draft by crossing out the incorrect commas and writing the commas where they are needed.

March, 8 2018,

Dear Ella

I'm starting a community project. Would you like to help me clean up the park? There is a lot of trash and weeds. I want to make it a prettier place to enjoy.

Sincerely

Thomas

My Learning Goal

I can use elements of narrative nonfiction to write a personal narrative.

Sequence of Events

An author organizes the events of a personal narrative in the order, or **sequence,** in which they happened. The author uses time-order words like these to help show the sequence:

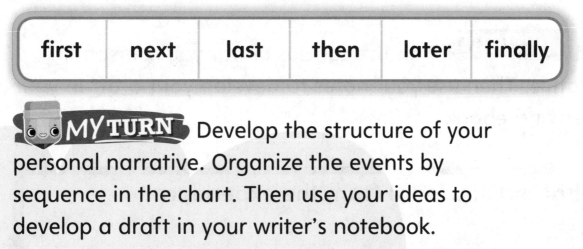

| first | next | last | then | later | finally |

MY TURN Develop the structure of your personal narrative. Organize the events by sequence in the chart. Then use your ideas to develop a draft in your writer's notebook.

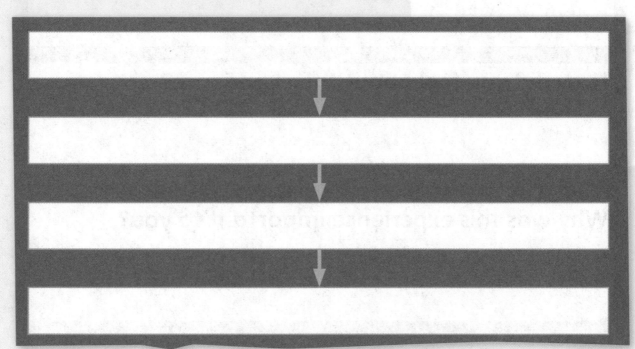

Conclusion

An author writes a **conclusion** to a personal narrative. The conclusion wraps up the story in an interesting way. In the conclusion, authors may

- share something they learned from the experience.
- tell how they feel about the experience.
- tell why the experience was important to them.

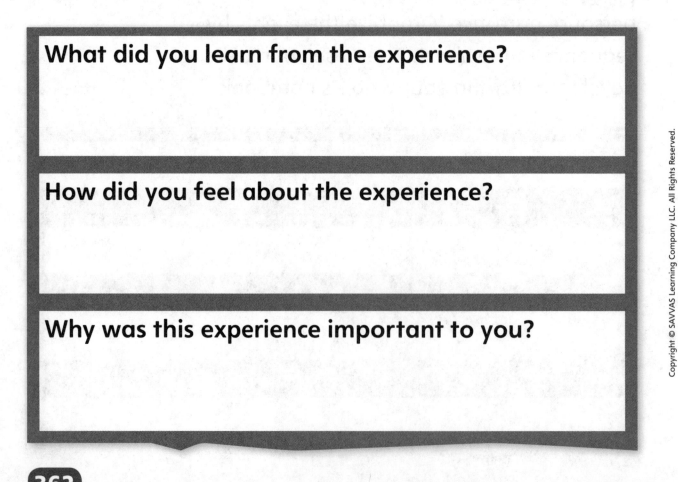 **MY TURN** Plan the conclusion for your personal narrative. Then use your notes to develop your draft in your writer's notebook.

What did you learn from the experience?

How did you feel about the experience?

Why was this experience important to you?

Details

An author uses words and visuals to add details to a personal narrative. These details help readers picture the experience. Interesting and sensory details describe what is happening and tell a narrator's actions, thoughts, and feelings.

MY TURN Write details to include in your personal narrative. Add visuals to make your ideas, thoughts, and feelings clear. Share your draft and visuals in Writing Club. Listen for feedback.

Outer Details	Inner Details
I saw	I thought
I heard	
I smelled	I felt
I touched	
I tasted	

Old Stuff, New Uses

After you use something, you might throw it away. But there's already too much trash in the world. Why not find another way to use it?

Use old cans to store art supplies.

Use an old ketchup bottle to squirt perfect pancakes.

Use an egg carton to plant seeds.

Use an old milk jug to water your plants.

Weekly Question

How can people work together to solve a problem?

 TURN and TALK

Too much trash is a problem. Use sources you have read to help you decide how to solve that problem. How might you get others to help solve it? Write down some ideas.

Use your old toys to create a robot.

Prefixes un-, re-, pre-, dis-

A prefix is a group of letters that is added to the beginning of a base word to make a new word. The prefix adds its meaning to the base word.

un-	re-	pre-	dis-
not, or the opposite of	again, or back	before	not, or the opposite of

untrue = not true

retie = tie again

prepay = pay before

distrust = not trust

MY TURN Read, or decode, the words with prefixes below. Find the prefix in each word and circle it. Underline the base word.

un-	re-	pre-	dis-
unlock	replay	preschool	dislike

TURN and TALK Reread the words in the chart with a partner. Identify the meaning of each word. Take turns using the words in sentences.

Prefixes un-, re-, pre-, dis-

The prefixes **un-**, **re-**, **pre-**, and **dis-** are added to the beginning of base words to make new words.

MY TURN Read each sentence. Find the word in **bold** type and circle the prefix. Under each sentence, circle the letter next to the word's meaning.

1. The river is muddy and looks **unclean.**

Unclean means: a. clean again b. not clean

2. You must **preheat** the oven before baking the cake.

Preheat means: a. heat before b. not heat

3. Sam used the wrong color, so he will **repaint** the wall.

Repaint means: a. paint again b. paint before

4. Kate did not want to **disobey** her mom and break the rule.

Disobey means: a. obey before b. not obey

Look to see if an unfamiliar word has a prefix and a base word that you know.

My Words to Know

MY TURN Read the words in the box. Then complete each sentence using the words.

color	questions	area

1. Red is my favorite _____.

2. The park covers a large _____.

3. I have the answers to your _____.

TURN and TALK Work with a partner. Follow the directions. Take turns.

1. Name your favorite color. Then name something that has your favorite color.

2. Describe the area in the playground you like best. Tell why you like it. Use the word **area**.

3. Write down two questions to ask your partner. Label them Question 1 and Question 2.

Cleaning the Beach

People disliked the beach in Joe's town. It was dirty. This made Joe unhappy.

Joe needed a plan. He went to the beach to preview the area. There was trash everywhere.

Joe gathered his friends and their parents too. Everyone worked hard to get rid of the trash. Later, they chose to regroup and have a party on their clean, beautiful beach.

1. Why was Joe unhappy?

_____

_____

2. How was Joe able to fix the problem?

_____

_____

3. Find one word with each prefix: **un-**, **re-**, **dis-**, and **pre-**. Write them.

_____

_____

My Learning Goal

I can read a biography and understand its text structure.

Spotlight on Genre

Biography

A **biography** is the story of a real person's life that is told from the point of view of another person.

- It tells about all or part of a person's life.

- It tells about **real events**.

- It is often told in **chronological order,** or time order, with words like **first, then,** and **finally**.

- It tells about something **important** the person did, such as how she or he solved a **problem**.

- It is told from a **third-person** point of view. The narrator uses the pronouns **he** and **she.**

> **TURN and TALK** Tell about a real person you have read about. Who was the person? What did you find out about his or her life?
>
> **Establish Purpose** Before you read, look at the first few pages of *One Plastic Bag*. What do you want to find out from this text?

Biography Anchor Chart

Purpose

To give information about the life of a real person

Elements

- is written by someone else
- is about all or part of the person's life
- tells how the person affected others

Rosa Parks worked to give African Americans the same rights as others.

Text Structures

- Chronological order, or time order
- Descriptive
- Cause and effect
- Problem and solution

One Plastic Bag: Isatou Ceesay and the Recycling Women of the Gambia

Preview Vocabulary

Look for these words as you read *One Plastic Bag*.

scents	useless	crumble	plastic	garbage

First Read

Look through the text. Make two predictions.

Read for the purpose you set.

Ask whether your predictions matched the text. Correct or confirm your predictions.

Talk about how this text answers the weekly question.

Meet the Author

Miranda Paul once used a cereal box to make a holiday ornament. She got the idea to write *One Plastic Bag* when she was a teacher in Gambia.

ONE PLASTIC BAG

Isatou Ceesay and the Recycling Women of the Gambia

by Miranda Paul
illustrated by Elizabeth Zunon

AUDIO
Audio with Highlighting

ANNOTATE

CLOSE READ

Njau, Gambia

1   Isatou walks with her chin frozen. Fat raindrops pelt her bare arms. Her face hides in the shadow of a palm-leaf basket, and her neck stings with every step.

scents strong smells, good or bad

2   Warm scents of burning wood and bubbling peanut stew drift past. Her village is close now. She lifts her nose to catch the smell.

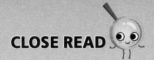

3   The basket tips.

4   One fruit tumbles.

5   Then two.

6   Then ten.

7   The basket breaks.

8   Isatou kicks the dirt.

Identify Text Structure

<u>Underline</u> the sentences that tell what happens after the basket starts to fall. What time-order word shows the sequence, or order, in which those things happen?

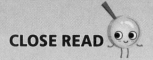

Confirm or Adjust Predictions

Highlight the words that helped you make a prediction about how Isatou would feel about this kind of bag later.

9 Something silky dances past her eyes, softening her anger. It moves like a flag, flapping in the wind, and settles under a tamarind tree. Isatou slides the strange fabric through her fingers and discovers it can carry things inside. She gathers her fruits in the bag.

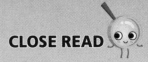

10   The basket is useless now. She drops it, knowing it will crumble and mix back in with the dirt.

11   Four goats greet Isatou as Grandmother
Mbombeh emerges from her kitchen hut.
"Hurry in before the rain soaks your
beautiful *mbuba*!"

12   Isatou scurries in, and Grandmother serves spicy rice and fish. Rain drums on the creaking aluminum roof.

13   "I... broke your basket," Isatou confesses. "But I found this."

14   "Plastic," Grandmother frowns.

15   "There's more in the city."

plastic a light, strong material that can be made into things

Identify Text Structure

<u>Underline</u> the phrase that tells when Isatou's neighbors use plastic bags.

16   Day after day, Isatou watches neighbors tote their things in bright blue or black plastic bags. Children slurp water and *wanjo* from tiny holes poked in clear bags. Market trays fill with *minties* wrapped in rainbows of plastic.

17   The colors are beautiful, she thinks. She swings her bag high. The handle breaks.

18   One paper escapes.

19   Then two.

20   Then ten.

21   Isatou shakes sand off her papers. Another plastic bag floats by, and she tucks her things inside.

22   The torn bag is useless now. She drops it to the dirt, as everyone does. There's nowhere else to put it.

CLOSE READ

Confirm or Adjust Predictions

Highlight words that tell what Isatou thinks of plastic bags now. Use text features and genre characteristics.

23 Day after day, the bag she dropped is still there.

24 One plastic bag becomes two.

25 Then ten.

26 Then a hundred.

27 Plastic isn't beautiful anymore, she thinks. Her feet step down a cleaner path, and the thought floats away.

28 Years pass and Isatou grows into a woman. She barely notices the ugliness growing around her . . .

29 until the ugliness finds its way to her.

30 Isatou hears a goat crying and hurries toward Grandmother's house. Why is it tied up? Where are the other goats?

31 Inside, the butcher is speaking in a low voice.

32 "Many goats have been eating these," he says. "The bags twist around their insides, and the animals cannot survive. Now three of your goats and so many other goats in the village have died!"

33 Grandmother Mbombeh's powerful shoulders sag. Isatou must be strong and do something. But what?

34 Isatou's feet lead her to the old, ugly road. A pile of garbage stands as wide as Grandmother's cooking hut. Mosquitoes swarm near dirty pools of water alongside the pile. Smoke from burning plastic stings her nose. Her feet back away.

35 Goats scamper past. They forage through the trash for food. Her feet stop. She knows too much to ignore it now.

36 Holding her breath, she plucks one plastic bag from the pile.

37 Then two.

38 Then ten.

39 Then a hundred.

CLOSE READ

Confirm or Adjust Predictions

Highlight the sentences that helped you make a prediction about what Isatou would do with the plastic bags later.

garbage scraps of things thrown away

40 "What can we do?" Isatou asks her friends.

41 "Let's wash them," says Fatim, pulling out *omo* soap. Maram grabs a bucket, and Incha fetches water from the well. Peggy finds clothespins, and they clip the washed bags on the line.

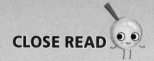

42   As the bags dry, Isatou watches her
sister crochet. "Can you teach me?"

43   "*Waaw*—yes." Her sister shows Isatou
the stitches, then hands her a metal tool.
Isatou's fingers busy themselves … in …
out … around. "*Jerejef*—thank you."

Identify Text Structure
<u>Underline</u> the words that tell **when** Isatou watched her sister crochet.

44   Isatou finds a broomstick and carves her own tool from its wood.

45   "What's that for?" Fatim asks.

46   Isatou pauses. She and Peggy have an idea. But will their friends think it's crazy? Will the idea even work?

47   Nervously, she explains the plan.

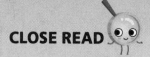

48 One friend agrees to help.

49 Then two.

50 Then five!

51 The women cut bags into strips and roll them into spools of plastic thread. Before long, they teach themselves how to crochet with this thread.

Confirm or Adjust Predictions

Highlight the words that tell what is done with the plastic bags Isatou took from the garbage pile. Use text features and genre characteristics.

CLOSE READ

Vocabulary in Context

Underline sentences that show what **mock** means.

52   "*Naka ligey be?*" asks Grandmother. "How is the work?"

53   "*Ndanka, ndanka,*" answers Isatou. "Slow. Some people in the village laugh at us. Others call us 'dirty.' But I believe what we are doing is good."

54   The women crochet by candlelight, away from those who mock them . . .

55   until a morning comes when they will no longer work in secret.

56 Fingers sore and blistered, Isatou hauls the recycled purses to the city.

57 One person laughs at her.

58 Then two.

59 Then ten.

60 Then . . .

CLOSE READ

Identify Text Structure

<u>Underline</u> the time-order word that shows how long it takes to sell the purses.

61 One woman lays dalasi coins on the table. She chooses a purse and shows it to one friend.

62 Then two.

63 Then ten.

64 Soon everyone wants one!

65   Isatou fills her own purse with dalasi. She zips it shut and rides home to tell Grandmother she has made enough to buy a new goat.

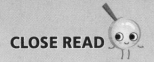

Identify Text Structure

Underline the time-order words in this text.

66   When she passes by the pile of rubbish, she smiles because it is smaller now. She tells herself, one day it will be gone and my home will be beautiful.

67   **And one day . . .**

68 ... it was.

Develop Vocabulary

 MY TURN In your own words, write what each word means. Then find each word in *One Plastic Bag*. Check the definition in the margin. Revise your chart if needed.

Word	Meaning
scents	strong smells that can be good or bad
useless	
crumble	
plastic	
garbage	

Check for Understanding

MY TURN Look back at the text to answer the questions. Write the answers.

1. This text is a biography. What does that tell you about this text? Is it first person or third person?

_____

_____

2. How do the illustrations of the women making and selling the purses help you better understand the text?

_____

_____

3. What do you think would have happened if Isatou had not thought of a way to recycle plastic bags?

_____

_____

_____

Many of our toys and containers are also made of plastic.

Identify Text Structure

A chronological, or time-order, structure of an informational text puts events in the order in which they happen. Time-order words like **first** and **then** state the order explicitly.

MY TURN Go to the Close Read notes. Underline words that show time order. Use what you underline and other text evidence to complete the chart.

First,	
Day after day,	
When goats die from eating bags,	
Soon after women make purses from bags,	
One day	

Make and Confirm Predictions

Use characteristics of a genre to make predictions. At the beginning of a biography, predict how the person will think or act. As you read, if your prediction is right, you can confirm. If your prediction is not right, you can correct your prediction to match events.

MY TURN Go back to the Close Read notes. Underline words that helped you make and correct or confirm predictions. Then complete the chart.

Paragraphs	I predicted . . .	When I read . . .,
9 and 27		
36–39 and 51		

Reflect and Share

Write to Sources

You read about how Isatou Ceesay saw a problem and solved it. On a sheet of paper, retell the text about Isatou Ceesay. Describe how she made a difference in her community.

Retell a Text

When you retell a text, keep the meaning and order of the text.

- Write the events in order. Start with what happened first. End with what happened last.
- Tell only the important parts.

Weekly Question

How can people work together to solve a problem?

I can use language to make connections between reading and writing narrative nonfiction.

My Learning Goal

Academic Vocabulary

Word parts can help you figure out a word's meaning. The prefix **un-** means "not." Adding the prefix **un-** to a word makes a word that means the opposite.

un-   +   equal   =   unequal

(prefix)   (word)   (new word)

Adding the prefix **un-** to **equal** makes the new word **unequal**, which means "not equal."

MY TURN Add the prefix **un-** to each word to build a new word. What does each word mean?

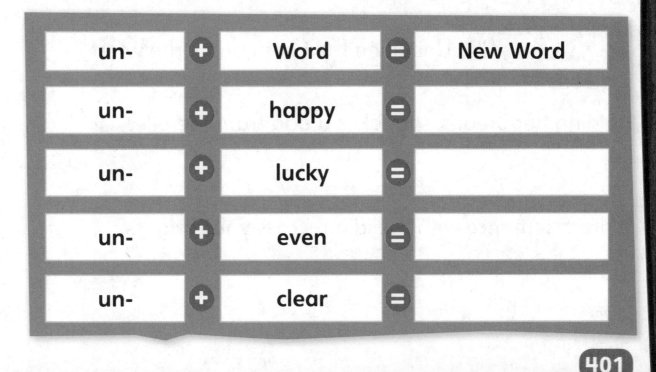

un-	+	Word	=	New Word
un-	+	happy	=	
un-	+	lucky	=	
un-	+	even	=	
un-	+	clear	=	

401

Read Like a Writer, Write for a Reader

Authors use literal and figurative language. In **literal** language, words have their normal meanings. In **figurative** language, words have different meanings than usual. **Idioms** are common phrases that use figurative language.

Author's Words	What the Words Mean
"Something silky dances past her eyes."	She sees something moving past her face. (figurative)
"Grandmother serves spicy rice and fish."	Grandmother serves dinner. (literal)

TURN and TALK Discuss the author's use of literal and figurative language. Why did the author use these words?

MY TURN Underline the idiom and write what it means.

Holding her breath, she takes a bag from the pile.

_____

Write a sentence with the idiom **cross your fingers**.

_____

Spell Words with Prefixes un-, re-, pre-, dis-

To spell words with prefixes, spell the prefix and then think about how the base word is spelled. For example, **un** + **fair** make the word **unfair**.

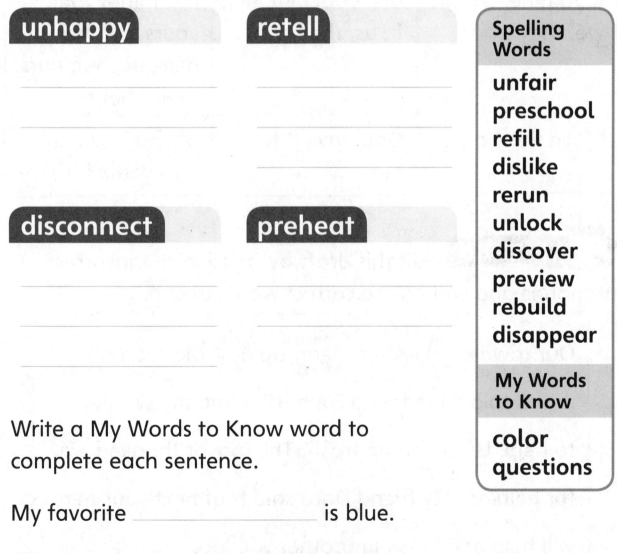

MY TURN Write words from the list that have the same prefix as each word below.

unhappy

_____

_____

retell

_____

_____

_____

disconnect

_____

_____

_____

preheat

_____

_____

Spelling Words

unfair
preschool
refill
dislike
rerun
unlock
discover
preview
rebuild
disappear

My Words to Know

color
questions

Write a My Words to Know word to complete each sentence.

My favorite _____ is blue.

We asked our teacher a lot of _____.

Pronouns

A **subject pronoun** can be the subject of a sentence. An **object pronoun** is used after an action verb or a preposition and is not used as a subject. A **possessive pronoun** shows ownership.

Subject Pronouns	Object Pronouns	Possessive Pronouns
I, you, he, she, it, we, they	me, you, him, her, it, us, them	my, mine, your, yours, his, her, hers, its, our, ours, their, theirs
I love this book.	Dad gave it to me.	My book is here, and yours is there.

MY TURN Edit this draft by crossing out incorrect pronouns and writing the correct words above.

Our town organized a clean-up day. Me read about it and told mine friend John. Him and me wanted to help. Us picked up trash. The mayor thanked we for helping. My friend Dora said that next year her will help and hers big brother will too.

I can use elements of narrative nonfiction to write a personal narrative.

My Learning Goal

Edit for Capitalization and Commas

Capitalize the names of people, places, months, and days of the week. Capitalize the greeting and conclusion in a letter. Use a comma in dates. Authors edit their writing to make sure they have used capital letters and commas correctly.

> May   ,   Sunday Tim   Florida
> Today is ~~may~~ 4 2020. On ~~sunday~~, ~~tim~~ leaves for ~~florida~~.

MY TURN Edit the letter. Use capital letters and commas correctly. Then edit the draft of your personal narrative for capital letters and commas.

november 14 2020

dear Grandma,

It is a dark and dreary saturday. I am lonely because my best friend lisa is away on a trip to austin.

love,

Coby

Edit for Pronouns

A **subject pronoun** can be the subject of a sentence. An **object pronoun** is used after an action verb or a preposition, not as a subject. A **possessive pronoun** shows ownership.

A pronoun must **agree** with the person or thing it refers to. **Dad** took off **his** hat. (Not **her** hat.)

Authors edit their writing to make sure they have used subject, object, and possessive pronouns correctly.

> I
> My sister and ~~me~~ were so tired. We had looked all over
>   him
> town for ~~he~~. We finally gave up and went home. There he
>   our
> was, ~~ours~~ lost puppy!

 MY TURN Edit the sentences. Cross out the incorrect pronoun. Write the correct pronoun above it. Then edit the draft of your personal narrative to be sure you used subject, object, and possessive pronouns correctly.

> Diego invited I to come for lunch. Her mother made
>
> we corn tortillas. Us filled them to make us own tacos.

Edit for Compound Subjects and Predicates

Authors often edit two sentences to form one. Use the coordinating conjunction **and** between two subjects to form a compound subject. Use **and** between two predicates to form a compound predicate.

> ~~~~~~and Ana play~~~~~~
> Josh ~~plays~~ kickball often. ~~Ana plays kickball often.~~
>
> ~~~~~~and~~~~~~
> Sara sings ~~in the play. Sara~~ dances in the play.

MY TURN Edit the sentences to form compound subjects or compound predicates. Cross out words or sentences you do not need. Then edit the draft of your personal narrative for compound subjects and compound predicates.

> The Clarks went to the beach. The Lees went to
>
> the beach. They enjoyed swimming.
>
> They enjoyed playing in the sand. They built a
>
> big sand tower together.

Look What We Can Do!

Children go to school and learn, of course. They also play and help at home. But that's not all children can do.

Children start their own businesses. Some make and sell lemonade. Others make clothes and sell them online.

Children raise money for charity to help other children around the world.

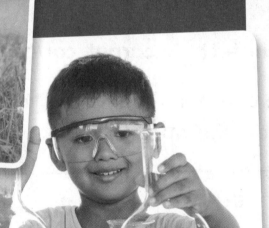

Children help younger children. They teach them, care for them, and protect them.

Children are scientists. One girl discovered an exploding star. One boy found a chemical that will help protect Earth.

Children play in children's orchestras to make beautiful music together.

Weekly Question

How can you get involved to improve your community?

Quick Write Think of one thing you can do. Think of one thing you would like to do. Write them here.

Syllable Pattern VCCV

Each syllable in a word has one vowel sound. When two vowels are separated by two consonants (VCCV), the syllables break between the consonants (VC/CV). The vowel sound in the first syllable is usually short. Sometimes it is an **r**-controlled vowel.

tablet tab/let   **insect in/sect**   **carpet car/pet**

MY TURN Draw a line between the syllables in each word. Then read, or decode, the words.

basket	reptile	sister	contact	public
trumpet	market	orbit	circus	napkin

TURN and TALK With a partner, check where you drew the lines to divide the syllables. Then read the words together again, blending the syllables.

The second syllable can have a short, long, or r-controlled vowel. Look for syllable patterns you've learned.

Syllable Pattern VCCV

MY TURN Write the syllables of each word in the boxes next to it. Then read the word.

1. expert

2. invent

3. object

4. plastic

5. publish

6. perfect

7. garden

8. custom

My Words to Know

MY TURN Read the words in the box. Then identify and write the word that completes each sentence.

horse	problem	complete

1. Rena likes to ride her _____ through the woods.

2. Curt had a hard time with the math _____.

3. Taki wanted to _____ all his homework before dinner.

TURN and TALK Work with a partner. Take turns answering these questions. Use the My Words to Know words in your answers.

1. Would you like to have a **horse?** Why or why not?

2. Name a **problem** you wish you could solve.

3. What chores do you need to **complete** each day?

Kent's Idea

At school, Kent always completed his lessons before other students completed their lessons. For him, this was a problem. He wanted more to do.

Then he had a splendid idea. "Can I read to the first graders?" he asked. His teacher said yes.

Now Kent reads chapter books to the first graders every week. They love him!

1. What was Kent's problem? _____

_____

2. How did he solve his problem? _____

_____

3. Divide these words into syllables and read them.

lessons   splendid

problem   chapter

My Learning Goal

I can learn about making a difference by reading a persuasive text.

Persuasive Text

Persuasive text uses facts and opinions to get readers to think or act a certain way.

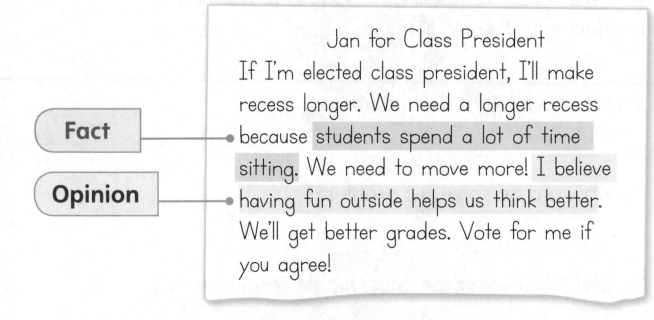

Fact

Opinion

Jan for Class President
If I'm elected class president, I'll make recess longer. We need a longer recess because students spend a lot of time sitting. We need to move more! I believe having fun outside helps us think better. We'll get better grades. Vote for me if you agree!

TURN and TALK Talk with a partner. Describe how biographies and persuasive text are alike. Then tell how they are different.

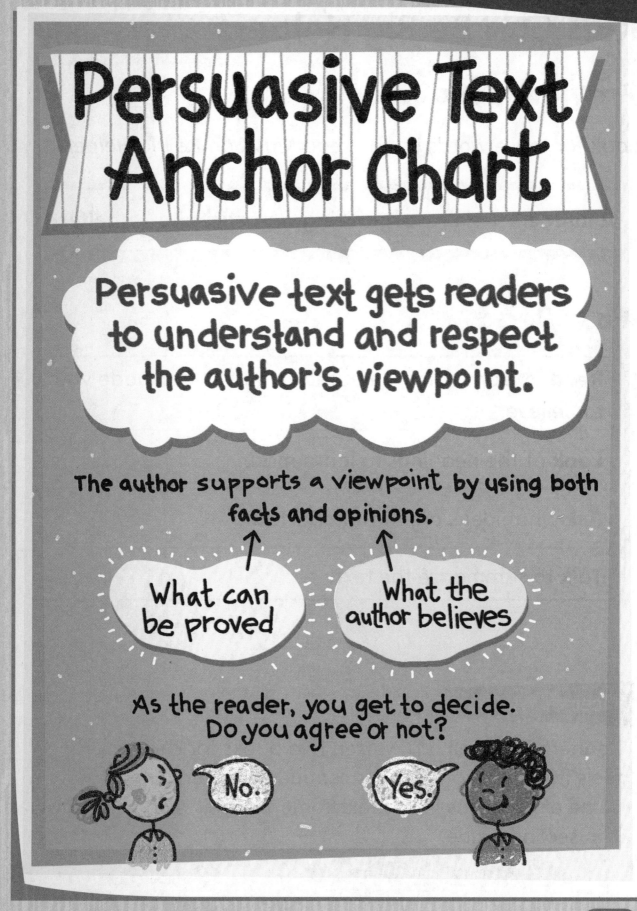

Persuasive Text Anchor Chart

Persuasive text gets readers to understand and respect the author's viewpoint.

The author supports a viewpoint by using both facts and opinions.

What can be proved

What the author believes

As the reader, you get to decide. Do you agree or not?

No.

Yes.

Kids Can Be Big Helpers

Preview Vocabulary

Look for these words as you read *Kids Can Be Big Helpers*.

volunteers	skill	organizing	participate	shelter

First Read

Read to learn what the author wants to persuade you to believe.

Look at the headings to learn more.

Ask what ideas are most important.

Talk to summarize the text.

Meet the Author

Kenneth Braswell has written two books for children. He feels that helping out in his community is very important. Some of the ideas in this text came from his own son, who is in second grade.

Genre Persuasive Text

Kids Can Be BIG Helpers

by Kenneth Braswell

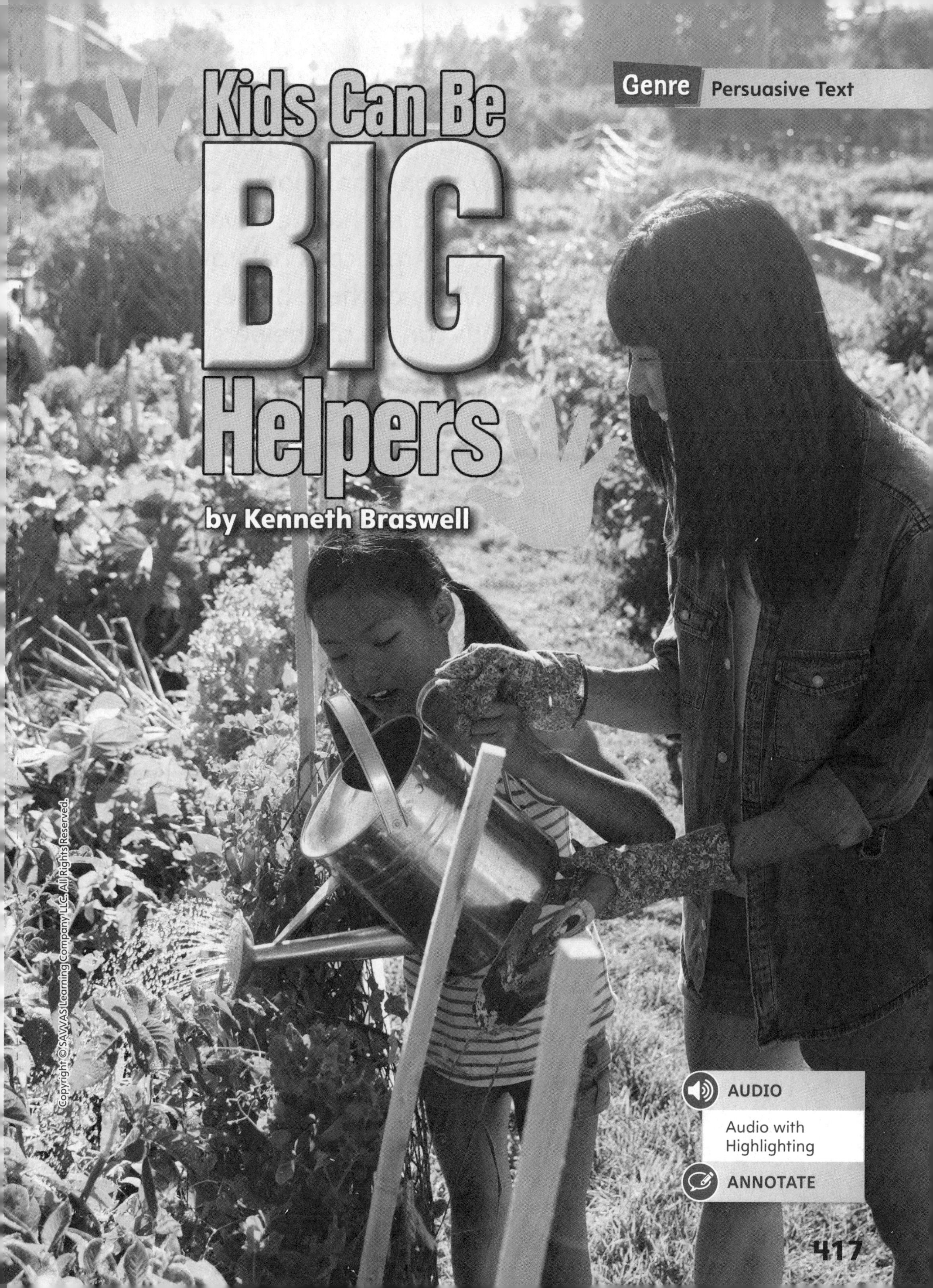

AUDIO

Audio with Highlighting

ANNOTATE

Understand Persuasive Text

Underline words that tell what the author wants to persuade the reader to believe.

1   There are more than 320 million people living in the United States. How can so many people get along? One way is by helping each other. Every day, millions of Americans help other Americans. Many of these helpers are students. Kids can be big helpers.

Helping Others at Home and at School

2 You see people being helpful every day. At home, family members carry groceries or help do the dishes. At school, students help teachers clean up. Students help classmates with school work.

Helping Others in the Community

3   You see people helping in your community, too. Some people help as part of their jobs, such as police officers. Some helpers are volunteers. A volunteer is someone who is not paid to do a job. Volunteers help to make their communities better places to live. Volunteers make a difference.

volunteers people who do jobs without getting paid

4   Volunteering and helping others makes people feel good. Grown-ups volunteer. Young people can volunteer, too. Everyone should volunteer. Keep reading to find out why.

Some Jobs Volunteers Can Do

- Read to young children
- Raise money for special causes
- Clean up litter in outdoor areas
- Collect books or clothing for people who need them
- Visit a senior center to brighten the day of an older person

Monitor Comprehension

One way to monitor comprehension is to look for pictures that help you understand the text. Reread the list of jobs volunteers can do. Highlight the job that is shown in the picture.

Understand Persuasive Text

<u>Underline</u> one reason the author gives in the paragraph to convince you that kids should help others.

Reason 1

Helping Others Makes Good Citizens

5   Helping others is an important way to be a good citizen. Good citizens pay attention to issues, or problems, in their community. For example, some people might not have enough food to eat. Or maybe children don't have a place to play outside. Different communities have special problems. Volunteers can work together to help in a variety of ways.

6   When people volunteer, they learn to be responsible. They take action and try to fix problems. Being responsible also means being trustworthy.

People Who Are Responsible . . .

- Show up on time.
- Do what they say they are going to do.
- Stay until the job is finished.

CLOSE READ

Monitor Comprehension

Reread the text. Highlight the first problem students in the example need to solve. Then highlight how they solve it.

skill something a person does well

Reason 2

Helping Others Teaches Useful Skills

7   When people volunteer and help others, they learn new skills. One important skill is problem solving. Volunteers often work to solve problems. Here's an example: A group of students wants to raise money for the local animal shelter. The first problem is how to raise money. The students come up with the idea of having a pet fair. Then comes the next problem: figuring out how to put the whole event together!

8 First, the students ask for help from other students and from parents. Some helpers make homemade dog treats. Other helpers make cat toys. Other helpers make posters. They also send messages on social media. Talking to people, organizing things, and working with others are all important skills!

organizing planning so things run smoothly

Pet Treats

Pet Toys

Pet Costumes

Understand Persuasive Text

Underline a reason the author gives in the text for helping people.

Reason 3

Helping Others Is Good for People

9 Believe it or not, helping others is good for your health. Experts say that helping others makes people happier. They feel good about themselves. Happy people who feel good about themselves are usually healthier. Volunteering can also make you more successful. According to one expert, students who volunteer do better in school.

Reason 4

Helping Others Is Fun!

10   Another good reason to help others is because it can be fun. You can volunteer to do things you enjoy. You can work with friends. People often make new friends when they volunteer. Think how nice it would be to help someone and laugh with a friend all at the same time.

CLOSE READ

Vocabulary in Context

<u>Underline</u> words in the text that help you understand what **donate** means.

participate take part; join

Ways to Help Others

11 One way to help others is to participate in a drive. In a penny drive, students ask classmates and parents to donate, or give, pennies. They collect lots of pennies. Over time, those pennies add up. Then the money is donated to people who need help. A penny drive is a great way to learn about money while helping others.

CLOSE READ

12   Many families volunteer in places such as shelters. A shelter is a place where people live and receive help while they are looking for another home. Volunteers help by preparing and serving food. Volunteers might also talk and play games with people who need a friend.

shelter a home for a short time

13   You can also help your community in small ways every day. Be a good example to others. Don't litter. Clean up after yourself. Be courteous to workers such as waiters and store clerks. All of these actions are part of being a good citizen.

Start Helping!

14   There are many ways kids can be big helpers. You can help out at home or at school. You can volunteer in your community. Helping others can happen almost anywhere. There are many good reasons to help other people. Not only is it good for them, it's good for you, too.

15   Find a way to help someone today— and every day!

Monitor Comprehension

Highlight something in the text that you don't understand. Think about a question you could ask about it.

Develop Vocabulary

MY TURN Use the definitions from the Close Read notes to write what each word means. Use a print or digital dictionary to determine, or figure out, how to pronounce, or say, the words.

Word	Meaning
volunteers	
skill	
organizing	
participate	
shelter	

Check for Understanding

MY TURN Look back at the text to answer the questions. Write the answers.

1. What is the author of this persuasive text trying to convince readers to do?

_____

_____

_____

2. Why do you think the author used section headings in this text?

_____

_____

_____

3. Do you agree with the author's argument? Why or why not?

_____

_____

_____

Understand Persuasive Text

A writer uses persuasive text to try to convince readers to think or act a certain way. The **argument** is the main idea. It is what the author wants readers to think or do. The author supports the argument with **reasons, evidence,** and **examples.**

MY TURN Go to the Close Read notes. Underline the reasons the author uses to support his argument. Use what you underlined and other text evidence to complete the chart.

Main Argument			
Reason 1	**Reason 2**	**Reason 3**	**Reason 4**

Monitor Comprehension

As you read, stop to monitor comprehension, or think about whether you understand what you just read. If you do not understand something, you may need to make adjustments to understand more. You can:

- **Reread** parts of the text you did not understand.

- **Use background knowledge** (what you already know).

- **Check for visual cues** in the illustrations or photos.

- **Ask questions** about what you don't understand.

MY TURN Go back to the Close Read notes and follow the instructions to highlight the text. Then use what you highlighted to complete the chart.

Parts of the Text I Did Not Understand	Strategy I Used to Understand

Reflect and Share

Talk About It

Discuss the texts you've read that tell how children can make a difference in a community. What ideas have the texts given you? Describe your personal connection to these texts, or what they mean to you.

Take Turns

It's important to take turns in a discussion. Sometimes you might feel like you have something really important to say, but you need to wait until the person talking has finished.

- Make your point and then give others a chance to respond.

- If you interrupt someone by accident, say you're sorry and let them finish.

I'm sorry. I didn't mean to interrupt. Please finish what you were saying.

Weekly Question

How can you get involved to improve your community?

I can develop knowledge about language to make connections between reading and writing.

My Learning Goal

Academic Vocabulary

You have learned many different words during this unit. Choose six new words you learned that could help you answer the Essential Question: **Why is it important to connect with other people?** Write them in the blanks below.

_____

_____

_____

_____

_____

TURN and TALK Tell your partner why you chose the words you did. Then use the words to answer the Essential Question.

Read Like a Writer, Write for a Reader

Authors choose words to persuade readers to think or act a certain way.

Author's Words	What It Makes Me Think or Want to Do
"You can volunteer to do things you enjoy. You can work with friends. People often make new friends when they volunteer. Think how nice it would be to help someone and laugh with a friend all at the same time."	These words make me think that volunteering is fun and it is something I'd like to do.

MY TURN Write three or four sentences to persuade readers of something. It could be why you should get a pet, why your bedtime should be later, or why people should not litter. Choose your words carefully.

Choose a topic you feel strongly about.

Spell Words with Syllable Pattern VCCV

MY TURN A dictionary has **guide words** that tell the first and last words on each page. Write the Spelling Word you would find on a dictionary page with each pair of guide words.

1. hit–hump _____

2. vase–vest _____

Write the rest of the Spelling Words and the My Words to Know words in alphabetical order. To help you write the words in ABC order, say the alphabet to yourself. If two words start with the same letter, look at the second and third letters. Hint: **complete** comes before **contest** because **m** comes before **n**.

1. _____   **6.** _____

2. _____   **7.** _____

3. _____   **8.** _____

4. _____   **9.** _____

5. _____   **10.** _____

Spelling Words

magnet

hornet

bandit

signal

velvet

dentist

doctor

sister

harvest

contest

My Words to Know

problem

complete

Reflexive Pronouns

A **reflexive pronoun** refers back to the subject of the sentence. Reflexive pronouns end in **-self** or **-selves**.

I see myself in the mirror. They see themselves in the mirror.

Reflexive Pronouns	
myself refers to **I**	**ourselves** refers to **we**
yourself refers to **you**	**yourselves** refers to **you**
himself refers to **he** or a noun **herself** refers to **she** or a noun **itself** refers to **it** or a noun	**themselves** refers to **they**

MY TURN Write the correct reflexive pronouns to complete this story.

I made breakfast _____ today. When Dad came into the kitchen, I said, "You can help _____." We ate by _____ because Mom was still asleep. After breakfast, Dad cleaned up by _____. Later we all went for a walk and saw children playing ball. They were really enjoying _____!

I can use elements of narrative nonfiction to write a personal narrative.

My Learning Goal

Edit for Adjectives and Adverbs

Authors edit their writing to check that they have used adjectives, including articles, and adverbs correctly.

MY TURN Edit this draft. Read it once to look for ways you can add adjectives and adverbs to make the writing more interesting. Read it again to look for mistakes in the use of adjectives, including articles, and adverbs.

Our class went on a trip to a awesome pumpkin farm. There were hundreds of pumpkins! I could hard decide which one to pick. So I picked two. First, I chose the tall, oval pumpkin. Then I chose a small one. I'm going to paint a face on each one.

MY TURN Edit your personal narrative for adjectives, including articles, and adverbs.

Edit for Spelling

Authors use spelling patterns and rules as they edit to make sure they have spelled words correctly. Here are some tips for spelling words correctly:

- Think about the base word, or main part, of long words. For example, **helper** has the word **help** in it.
- Some common words, such as **people** and **because**, are hard to spell. You will have to learn them.
- You can add endings to word parts to make other words.

 MY TURN Edit this draft to fix mistakes in spelling.

> Last month, my class wanted to help peeple in our
>
> community. So we decidid to have a food drive. We had a
>
> contst to see who could collect the most food. Everbody
>
> brought in something. Our teecher was very proud of us!

 MY TURN Edit your personal narrative for the correct spelling of words.

Assessment

In this unit, you learned to write a personal narrative. Rate how well you understand each skill. Review any skill you mark "No."

1. How to generate ideas for a personal narrative	YES NO
2. How to plan a personal narrative	YES NO
3. How to write a setting	YES NO
4. How to develop a sequence of events with a problem and a resolution	YES NO
5. How to add details	YES NO
6. How to write a conclusion	YES NO
7. How to proofread and edit for: • capitalization and commas • pronouns • compound subjects and predicates • adjectives and adverbs • spelling	YES NO

UNIT THEME

Making a Difference

TURN and TALK I Spy

With your partner, write an example from each text of one person connecting with another or with a group of people. Use your notes to help you answer the Essential Question.

WEEK 3

The Garden of Happiness

_____

_____

BOOK CLUB

WEEK 2

Building on Nature

_____

_____

BOOK CLUB

WEEK 1

Who Says Women Can't Be Doctors?

_____

_____

★ **BOOK** CLUB

One Plastic Bag

_____
_____
_____

ONE PLASTIC BAG

WEEK
4

★ **BOOK** CLUB

WEEK
5

Kids Can Be Big Helpers

_____
_____

Kids Can Be BIG Helpers

Essential Question

MY TURN

In your notebook, answer the Essential Question: Why is it important to connect with other people?

★ **BOOK** CLUB

Project

WEEK
6

Now it is time to apply what you learned about connectons in your **WEEK 6** **PROJECT: Time Capsule!**

445

Consonant Patterns kn, wr, gn, mb, lf

Sometimes letters can be silent when they are in certain consonant patterns.

MY TURN Look at this chart. Read, or decode, the example words aloud.

Silent Consonants	Examples
k in **kn**	know
w in **wr**	write
g in **gn**	gnat, sign
b in **mb**	thumb
l in **lf**	half

TURN and TALK Read these sentences with a partner. Tell which consonants are silent. Then choose one of the words and use it in a sentence. Share your sentence with your partner.

I knew the word on the sign was wrong.

A lamb and a calf climb the hill.

Consonant Patterns kn, wr, gn, mb, lf

These letters are silent: **k** in **kn**, **w** in **wr**, **g** in **gn**, **b** in **mb**, and **l** in **lf**.

MY TURN Write the word from the box to match each clue. Circle the silent letter. Then read the word.

calf	knock	lamb
sign	wrong	knife

1. make a noise on a door _____

2. the opposite of **right** _____

3. where you see the word STOP _____

4. a baby sheep _____

5. something sharp to cut with _____

6. a baby cow _____

MY TURN Use two of the words from the box in a sentence. Read your sentence aloud.

_____

My Words to Know

MY TURN Read the high-frequency words in the box. Identify and <u>underline</u> the words in the paragraph. Then read the paragraph.

since	usually	friends

    Dana has lots of friends. She usually plays with them at the park. Since she has a lot of friends, she is never lonely.

Write each word next to its meaning.

1. most of the time _____

2. people you like to spend time with _____

3. another word for **because** _____

TURN and TALK Work with a partner. Make up new sentences that use each word.

Spell Words with kn, wr, gn, mb, lf

MY TURN The Spelling Words have consonant patterns with silent letters. Write the missing letter to make a spelling word from the list. Then write the word.

1. clim__ _____

2. ca__f _____

3. __nife _____

4. __rong _____

5. si__n _____

6. thum__ _____

7. __nat _____

8. __rite _____

9. com__ _____

10. __now _____

Spelling Words

wrong
thumb
calf
gnat
know
climb
comb
knife
sign
write

My Words to Know

usually
friends

Write a My Words to Know word to complete each sentence.

11. She _____ has cereal for breakfast.

12. I like to play with my _____.

Time Capsule

Activity

A time capsule is a way to connect with people in the future. Create a group time capsule you could bury that would help future generations understand your life today.

Let's Read!

This week you will read three articles about connecting with other people. Today's article will give you information about time capsules.

1. **Time Capsules**

2. **Let's Connect!**

3. **Connecting for a Cause**

Generate Questions

COLLABORATE With a partner, list two keywords or terms to use to guide your search in learning more about time capsules.

Use Academic Words

COLLABORATE What would you like people in the future to know about your life today? How could you tell those people what your life is like? Talk with your partner. Take turns listening and speaking. Try to use the Academic Vocabulary words.

Academic Vocabulary

connect	improve
discuss	responsible
equal	

Time Capsule Research Plan

Create and follow a research plan with help from your teacher.

Day 1 Generate key words for research.

Day 2 _____

Day 3 _____

Day 4 Write and revise a list of items in your time capsule. Include reasons for each.

Day 5 _____

Just the Facts

An informational text has

- one main idea.

- key details that provide supporting evidence.

- facts, examples, and definitions if needed.

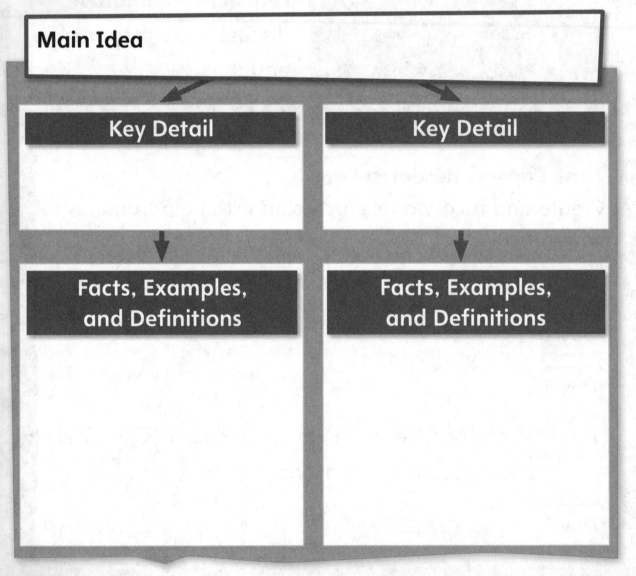

COLLABORATE Read "Let's Connect!" Then fill in the chart with information from the text.

Main Idea

Key Detail

Key Detail

Facts, Examples, and Definitions

Facts, Examples, and Definitions

Use a Web Site

A Web site often has different pages. Web pages on a Web site are linked. Each Web page has different information.

The home page of a Web site shows its Web pages as links you can click on. There are ways to identify the links. The text may be a different color, or it may turn a different color when you put the cursor over it.

http://today'stimecapsule.com

TODAY'S TIME CAPSULE

About
Get Started
FAQ
Photo Gallery
Contact

COLLABORATE Work with your partner to follow your research plan. Name the Web pages linked to the home page above. Then find a Web site to help you research time capsules. Find information on the Web pages. Record the name of the Web site and its URL.

List with Reasons

Write a list of what you would put in your time capsule. Include your reasons for including these items.

Items in My Time Capsule •————— Topic
to Be Opened in 2050

- recording of my favorite songs
  I want people in the future to •—————┐
  hear today's music.   │
- daily newspaper   Reasons
  People can read about today's   │
  important events. •—————————————————┘

- my favorite book
  Books in print may not exist in the future.

- a picture of my soccer team
  Sports jerseys and hairstyles will change.

- a copy of my daily schedule
  People may want to know how children
  spent their days.

Primary and Secondary Sources

COLLABORATE A **primary source** is made by someone who was at an event. It could be a letter, a blog or diary, or a recording. A **secondary source** is made by someone who got information from other sources. It could be a textbook or a book.

As you research time capsules, identify the items included as primary or secondary sources. Record two of each below.

Primary Sources	Secondary Sources

COLLABORATE With your group, decide on two primary sources and one secondary source for your time capsule.

Primary source: _____

Secondary source: _____

Write a Letter

A friendly letter has five parts. Note how each part is punctuated and capitalized.

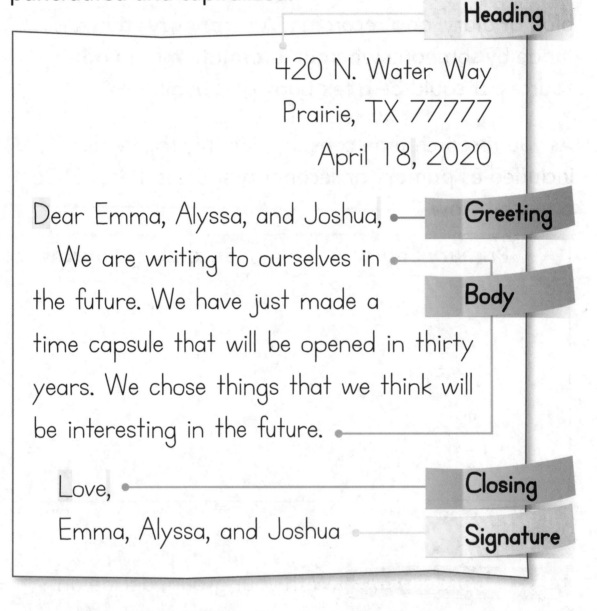

Heading

420 N. Water Way
Prairie, TX 77777
April 18, 2020

Dear Emma, Alyssa, and Joshua, **Greeting**

We are writing to ourselves in **Body**
the future. We have just made a
time capsule that will be opened in thirty
years. We chose things that we think will
be interesting in the future.

Love, **Closing**

Emma, Alyssa, and Joshua **Signature**

COLLABORATE With your group, write a letter to yourselves in the future. Tell about your thoughts and choices while creating the time capsule.

Revise

COLLABORATE This week your group created a time capsule to connect with people in the future. Reread your list with the reasons why you included the items. Do you need to add or change any items?

My list has...

☐ a title

☐ the name of each item in the time capsule

☐ a reason explaining why we chose each item

Edit

COLLABORATE Now it is time to edit your list. Check that these are correct:

☐ spelling

☐ punctuation

☐ capitalization of names and places

Share

COLLABORATE With your group, present your time capsule to another class. Use your list to identify and explain each item. Work collaboratively with your group to get ready to present.

- Divide the list equally among members of the group so that everyone will contribute to your talk.

- Agree on rules for discussion, such as listening to others and speaking when recognized.

- Build on each other's ideas as you make your contributions.

Reflect

MY TURN Complete the sentences.

I enjoyed working with the group on the time capsule because _____

_____

_____

One thing I found challenging was _____

_____

_____

Reflect on Your Goals

Look back at your unit goals. Use a different color to rate yourself again.

MY TURN Complete the sentences.

Reflect on Your Reading

From my independent reading in this unit, I most

liked _____

_____

because _____

_____

Reflect on Your Writing

From my writing in this unit, I most enjoyed writing

_____

_____

because _____

_____

Our Incredible Earth

Essential Question

How does Earth change?

▶ Watch

"Our Changing Earth" to see how many ways Earth can change.

TURN and TALK What kinds of changes did you see in the video?

Reading-Writing Bridge

- Academic Vocabulary
- Read Like a Writer, Write for a Reader
- Spelling • Language and Conventions

Writing Workshop

Procedural Text

- Introduce and Immerse
- Develop Elements • Develop Structure
- Writer's Craft • Publish, Celebrate, and Assess

Project-Based Inquiry

- Inquire • Research • Collaborate

Independent Reading

Reading on your own is a good way to become a better reader. The more you read, the easier it will become. When choosing a book, first decide what your purpose is for reading. Then select a book that matches that purpose.

Choose a book on something you want to know more about.

After you have read a book, review it. Think about the answers to these questions:

- What did I like about the book?
- What didn't I like about the book?
- Did the book meet my purpose for reading?
- Overall, did I like this book? Would I suggest it to a friend?

My Reading Log

Date	Book	Pages Read	Minutes Read	My Ratings
				🙂 😐 🙁
				🙂 😐 🙁
				🙂 😐 🙁
				🙂 😐 🙁
				🙂 😐 🙁
				🙂 😐 🙁

Unit Goals

In this unit, you will

- read informational text
- write a procedural text
- learn about changes on Earth

 **MY TURN** **Color** the pictures to answer.

I know about different types of informational text and understand their features and structures.	👍	👎
I can use language to make connections between reading and writing informational text.	👍	👎
I can use elements of informational text to write a procedural text.	👍	👎
I can talk with others about how Earth changes.	👍	👎

Academic Vocabulary

destroy	environment	reaction	balance	resources

In this unit, you will read about the changing **environment** on Earth. You will learn how forces of nature act on the Earth and the **reaction** they cause when landforms move and change. You'll read how volcanoes **destroy** things around them when they erupt. You may wonder how the Earth keeps itself in **balance**. You may also think about how these changes affect **resources** on Earth.

TURN and TALK Use the Academic Vocabulary words to talk with your partner about ways Earth can change. The picture will help you.

Earth's Features

Earth has many features. Here are just a few.

Earth's air is just right for us to breathe. The air protects us from harmful light and objects in space.

Most of Earth is covered by water. Ocean water is salt water. Water in most lakes and rivers is fresh water.

Clouds are water in the air. They drop rain and snow on Earth.

Weekly Question

What are some of Earth's changing features?

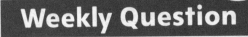

Look at the photo. How do you think the rocks on shore got their shapes?

Land on Earth takes many forms. Tall mountains, grassy plains, and sandy coasts are all landforms.

Homographs

Homographs are words that are spelled the same but have different meanings.

Can means "able to": I **can** ride a bike.

Can may also mean "a metal container": The soup is in a **can**.

Look at the words around a homograph in a sentence to figure out its meaning.

MY TURN Read the words and their meanings.

bat ─┬─ a flying animal
     └─ what you use to hit a ball in baseball

fall ─┬─ go or move down
      └─ the season after summer

TURN and TALK Read the sentences with a partner. Decide which meaning is used. Then use the word **bat** in two sentences with two different meanings. Then identify two other homographs.

1. **Bats** fill the sky in the evening.

2. The leaves turn yellow in the **fall**.

Homographs

Homographs are spelled the same but have different meanings. The context of the sentence will help you identify which meaning of the homograph is being used.

MY TURN Read each sentence. Circle the meaning of each homograph in **bold** print.

1. I **saw** a good movie.

   a. past tense of **see**   b. a tool to cut wood

2. The toy boat can't **sink**.

   a. where you wash up   b. go under water

3. Marsha **left** her keys at home.

   a. the opposite of **right**   b. let stay behind

4. A big **wave** washed away Ted's sand castle.

   a. move your hand to greet   b. a ridge of water

TURN and TALK Use the word **fly** in a sentence. Then have your partner use the word in a sentence in which it has a different meaning. Then identify another pair of homographs, and repeat the activity.

My Words to Know

Some words are used often. These words are called high-frequency words. You will have to remember these words. Often, you can't sound them out.

MY TURN Read the words in the box. <u>Underline</u> each word in the sentences below. Read the sentences. Then write a sentence that uses each word. Form the letters correctly as you write each word. Use connecting strokes to connect the letters.

heard	door	sure

Mark heard someone knocking. He went to the door. He wasn't sure who it was, so he asked, "Who's there?"

1. _____

2. _____

3. _____

TURN and TALK Work with a partner. Read each other's sentences. Help with any corrections.

The Best Place

Abby lives on the coast. From the beach, she sees crashing waves and tall cliffs. She is sure this is the best place on Earth.

Dale lives in the mountains. When he stands on the rocks, he sees their snowy tops. He is sure this is the best place.

Who is right? They both are! To Abby and Dale, where they live is the best.

1. Where do Abby and Dale live? _____

_____

2. How are Abby and Dale alike? _____

_____

3. Underline the words **rocks** and **tops** in the passage. Then circle the letter of the meaning used.

rocks: a. moves back and forth   b. large stones

tops: a. the highest points   b. toys that spin

My Learning Goal

I can read informational text and learn facts about a topic.

Spotlight on Genre

Informational Text

Science books and how-to texts are examples of informational text. Informational text:

- tells facts about people, animals, places, or events.

- may include text and graphic features that add or explain information.

- includes a main topic with details that support it.

Facts are bits of information that can be proved true.

 MY TURN Describe someone or something important to you. You might talk about a family member, your home, or a favorite place. Use facts.

Informational Text Anchor Chart

Facts about people
Dana Brown works at the state park.

Facts about places
In the Arctic, icebergs float in the open water.

Informational text tells facts about a topic.

Facts about animals
Many lizards live in trees.

Facts about events
People around the world watch the Olympics.

Introducing Landforms

Preview Vocabulary

Look for these words as you read *Introducing Landforms*.

| coast | plains | desert | canyons | volcano |

First Read

Read to learn about landforms.

Look at the photos to help you understand the text.

Ask questions to clarify information.

Talk about the text with a partner.

Meet the Author

Bobbie Kalman

Bobbie Kalman and **Kelley MacAulay** have written many children's books together. They have written about deserts, storms, zebras, reptiles, and karate. In this excerpt from *Introducing Landforms*, they focus on the many interesting features of planet Earth.

Introducing Landforms

by Bobbie Kalman and
Kelley MacAulay

AUDIO

Audio with
Highlighting

ANNOTATE

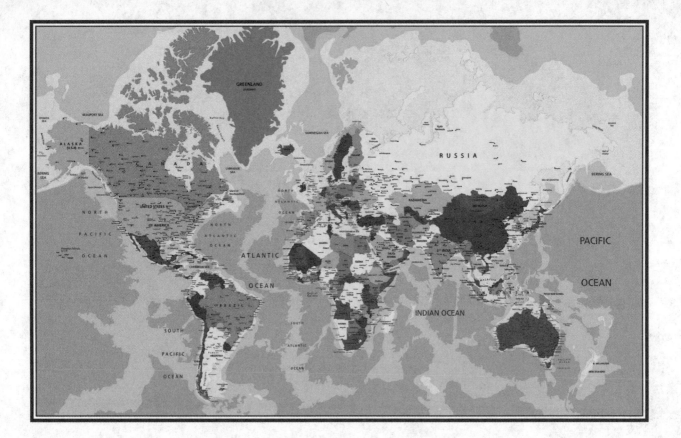

How Earth looks

1   There are seven huge areas of land on Earth. The areas of land are called **continents**. The continents are North America, South America, Europe, Asia, Africa, Australia and Oceania, and Antarctica. There are huge areas of water around the continents. The areas of water are called **oceans**.

What are landforms?

2   The continents are Earth's biggest **landforms**. Landforms are different shapes of land on Earth. In some places, the land is flat. In other places, the land is tall and steep. There are many kinds of landforms on Earth.

Wind and water shape rocks.

Fire shapes some mountains.

Ice creates many landforms.

What shapes the land?

3   Landforms are shaped by wind, fire, water, and ice. Landforms are also shaped by movements of the Earth under the ground. Some landforms are shaped by animals or people.

Small underwater animals created this island.

People created these peninsulas.

CLOSE READ

Describe Connections

<u>Underline</u> the words in paragraph 3 that tell what shapes the land.

Monitor Comprehension

Readers can make adjustments when their understanding breaks down. Highlight the sentences in the text that the larger picture helps you understand.

coast the land along the sea

The water in oceans is salt water. Salt water has a lot of salt in it. This girl is playing in shallow ocean water on a beach.

Ocean meets land

4   A coast is a landform. It is the edge of land where it meets an ocean. Coasts can be very different. Some are rocky with **cliffs**. A cliff is a tall, steep rock. Other coasts have beaches. A beach is an area of sand or **pebbles** next to water. The water at many beaches is shallow and clear.

cliff

cliff

This rocky coast has tall cliffs.

The coast and water

5   Peninsulas and sea caves are landforms that are parts of some coasts. Some coasts give the ocean waters near them different shapes. **Bays, coves,** and **harbors** are ocean waters that are shaped by coasts. They are shown below.

A sea cave is a large hole in the side of a cliff. The cave is made by waves that hit the cliff many times.

1. A peninsula is land that has water around three sides.

2. A bay is water that has land almost all around it.

3. A cove is a small bay.

4. A harbor is an area of water near a coast where boats are protected from the wind and waves.

Describe Connections

<u>Underline</u> sentences that describe how rivers and lakes are connected.

Rivers and lakes

6 **Rivers** and **lakes** are bodies of water that are on continents. A river is a large stream of water that flows into a lake or an ocean. A lake is a body of water that has land all around it. The water in rivers and lakes is **fresh water**. Fresh water does not have very much salt in it.

Most rivers start high up on mountains and flow downhill. Some rivers crash over cliffs in waterfalls. As the rivers flow, they carry rocks and dirt with them. Over time, rivers wear away the land. Rivers can even cut through mountains! In this way, rivers help shape the land on Earth.

What makes lakes?

7   Lakes form in large **basins** in the Earth. A basin is like a bowl. Many lakes form from melting **glaciers**. A glacier is a slow-moving river of ice. The water in lakes comes mainly from the rivers and streams that flow into them. Some of the water comes from rain and melting snow.

glacier

mountain

glacier

river

lake

When glaciers melt, the water flows down mountains in rivers. Some of the rivers empty into lakes.

Monitor Comprehension

Highlight the words that help you think about something you may have done that relates to the topic of this section.

High mountains

8   Have you ever climbed a mountain? A mountain is a very high area of rocky land. It is wide at the bottom and narrow at the top. It has steep sides. Mountains that are small and not steep are called hills.

This girl has climbed a mountain. The mountain is rocky and steep. How did she get up there?

The weather is cold high on mountains. Few plants and animals live there.

Some mountain ranges are very long. The Rocky Mountain range stretches from British Columbia, Canada, to New Mexico in the United States.

Alone or in groups?

9   Some mountains stand alone. A mountain that stands alone does not have other mountains around it. Most mountains are in groups. A group of mountains is called a **mountain range.** There are many mountain ranges on Earth.

Mount Fuji is a mountain in Japan. There are no other mountains around it.

CLOSE READ

Monitor Comprehension

Highlight the words that the picture helps you understand.

The valleys below

10   **Valleys** are low landforms that are between mountains. They are also below mountains. Some valleys have curved sides. Valleys with curved sides are U-shaped. Other valleys have steep sides. Valleys with steep sides are V-shaped. This picture shows a V-shaped valley.

Down in the valley

11   The weather is warmer in valleys than on the mountains around them. Trees, grasses, and flowers grow in valleys. There are rivers, too. Elk, rabbits, chipmunks, and hawks live in valleys. This horse has found food to eat in a valley.

This elk finds food and water in this valley river.

Describe Connections

Underline words that describe what plains are like in different places.

plains flat areas of land

Wide, flat plains

12   Much of the land on Earth is made up of **plains**. Plains are huge areas of nearly flat land. Some plains are covered in bushes or **forests**. Forests are areas with many trees. Other plains are covered in grasses and flowers. They are called **grasslands** or **prairies**.

Rabbits live in grasses on plains. This rabbit is hiding in the long grass.

These deer live on a plain with a forest. They are drinking from a river that flows through the plain.

These sheep are grazing, or eating grass, on a plain. Cows and horses also graze on plains.

Good for farming

13   The soil on plains is good for growing **crops**. Crops are plants that people grow for food. Plains are also good places to raise farm animals. On plains, there is plenty of grass to eat for cows, horses, and sheep.

corn

These palms are growing in a desert oasis.

CLOSE READ

desert a dry, sandy area of land without water and trees

Desert landforms

14   Deserts are dry areas that get very little rain. Strong winds blow in deserts. The winds push sand into huge piles called **dunes**. Dunes are desert landforms.

Desert oasis

15   In some parts of deserts, there is water under the ground. When the water comes up from the ground, it makes an **oasis**. An oasis is an area in a desert where plants grow.

dunes

Mesas and buttes

16   Mesas are other desert landforms. Mesas are hills and mountains with flat tops and very steep sides. Wind blows sand against the sides of mesas. Over time, the mesas become very narrow. When they become narrow, the mesas are called buttes.

These buttes are called the "Three Sisters."

Vocabulary in Context

Underline words that help you understand what **buttes** are.

The Colorado River flows through the Grand Canyon. The Grand Canyon is a huge, wide canyon.

canyons narrow valleys with high, steep sides, often with a stream at the bottom

Deep canyons

17   Canyons are landforms that are also found in dry areas. Canyons are much deeper than the land around them is. Many canyons have rivers running through them. The rivers wear away the rocks in the canyons. Over time, the rivers change the shapes of the canyons.

Some canyons are very narrow.

Strange shapes

18 Some canyons have **hoodoos**. Hoodoos are thin rocks that rise up from the ground in dry areas. They have interesting shapes. Some hoodoos look like giant mushrooms. Other hoodoos look like weird creatures.

Vocabulary in Context

Find the picture that helps you understand the meaning of **creatures**. Underline that picture's caption.

These hoodoos are in Goblin Valley, Utah. What are goblins?

hoodoo

There are more hoodoos in Bryce Canyon, Utah, than in any other place on Earth. The hoodoos were formed by wind, water, and ice. People see many shapes in the hoodoos. What do you see?

opening

lava

This volcano is erupting. Hot lava is pouring down the sides of the volcano.

CLOSE READ

Describe Connections

<u>Underline</u> words that help you describe what dried lava does to volcanoes.

volcano an opening in the Earth's crust through which steam, ashes, and lava are sometimes forced out

What is a volcano?

19   A **volcano** is an opening in the Earth's surface. Some volcanoes are **active**, and some are **dormant**, or not active. An active volcano still erupts, or explodes. Smoke, ash, and lava shoot out from its opening. Lava is hot liquid rock. After lava pours out, it dries and gets hard. Each time a volcano **erupts,** the dried **lava** builds up. The volcano gets bigger and bigger.

Mountains of lava

20   Dried lava can get so tall that it makes a mountain! Some volcanoes erupt every day, and the mountains keep growing. Volcanoes that erupt under water become mountains, too. They grow until their tops reach above the surface of water. Their tops become islands.

These mountains formed from dried lava.

Wizard Island is a volcano that formed in the water. It is found in a lake in Oregon.

Develop Vocabulary

 MY TURN Write the meanings of these words from *Introducing Landforms*. Then write an example of each kind of landform.

Word	Meaning	Example
coast		
plains		
canyons		
volcano		
desert		

Check for Understanding

MY TURN Look back at the text to answer the questions. Write the answers.

1. What makes this text informational?

_____

2. Many of the words in this text are in bold print. Why do you think the author did this?

_____

_____

3. Which type of landform is most interesting to you? Why?

_____

_____

_____

The author of *Introducing Landforms* used headings to tell me what the paragraph under each heading is about.

Describe Connections

You can connect details to key ideas. Understanding the connection between ideas in a text can help you figure out what the text is all about.

MY TURN Go to the Close Read notes. Follow the directions to underline the text. Use the details you underlined to complete the chart.

Section Title	Key Ideas
What shapes the land?	Land is shaped by wind, fire, water, ice, movements of Earth, animals, and people.
Rivers and lakes	
Wide, flat plains	
Mountains of lava	

Describe how the ideas you underlined are connected.

Monitor Comprehension

As you read, stop to monitor comprehension, or think about whether you understand what you read. If you don't understand something, try making these adjustments:

- Reread the part you didn't understand.

- Use background knowledge.

- Check for visual cues in illustrations or photos.

- Ask questions.

MY TURN Go back to the Close Read notes and follow the instructions to highlight the text. Then complete the chart.

Parts of the Text I Did Not Understand	Strategy I Used to Understand It

Reflect and Share

Talk About It

Discuss the landforms you learned about this week. Talk about the ones you've seen and the ones you'd like to see. Use examples from the texts to support your response.

Ask for Clarification

You can develop social communication, or learn how to discuss, by knowing when to ask a question and when to tell something you know.

- Wait until the other person stops talking.

- Ask politely what he or she meant.

When you are speaking, other people may request clarification. This is your chance to explain what you meant.

- Use words that will make what you said easier to understand.

- Produce complete sentences.

Weekly Question

What are some of Earth's changing features?

I can use language to make connections between reading and writing informational texts.

My Learning Goal

Academic Vocabulary

Related words often share word parts. Their meanings may change depending on the word parts.

MY TURN For each vocabulary word, write a word that is related to it.

Word	Related Word	How Word Changed
destroy		
reaction		
balance		
resources		

Read Like a Writer, Write for a Reader

Authors use graphic features such as maps, photographs, pictures, and diagrams to help readers understand information in the text. In *Introducing Landforms*, the author used a map and many photographs.

Graphic Features	Why the Author Included It (Author's Purpose)
map in the section "How Earth Looks"	to help me see where continents and oceans are
photographs in the section "Strange Shapes"	to show me what hoodoos look like

MY TURN Suppose you are writing about landforms where you live. What graphic features would you include?

_____

_____

_____

_____

_____

_____

Spell Words That Are Homographs

Homographs are spelled the same but have different meanings. Sometimes they are pronounced differently.

MY TURN Write a Spelling Word to finish each sentence. Then write the My Words to Know words.

1. The bad news _____ me.

2. The _____ blew the leaves.

3. She _____ her homework after dinner.

4. He came in _____, not first.

5. Try not to _____ the paper.

6. Follow me and I'll _____ you.

7. The opposite of up is _____.

8. He _____ the string around the box.

9. Two things that look the same are a _____.

10. I can stand on one _____.

11. I _____ the bell ring.

12. Are you _____ you want to go?

Spelling Words
lead
wind
down
foot
upset
does
wound
match
tear
second

My Words to Know
heard
sure

Prepositions and Prepositional Phrases

A **preposition** is a word that shows how a noun and another word in a sentence are related. A preposition is the first word in a group of words called a **prepositional phrase**.

Sentence	Prepositional Phrase
The dog is in the house.	in the house
I left my book at school.	at school
We go to gym after lunch.	after lunch

MY TURN Edit this draft. Cross out each incorrect preposition. Write the correct preposition above it.

Every summer we go at the mountains. To get there, we drive across a tunnel. Then we drive toward a winding road. We stay in a cabin in a lake. We enjoy boating in the lake. We have fun swimming on the lake, too.

My Learning Goal

I can use elements of informational text to write a procedural text.

How-To Text

A **how-to text** is a kind of procedural text. In a **procedural text**, an author tells how to do something. The author includes step-by-step directions and sometimes graphic features to show what to do.

How to Make a Straw Painting

You Need: newspaper, paint, straws, plastic spoons, paper

What to Do

1. Cover your work area with newspaper.

2. Drop small blobs of paint on your paper with a spoon.

3. Blow air through the straw to spread the paint.

4. Move the straw for different patterns.

5. Try different paint colors and amounts.

Graphics

Command

Precise Instructions

Generate Ideas

Drawing is one way an author generates, or thinks of, ideas before beginning to write.

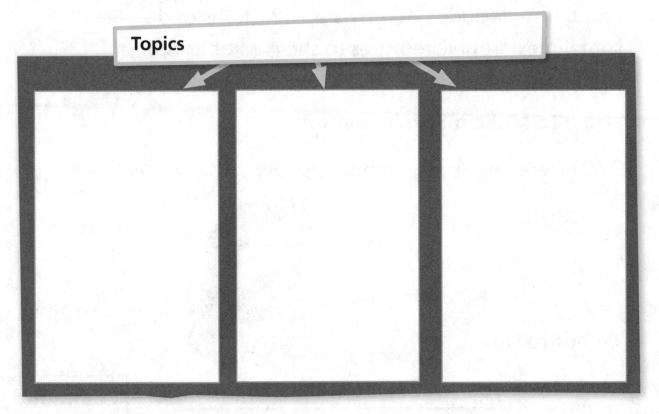 **Draw pictures to show three topics you might write about for your how-to text.**

Topics

Use this checklist to help decide which topic to use:

☐ This topic is something I know a lot about.

☐ I can break the procedure into simple steps.

☐ I can present each step in order.

☐ I will enjoy writing about this topic.

Plan Your How-To Text

Now focus on the topic of your procedural text and how to break down the procedure into simple steps.

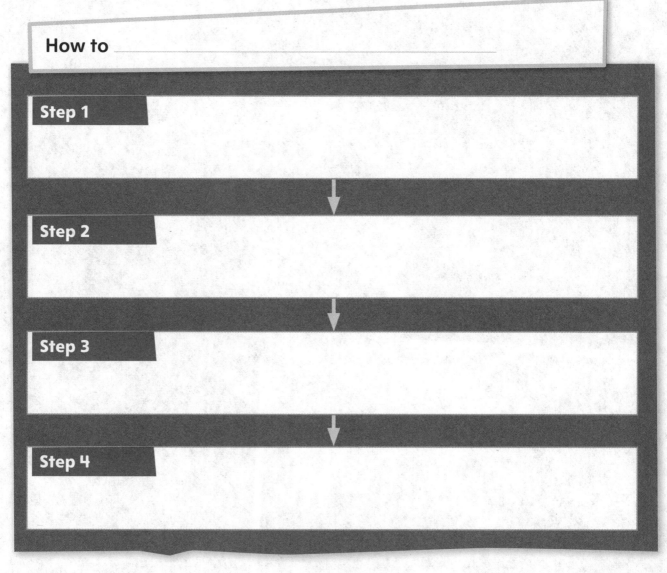 **MY TURN** Use the organizer to plan the step-by-step directions. Give the instructions orally and have others follow them. Help a classmate with his or her sequence of actions by following his or her instructions. Tell your ideas in Writing Club and ask for feedback.

How to _____

Step 1

Step 2

Step 3

Step 4

The Grand Canyon

The Grand Canyon is a natural treasure. In the canyon, you will find a mighty river and beautiful rock layers, signs of long-ago life, and fun things to do and explore.

Weekly Question

How do natural events change the Earth?

 **TURN and TALK**

How do you think the river and the canyon are connected? Talk about your ideas with a partner.

Double Consonants

A word with a VCCV pattern has two consonants. The word has a double consonant when the two consonants are the same. The syllables break between the double consonants (VC/CV). The first syllable is closed and usually has a short vowel sound.

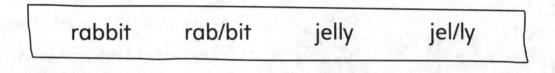

| rabbit | rab/bit | jelly | jel/ly |

MY TURN Draw a line between the syllables in each word. Then read, or decode, the words.

| happen | lesson | pillow | cotton | butter |

TURN and TALK With a partner, check where you drew the lines to divide the syllables. Then read the words together, blending the syllables.

The second syllable can have a short, long, or r-controlled vowel.

Double Consonants

MY TURN Write the syllables of each word in the boxes next to it. Then read the word.

1. tennis

2. tunnel

3. kitten

4. bottom

5. traffic

6. hippo

7. button

8. rabbit

My Words to Know

MY TURN Read the words in the box. <u>Underline</u> the words in the sentences, and read the sentences. Then write your own sentence for each word.

become	across	during

1. Ida wants to become a scientist.

2. We stopped to rest during the long bike ride.

3. Joe lives across the street from Jen.

_____

_____

_____

_____

_____

TURN and TALK Read your sentences aloud with a partner. Help each other with any corrections.

The Changing River

Sam lives in the river valley. During Sam's life, he has seen much happen. The river has changed. When Sam was little, he could step on stones to walk across the river. Seeing fish at the bottom was common. But over time, the river has become wider and deeper. Now Sam uses a boat to cross the river.

1. How did Sam cross the river when he was little?

_____

2. How did the river change? _____

_____

3. Draw a line to divide these words into syllables. Read them. Then underline them in the story.

| valley | happen | common | bottom |

I can read informational texts and learn facts about a topic.

Spotlight on Genre

Informational Text

Authors write informational text to inform, or to give facts. They try to make the topic interesting or engaging for the reader. They often include:

- detailed photographs
- interesting words and descriptions
- information about unusual sights or events

You can learn more when text looks interesting and exciting.

Establish a Purpose Setting a purpose helps you understand more as you read. Your purpose for reading informational texts could be to learn about a topic.

TURN and TALK With a partner, look through *How Water Shapes the Earth* and *How Earthquakes Shape the Earth*. Read the heads and look at the pictures. Write two things you want to learn.

Informational Text Anchor Chart

The purpose of an **inform**ational text is to inform.

To inform means to give facts or teach something.

facts you didn't know

new words about the topic

Things you can learn from Informational Text

information about things you may never see or do

what you want to learn more about

How Water Shapes the Earth

Preview Vocabulary

Look for these words as you read *How Water Shapes the Earth.*

flows	disasters	ruin

First Read

Read to learn about how water shapes the Earth.

Look at the photos to help you understand the text.

Ask which ideas are most important.

Talk to summarize the text.

Meet the Author

Jared Siemens loves to read just about anything—poetry, stories, music blogs, and anything about Antarctica. He has written mainly newspaper articles and children's informational books. He has also written the scripts for two short films.

Genre Informational Text

AUDIO

Audio with Highlighting

ANNOTATE

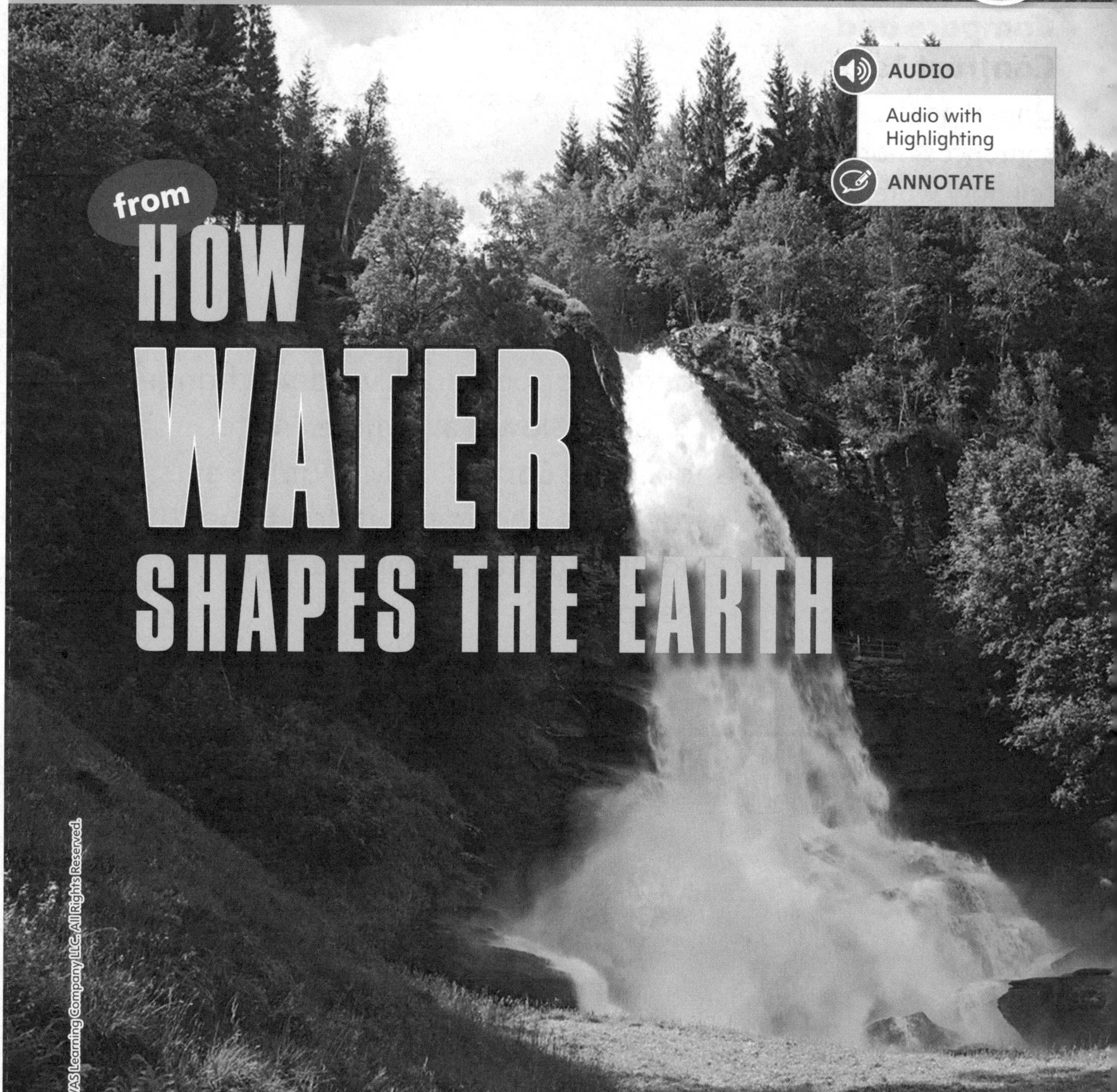

from HOW WATER SHAPES THE EARTH

by Jared Siemens

Compare and Contrast Texts

Underline the sentences that tell how water shapes the Earth. Reread paragraph 3, "What shapes the land?" in *Introducing Landforms.* Compare the ideas that the two texts present.

flows moves along smoothly

HOW DOES WATER SHAPE THE EARTH?

1   The Earth is always changing. Some changes happen quickly. Some changes take place slowly over time. Water shapes the Earth slowly. Water wears away rocks and soil as it flows over the land. It also moves soil and rocks to other places.

Create New Understandings

Highlight a detail that tells how water can change the land.

HOW DOES WATER CARVE THROUGH LAND?

2   Rivers and streams flow over land. They flow from high places to low places. Rivers can carve great valleys and canyons into the land over time. The Grand Canyon was made by the Colorado River about 5 million years ago.

Compare and Contrast Texts

<u>Underline</u> what happens when waves wear down the land. Then read paragraph 4 under "Ocean meets land" in *Introducing Landforms*. Compare and contrast the ideas in both texts.

HOW DO WAVES SHAPE THE LAND?

3   Moving water is very powerful. Ocean waves crash into land over and over again. The waves wear down the land. This shapes the coastlines and makes cliffs. Waves also break down rock into sand.

CLOSE READ

Create New Understandings

Highlight words that tell what waterfalls do.

HOW DO WATERFALLS SHAPE THE LAND?

4   A waterfall forms where a river or stream flows quickly over a high ledge of hard rock. Waterfalls move rock and soil into a pool below.

CLOSE READ

Compare and Contrast Texts

<u>Underline</u> the definition of **glaciers**. Compare that definition to the one in paragraph 7 in *Introducing Landforms*.

HOW DO GLACIERS SHAPE THE LAND?

5 Glaciers are large pieces of frozen water that move slowly over the land. They drag pieces of rock and soil along with them as they move. Sometimes when glaciers melt they leave large rocks behind. Some rocks break apart when water freezes in their cracks. This can change the shape of mountains and the land around them.

HOW DOES WATER DESTROY THE LAND?

6   Water changes the land quickly during natural disasters such as floods, hurricanes, and tsunamis. Floods destroy farmland by washing away the topsoil that helps plants grow. Hurricanes and tsunamis can ruin coastal cities and wash away the homes of people living there.

disasters events that cause great damage, loss, or suffering

ruin destroy or spoil something

How Earthquakes Shape the Earth

Preview Vocabulary

Look for these words as you read *How Earthquakes Shape the Earth*.

amount	damage

Read and Compare

Read to compare this text with *How Water Shapes the Earth*.

Look at the photographs to understand the text.

Ask questions to clarify information.

Talk about the most important ideas.

Meet the Author

Aaron Carr has written many science books for young readers, including *Tasmanian Tiger* and *Earthworms*. He also works as a reporter and photographer for newspapers. He lives in Vancouver, Canada. **Megan Cuthbert** has written books for young readers, such as *How Wind Shapes the Earth*. She also lives in Vancouver.

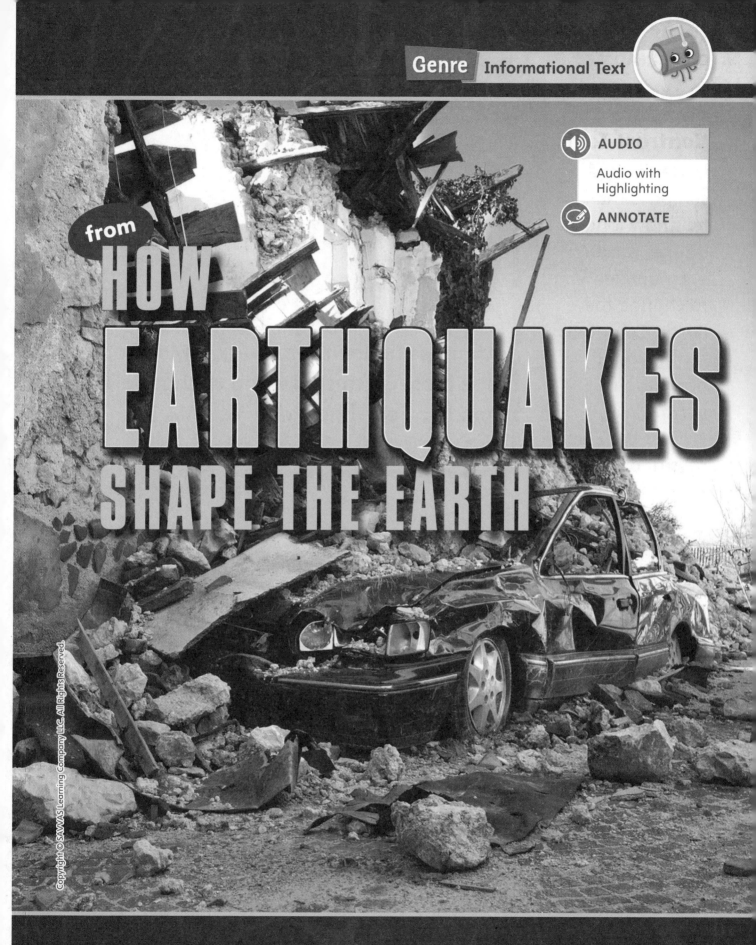

AUDIO
Audio with Highlighting

ANNOTATE

from

HOW EARTHQUAKES SHAPE THE EARTH

by Aaron Carr and Megan Cuthbert

Compare and Contrast Texts

<u>Underline</u> the sentence that tells how long it takes for an earthquake to change the Earth. Compare that to what paragraph 1 in *How Water Shapes the Earth* says about how long it usually takes water to change the Earth.

HOW DO EARTHQUAKES SHAPE THE EARTH?

1   The Earth is always changing. Some changes happen very quickly. Many of the most Earth-shattering changes are made by earthquakes.

Compare and Contrast Texts

<u>Underline</u> the main way earthquakes can shape Earth. Now look back at paragraph 5 in *How Water Shapes the Earth*. Compare and contrast ways glaciers and earthquakes shape the Earth.

Copyright © SAVVAS Learning Company LLC. All Rights Reserved.

2   Earthquakes can break apart the ground. People can feel the ground moving underneath them. This can be very scary.

529

Create New Understandings

Highlight two details that together help you understand what can happen when the ground shakes during an earthquake.

amount a quantity or number of something

damage harm

WHAT HAPPENS DURING AN EARTHQUAKE?

3 The shaking ground from an earthquake can cause a great amount of damage. It can make houses fall down or roads crack open. Floods can also be caused by earthquakes.

WHAT CHANGES CAN EARTHQUAKES CAUSE?

4   The strongest earthquakes can move large areas of land. Some of these strong earthquakes move land deep under water. This pushes water up to make giant waves. These giant waves are called tsunamis.

Create New Understandings

Highlight the sentences that explain what happens to waves when strong earthquakes move under water.

Vocabulary in Context

Underline words that help you understand the meaning of **aftershocks**.

WHAT IS AN AFTERSHOCK?

5   Small earthquakes may happen days or even weeks after an earthquake. They are called aftershocks. Aftershocks often add to the damage caused by the first earthquake.

Develop Vocabulary

MY TURN Complete each sentence below with a word from the box.

ruin   disasters   damage   flows   amount

1. Floods and hurricanes are _____ that cause great loss and suffering.

2. Floods can cause a large _____ of farmland to be washed away.

3. Earthquakes cause a lot of _____ because the ground shakes and breaks apart.

4. Tsunamis and hurricanes can _____ coastal cities by washing away homes.

5. Use the word **flows** to describe how water can change landforms.

Florida and Texas have had more hurricanes than any other state.

Check for Understanding

MY TURN Look back at the text to answer the questions. Write the answers.

1. What makes these informational texts?

_____

_____

_____

2. Why did the authors of both texts use section headings?

_____

_____

_____

3. How are earthquakes and rivers alike?

_____

_____

_____

Compare and Contrast Texts

When you **compare**, you tell how two things are alike. When you **contrast**, you tell how they are different. You can compare and contrast important points in two texts about the same topic.

MY TURN Go to the Close Read notes. Follow the directions to underline the texts. Use what you underlined and what you read to complete the chart with information that compares and contrasts water and earthquakes.

Water	Both	Earthquakes

Create New Understandings

When you read more than one text about the same topic, use what you learned from those texts to form a better understanding of the topic. Using what you learned to create new understanding is called synthesizing.

MY TURN Go back to the Close Read notes. Follow the instructions to highlight the text. Use what you highlighted and read to complete the chart and create a new understanding.

Ideas from *How Water Shapes the Earth*	Ideas from *How Earthquakes Shape the Earth*	New Understanding or Synthesized Idea

Reflect and Share

Write to Sources

This week you read how water and earthquakes shape and change the Earth. On a sheet of paper, write a paragraph with brief comments explaining how one natural event shapes and changes the Earth. Support your ideas with examples from the texts.

Paraphrase Texts

When you paraphrase, you put the facts and details from sources in your own words. Be sure to

- Keep the same meaning as the words in the text.
- Keep the information in an order that makes sense.

Choose a natural event that you think causes the most change. Use facts, details, and examples from the texts to explain what happens.

Weekly Question

How do natural events change the Earth?

I can use language to make connections between reading and writing informational text.

My Learning Goal

Academic Vocabulary

Synonyms are words that mean the same thing. Writers choose synonyms to make their writing more interesting. Sometimes you can figure out the meaning of a word by looking for a synonym near it.

MY TURN Use a dictionary or a thesaurus to find a synonym for each of these words. Then, in your own words, explain the meaning of both words. On a piece of paper, use a word and its synonym in two sentences.

Word	Synonym	Meaning
destruction		
act		
environmental		

Read Like a Writer, Write for a Reader

Authors organize their ideas to help readers understand the information. Sometimes authors tell how one event (the cause) makes another event happen (the effect). This text structure is called cause and effect. An author may use a cause-and-effect clue word like **because** or **so**, but not always.

Cause and Effect	How the Text Structure Helps
"Ocean waves crash into land over and over again. The waves wear down the land. This shapes the coastlines and makes cliffs. Waves also break down rock into sand."	The first sentence tells the cause: ocean waves crashing into the land. The crashing waves cause these things to happen: they wear down the land, they make the shape of coastlines and cliffs, and they break rock into sand.

MY TURN Write two sentences using cause and effect. The first sentence tells the cause. The second sentence tells its effect.

_____

_____

_____

Spell Words with Double Consonants

Words that have double consonants in the middle are divided into syllables between the two consonants.

MY TURN Unscramble the letters to make a Spelling Word. Write the word, adding a line between the syllables. Then write the My Words to Know words.

1. lodlar _____

2. ppuser _____

3. tbeetr _____

4. ctati _____

5. usdend _____

6. drnien _____

7. msurme _____

8. rtietb _____

9. newinr _____

10. remismw _____

11. socras _____

12. ringdu _____

Spelling Words
dinner
attic
winner
sudden
dollar
supper
summer
swimmer
bitter
better

My Words to Know
across
during

Contractions

A **contraction** is made by putting two words together. Some letters are left out. An **apostrophe (')** takes the place of the missing letters. Read these contractions.

Contractions with Not	Contractions with Will	Contractions with Forms of Be
is + not = isn't	I + will = I'll	I + am = I'm
do + not = don't	you + will = you'll	you + are = you're
can + not = can't	she + will = she'll	he + is = he's
will + not = won't	we + will = we'll	it + is = it's

MY TURN Edit this draft. Cross out each incorrect contraction. Write the correct spelling of the word above it.

The school book fair starts today, but my class is'nt going until tomorrow. Jack told me its amazing how many books are there. Il'l have a hard time choosing a book. Kyle said hes going to buy two!

I can use elements of informational text to write a procedural text.

How to Write a Command

An author of a procedural text uses short sentences to tell how to follow a sequence of actions. Each sentence is written as a **command.** A command begins with a verb that makes the directions easy to follow. For example:

Cut the string into 12-inch pieces.

Mix the ingredients together.

To restate instructions, begin with a verb but put the commands in your own words.

MY TURN Fill in the chart using a how-to text from your library. Restate the directions orally. Then compose two commands for a procedural text in your notebook.

Title:
Two Commands

Writing Precise Instructions

In a procedural text, an author writes precise instructions. Precise instructions give details to make each step clear. Here are examples:

Instructions	Precise Instructions
Drop paint on your paper.	Drop small blobs of paint on your paper with a spoon.
Punch holes in the paper.	Punch one hole in each corner of the paper.
Add the flour.	Add the flour slowly as you mix.
Squeeze lemons.	Squeeze the juice from 8 lemons.
Put a cube on top.	Put a red cube on top.
Pour into a pan.	Pour into a large square pan.

 MY TURN Develop precise instructions for your how-to text. Use details to compose a draft in your writer's notebook.

Graphics

In a procedural text, an author usually includes graphics to help readers understand how to do something. Graphics include drawings, photographs, and diagrams.

MY TURN Read a how-to text in your classroom library. Draw or describe a graphic that makes it easier to understand how to do something. Then decide how you will use graphics in your procedural text. Draw or write your ideas in your writer's notebook.

Title:

Graphic

Lightning!

Have you ever walked across a carpet and felt a shock when you touched something metal? That shock is like lightning. Lightning is a giant electric spark. It is extremely hot. In fact, it's much hotter than the sun! The high heat makes the air expand, or stretch out, quickly. That expanding air vibrates and creates the sound of thunder.

Lightning Facts

- Count to one. In that time, about 100 lightning bolts hit Earth.

- A lightning bolt can be 5 miles long.

- Light travels faster than sound, so you see lightning first, and then you hear thunder.

Weekly Question

How does weather change Earth?

MY TURN Think about storms you have experienced. Think about other kinds of weather you have heard about. How can bad weather change a place? Draw two pictures of a place. Draw one before a storm and one after a storm.

Vowel Sound Spelled aw, au, augh, al

Say the name of this picture and listen for the vowel sound.

paw

The letter patterns **aw, au, augh,** and **al** can make the vowel sound you hear in the word **paw.**

MY TURN Read the words below. Listen for the vowel sound in each word.

aw	au	augh	al
law	sauce	taught	talk
yawn	auto	naughty	chalk

TURN and TALK Reread the words in the chart with a partner. Underline the letters that make the vowel sound you hear in **paw** in each word. Then choose one word from each spelling pattern and use it in a sentence. Take turns with your partner.

Vowel Sound Spelled aw, au, augh, al

MY TURN Read each word. (Circle) the words with the vowel sound you hear in **paw**. Then write the correct word from the box in each sentence.

hawk	caught	walks	people
fault	lunch	author	draw

1. Ricky likes to take long _____.

2. That _____ is a beautiful bird.

3. This _____ writes great stories.

4. I didn't do it! It's not my _____.

5. I want to _____ a picture of you.

6. Rosa went fishing with her dad and _____ a fish.

My Words to Know

Some words are used often. These words are called high-frequency words. You will have to remember these words. Often, you can't sound them out.

MY TURN Read the words in the box. Write the word from the box that goes in each sentence. Form the letters correctly as you write each word. Use connecting strokes to connect the letters. Then read the sentences.

hours	products	happened

1. You missed the race. It _____ two days ago.

2. The grocery store sells all kinds of dairy _____.

3. Ed wakes up two _____ before school.

TURN and TALK Work with a partner. Take turns answering these questions. Use the words from the box in your answers.

1. Do you think students should spend more **hours** in school? Explain.

2. Name your favorite **products** at the grocery store.

3. What is the funniest thing that ever **happened** to you?

A Small Tree in a Big Wind

Raccoon lived in a small tree. While she was away, a big gust of wind blew. Because the tree was weak, the wind broke off a branch. When Raccoon walked up to the tree, she saw what had happened.

"The wind taught me a lesson!" said Raccoon. "I'm moving to a bigger tree!"

"Good idea! I'll help you!" said Hawk.

1. Why did a branch come off Raccoon's tree?

   _____

2. What lesson did the wind teach Raccoon?

   _____

3. Find one word with each vowel pattern: **aw, au, augh, al**. Write them on the line.

   _____

553

I can read a readers' theater text and understand elements of drama.

Drama

A **drama** is a story written for people to act out. A drama has elements that include **characters**, **dialogue**, **setting**, and **stage directions**.

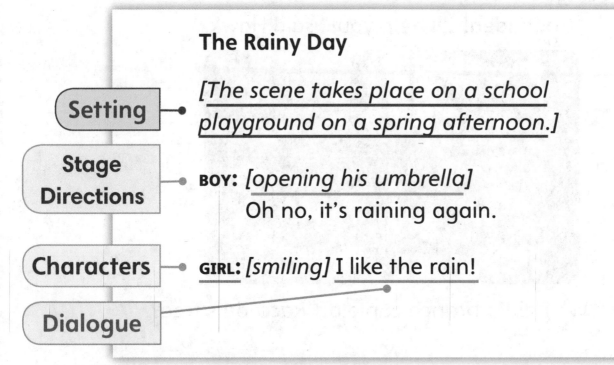

The Rainy Day

Setting • [*The scene takes place on a school playground on a spring afternoon.*]

Stage Directions • BOY: [*opening his umbrella*]
Oh no, it's raining again.

Characters • GIRL: [*smiling*] I like the rain!

Dialogue

Readers' theater is a kind of drama for people to read aloud. It does not involve acting on a stage.

TURN and TALK Discuss these questions: How are a drama and informational text different? How are they the same?

Drama Anchor Chart

Drama is
a story actors perform

has a description of
the setting

is sometimes divided
into scenes, or parts
with different settings

has dialogue, or
speech, that actors say

has stage directions
that tell how actors
should move or speak
their lines

Where Do They Go in Rain or Snow?

Preview Vocabulary

Look for these words as you read *Where Do They Go in Rain or Snow?*

| den | slippery | surface | underground | survive |

First Read

Look through these two readers' theater texts. Make predictions about characters and settings.

Read to see if the text matches your predictions.

Ask yourself what each drama is about.

Talk about the author's message in each drama.

Meet *the* Author

Melissa Stewart has cared about nature since she was a child. She even swam with sea lions and went to a rain forest to gather information for her books.

WHERE DO THEY GO IN RAIN OR SNOW?

READERS' THEATER

by Melissa Stewart
illustrated by Iole Rosa

AUDIO

Audio with
Highlighting

ANNOTATE

WHEN RAIN FALLS

1 **CHORUS 1:**   When rain falls in a forest...

2 **NARRATOR:**   A scurrying squirrel suddenly stops.

3 **SQUIRREL:**   *Tsst! Tsst! Tsst!* I pull my tail over my head. It makes a great umbrella.

4 **NARRATOR:**   Higher up, there's a hawk.

5 **HAWK:**   I puff out my feathers to stay warm and dry. *Ker-ree, ker-ree.*

6 **NARRATOR:**   What does a chickadee do?

7 **CHICKADEE:**   *Dee-dee, dee-dee.* I hide inside my tree hole home.

8 **NARRATOR:** A deer takes cover under a leafy tree canopy.

9 **DEER:** All the leaves and branches block the rain.

10 **NARRATOR:** Foxes nestle together inside a warm, cozy den.

den a wild animal's home or resting place

11 **Fox 1:** I could use a nap.

12 **Fox 2:** Me too. *[Big yawn.]*

13 **CHORUS 2:** **When rain falls on a field...**

14 **NARRATOR:** A plump little caterpillar crawls under a leaf.

15 **CATERPILLAR:** Time for a snack! *Munch, munch, munch.*

16 **NARRATOR:** An adult butterfly dangles from a nearby flower head.

17 **BUTTERFLY:** I don't mind hanging upside down.

18 **NARRATOR:** A raindrop knocks a ladybug off a slippery stem. It bounces into the air and tumbles to the ground.

19 **LADYBUG:** Don't worry about me. I have a hard exoskeleton.

slippery likely to cause slipping or sliding

20 **NARRATOR:**   A spider watches and waits as the rain beats down.

21 **SPIDER:**   Looks like I'll have to rebuild my web!

22 **NARRATOR:**   A little mouse crouches under a fallen leaf.

23 **MOUSE:**   *Squeak, squeak.* I don't like the rain.

24 **NARRATOR:**   What about bees and ants?

25 **BEE:**   I hide in my hive and stay bzzzz-y helping my friends make honey.

26 **ANT:**   I stay safe in my underground nest. There's always lots of work to do.

Confirm or Adjust Predictions

Highlight the new characters in lines 20–26. What other characters did you predict might appear? Confirm or correct your prediction.

27 **CHORUS 3:**	**When rain falls on a wetland...**
28 **NARRATOR:**	A turtle tucks in its tiny head and doesn't move an inch.
29 **TURTLE:**	I listen to the raindrops crashing down on my shell.
30 **EVERYONE:**	*Plop! Plop! Drip! Drop!*
31 **NARRATOR:**	A dragonfly swoops past the turtle and lands on a cattail.
32 **DRAGONFLY:**	I rest below the cattail's fluffy, brown top.

33 **NARRATOR:**	A whirligig beetle swims in circles on the water's surface.
34 **BEETLE:**	Yikes! Those crashing raindrops make it hard to stay afloat.
35 **NARRATOR:**	Where are the birds?
36 **SPARROW:**	*Clink, clink.* Here I am— hiding inside a thick bush.
37 **DUCK:**	*Quack, quack.* Not me! I keep on swimming—rain or shine. Raindrops slide right off my oily feathers.

CLOSE READ

Identify Elements of Drama

<u>Underline</u> the dialogue between the Narrator and the Sparrow.

surface the top or outside part of something

563

38	**CHORUS 4:**	**When rain falls in a desert...**
39	**NARRATOR:**	A rattlesnake squeezes into a rocky crevice.
40	**SNAKE:**	I curl up tight and fall as-s-s-s-s-s-s-leep.
41	**NARRATOR:**	Where does a tarantula go?
42	**TARANTULA:**	I crawl into a hole and hide.
43	**NARRATOR:**	Bats fly off to a hillside cave.
44	**BAT 1:**	*Teet! Teet! Teet! Teet!*
45	**BAT 2:**	We just hang around until the rain stops.

46 **NARRATOR:** A tiny elf owl peeks out of a hole in a cactus.

47 **ELF OWL:** *Da-da-da-da-dat-dat.* I like to watch the rain fall.

48 **NARRATOR:** A spadefoot toad only comes out in the rain. It digs to the surface, finds a mate, and lays its eggs.

49 **TOAD:** Then I dig back into the sand. *[Wave]* See you the next time it rains!

50 **EVERYONE:** **When the rain stops, animals living in fields and forests, wetlands and deserts return to their daily routines.**

51 **ALL ANIMALS:** *[Jump forward and make your animal sounds.]*

THE END

CLOSE READ

Confirm or Adjust Predictions

Identifying which character is speaking is part of knowing the structure of a play. Highlight the character names in lines 46–50. Confirm or correct your prediction.

UNDER THE SNOW

1 **CHORUS 1:** **Under the snow in a field...**

2 **NARRATOR:** Ladybugs pack themselves into a hole in an old stone wall.

3 **LADYBUG 1:** I like spending the winter with all my friends. It's like having a giant slumber party!

4 **LADYBUG 2:** Not me. I wish I had a little elbow room.

5 **NARRATOR:** A snake rests inside another hole in the same wall.

6 **SNAKE:** I curl up tight and fall a-s-s-s-sleep.

566

7	**NARRATOR:**	What does a vole do under the snow?
8	**VOLE:**	I tunnel through the white, fluffy stuff all winter long.
9	**NARRATOR:**	A chipmunk snoozes in an underground nest.
10	**CHIPMUNK:**	*Chip! Chip! Churp! Churp!* Sometimes I wake up to snack on nuts and seeds.

CLOSE READ

Vocabulary in Context

Sometimes you can figure out an unfamiliar word by finding words nearby that mean the opposite. Underline words that mean the opposite of **snoozes**.

underground
beneath the ground

Confirm or Adjust Predictions

Highlight the words that tell the setting of this part of the play. What prediction did you make about other settings that might appear in the rest of the drama?

survive continue to live

11 CHORUS 2: Under the snow in a forest...

12 NARRATOR: A mourning cloak butterfly rests in a pile of brush.

13 BUTTERFLY: I'm saving up all my energy for spring.

14 NARRATOR: What's inside that rotting log? Look, it's a centipede.

15 CENTIPEDE: Winter weather cools my body so much I can barely move.

16 NARRATOR: A bumblebee queen rests in a nearby crack.

17 BEE: It's nice to take a break after such a bzzzz-y summer.

18 NARRATOR: A wood frog hides in leaves on the forest floor.

19 WOOD FROG: *Quack, squawk, quack!* Winter doesn't bother me. I can freeze solid and still survive.

568

20 NARRATOR: A woolly bear caterpillar snoozes just a few inches away.

21 CATERPILLAR: I curl up my body, so my head almost touches my tail.

22 NARRATOR: Just below the ground, a spotted salamander waits out the coldest months of the year.

23 SALAMANDER: If winter's here, can spring be far behind?

24 NARRATOR: Deeper underground, a woodchuck sleeps soundly all winter long.

25 WOODCHUCK: *Chuck, chuck!* Do you think I'll see my shadow on February 2nd?

CLOSE READ

Identify Elements of Drama

<u>Underline</u> the words that the narrator says between lines 26 and 32.

26 **CHORUS 3:** Under the snow in a pond...

27 **NARRATOR:** A bluegill circles slowly through the chilly water.

28 **BLUEGILL:** *Glug! Glug!* I sure wish I had enough energy to catch that little bug.

29 **NARRATOR:** The water boatman swimming nearby has a different point of view.

30 **WATER BOATMAN:** Thank goodness that big fish can't chase me down!

31 **NARRATOR:** A carp rests quietly on the muddy bottom.

32 **CARP:** I wonder why that bluegill can swim, but I'm stuck down here?

33 **NARRATOR:**	Two tiny water striders lie just a few inches away.
34 **WATER STRIDER 1:**	Lucky for us that carp's totally pooped out.
35 **WATER STRIDER 2:**	You can say that again!
36 **WATER STRIDER 1:**	Lucky for us that carp's totally pooped out.
37 **WATER STRIDER 2:**	Oh, puh-lease!
38 **NARRATOR:**	A green frog and a painted turtle rest in the mud and wait for winter to end.
39 **FROG:**	Dude! Dude! I'm sick of this. How long until spring?
40 **TURTLE:**	Not much longer, I hope. My toes are getting wrinkled.

Confirm or Adjust Predictions

Highlight the words that tell the setting of this part of the readers' theater. Was your earlier prediction about settings correct?

41 **CHORUS 4:** Under the snow in a wetland...

42 **NARRATOR:** A beaver family huddles together inside a cozy log lodge.

43 **BEAVER 1:** *Whaaad, whaad, wat!* I could use a snack.

44 **BEAVER 2:** Me too. Let's swim over to our storage pile and grab a stick.

45 **NARRATOR:** Just below the wetland's icy surface, a red-spotted newt dodges and whizzes and whirls.

46 **NEWT:** *Wheee!* I don't mind if spring never comes.

47 **NARRATOR:** But everyone else is looking forward to warm, sunny days.

48 **CHORUS 1 & 2:**   And as time passes, the sun's rays slowly grow stronger.

49 **CHORUS 3 & 4:**   And each day is a little bit longer...

50 **EVERYONE:**   ...until finally, spring arrives.

51 **ALL ANIMALS:**   *[Jump forward and make your animal sounds.]*

THE END

CLOSE READ

Fluency

Speak in a different voice for each character as you read lines 27–47 several times with a partner. Use voices that show the different ways the animal characters feel about winter.

Develop Vocabulary

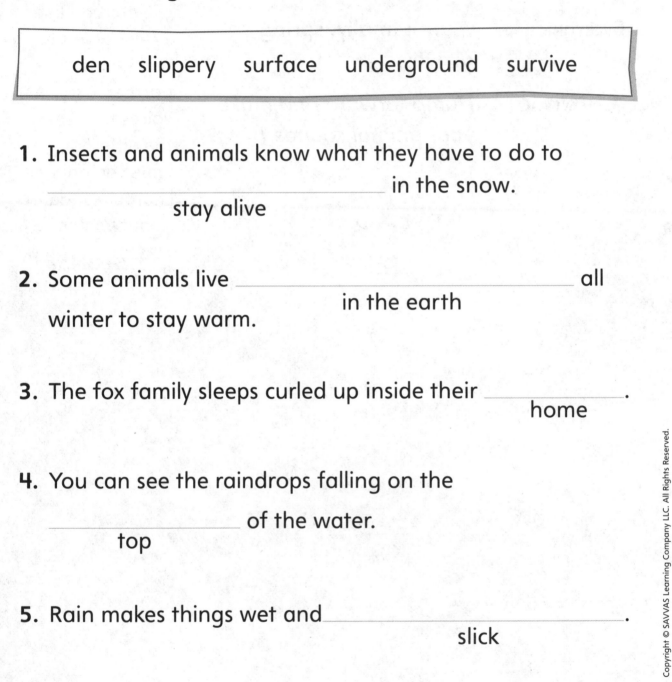 **MY TURN** Fill in each blank with a word that has a similar meaning to the word or words below the blank.

| den   slippery   surface   underground   survive |

1. Insects and animals know what they have to do to
_____ in the snow.
        stay alive

2. Some animals live _____ all
                                    in the earth
winter to stay warm.

3. The fox family sleeps curled up inside their _____.
                                                          home

4. You can see the raindrops falling on the
_____ of the water.
        top

5. Rain makes things wet and_____.
                                          slick

Check for Understanding

MY TURN Look back at the texts to answer the questions. Write the answers.

1. How can you tell these texts are dramas, or readers' theater texts?

_____

_____

2. Why do you think the author lists the character names down the left side of the page?

_____

_____

3. Would you rather be an animal in the rain or under the snow? Why?

_____

_____

When I read the
part of a mouse,
I use a high,
squeaky voice.

Identify Elements of Drama

Readers' theater is a drama that people read aloud in a way that helps others picture the action. Elements of any drama include **characters**, **setting**, and **dialogue**.

- **Characters** are the people or animals in the drama.

- **Setting** is where and when the story happens.

- **Dialogue** is the lines the characters say.

MY TURN Go to the Close Read notes. Follow the instructions to underline elements of drama. Use what you underlined and other text evidence to complete the chart. Discuss the elements in drama. How are these elements different than in a story?

Elements in Drama	When Rain Falls	Under the Snow
Characters (List 5)		
Settings (List all)		
Dialogue (List an example)		

Confirm or Adjust Predictions

Making, confirming, and correcting predictions helps you read for a purpose and remember what you read. Use the text structure, which is organized around characters and setting in a drama, to make predictions.

MY TURN Go back to the Close Read notes. Follow the directions to highlight the text. Use what you predicted and highlighted to complete the chart.

I predicted . . .	Now I know . . .

Reflect and Share

Talk About It

Discuss some of the ways different animals react to rain and snow. Use examples from the texts to support your response.

Recounting Ideas from a Text

When you share ideas and information you've read or heard, it is important to identify where the information came from.

- Share your own ideas and support them with text evidence.

- Identify the source of any ideas that are not your own.

Use these sentence starters to help you identify your own ideas and ideas that aren't your own.

I think that . . .
I read that . . .

Weekly Question

How does weather change Earth?

I can use language to make connections between reading and writing informational texts.

Academic Vocabulary

Context clues within and beyond a sentence can help you determine the meanings of unfamiliar words.

MY TURN (Circle) the clues that help you understand each bold word. Then complete the sentences.

1. Maria wants to be an **environmentalist** because she believes taking care of Earth is important.

   An **environmentalist** is a person who wants to

   _____.

2. Earthquakes and hurricanes cause a lot of **destruction**. It can take a community years to repair the damage.

   In this sentence **destruction** means

   _____.

3. A **balanced** meal includes foods from all food groups.

   If something is **balanced,** it

   _____.

Read Like a Writer, Write for a Reader

Authors choose words carefully to give their characters a voice. The words authors choose help express the personality of their characters—what they are like.

What the Character Says	What It Shows About the Character
Carp: I wonder why that blue gill can swim, but I'm stuck down here?	Carp sounds grumpy and envious that the blue gill can do something he can't.
Newt: *Wheee!* I don't mind if spring never comes.	Newt sounds cheerful and carefree.

What kind of person would say these words?

MY TURN Pick one of these words to describe a character's personality: brave, bossy, friendly, kind, shy. Write two sentences about something the character says, does, or thinks. Circle words that help a reader hear the character's voice.

Spell Words with aw, au, augh, al

The letter patterns **aw**, **au**, **augh**, and **al** all stand for the vowel sound you hear in **paw**.

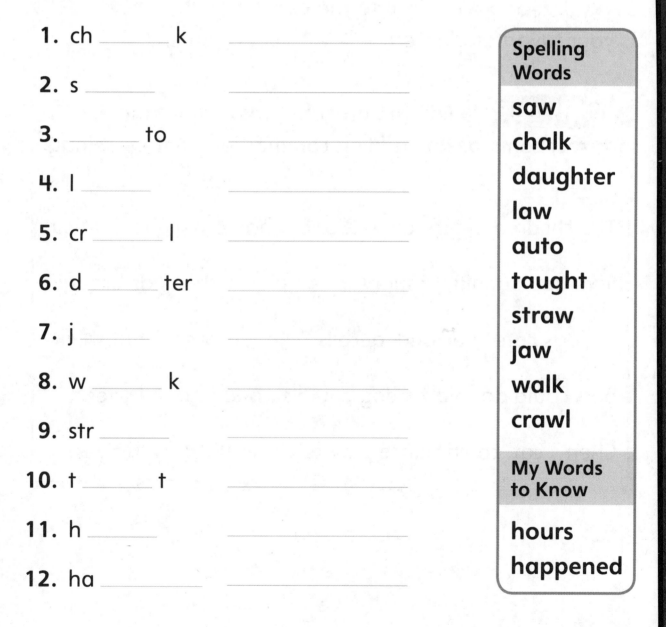 **MY TURN** Write the missing letters to make a Spelling Word. Write each word. Then write the My Words to Know words.

1. ch ____ k   _____

2. s _____   _____

3. ____ to   _____

4. l _____   _____

5. cr ____ l   _____

6. d ____ ter   _____

7. j _____   _____

8. w ____ k   _____

9. str _____   _____

10. t ____ t   _____

11. h _____   _____

12. ha _____   _____

Spelling Words

saw
chalk
daughter
law
auto
taught
straw
jaw
walk
crawl

My Words to Know

hours
happened

Commas in Sentences

When you list more than two items in a sentence, use commas to separate the items in the series. Put a comma after each item, except for the last one. Do not put a comma after **and** or **or**.

The characters in the play are Mouse, Bee, and Ant.
Becky, Liz, and Alex went to the beach.
Is your favorite color red, yellow, blue, or green?

MY TURN Edit this draft by crossing out the incorrect commas and adding commas where they belong.

The children in grades, 1, 2 and 3 had a pet show. Mica,

Sam and Sophia, brought in pet pigs. Other kids brought

in dogs cats birds and, gerbils. They showed what their

pets could do. Matt's dog could sit beg and roll over.

Chen's cat, could dance play fetch and give high fives.

I can use elements of informational text to write a procedural text.

My Learning Goal

Organize with Structure

In a procedural text, an author uses a structure to organize the information. Here is a common structure:

- head or title to identify the procedure, such as How to Make a Straw Painting
- list of materials or equipment
- steps listed in order to tell what to do
- graphics to show what to do

Sometimes the author includes subheads, such as these:

- What You Need
- What to Do

 **MY TURN** Compose a title for your procedural text.

How to _____

 **MY TURN** Develop a draft for your text by organizing your ideas in your writer's notebook.

Writing in Steps

In a procedural text, an author gives directions one step at a time in order. The steps may

- be in a bulleted (•) list or numbered in order.
- begin with time-order words such as **first**, **next**, **last**.

MY TURN Plan the structure of your procedural text. Write four steps in order. To make sure the steps are in the correct order, restate the directions orally to a classmate. Use these directions to develop a draft.

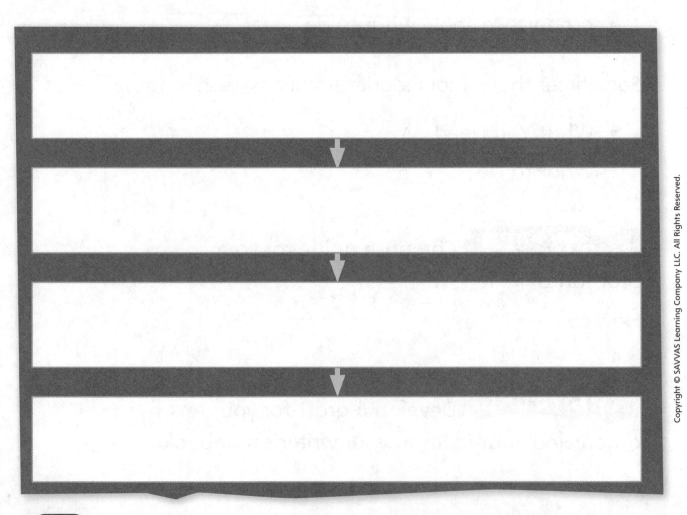

Introduction and Conclusion

An author may write an introduction and a conclusion to a procedural text. The introduction names the procedure and tells readers why they should do it. The conclusion may end with a good wish such as "Enjoy" or a final thought.

 **MY TURN** Plan the introduction and conclusion for your how-to text. Then compose them in your writer's notebook.

Title

Introduction

- What do you want readers to know?

- Why should they care about learning this?

Conclusion

- What do you hope readers will do?

- Do you have any advice for readers or final thoughts?

Earth Erupts

Deep underground, it is hot. A volcano is an opening that lets the heat out when it erupts. About 2,000 volcanoes are active on Earth. An active volcano is one that is likely to explode in the future.

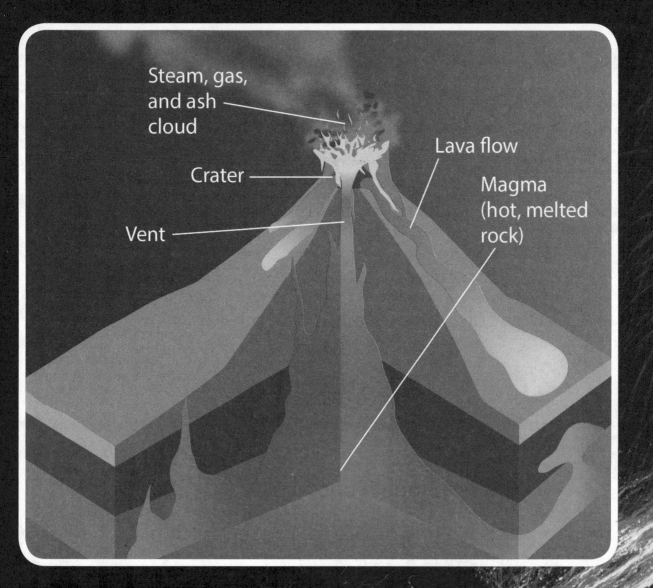

Steam, gas, and ash cloud

Crater

Vent

Lava flow

Magma (hot, melted rock)

Volcano erupts

Lava flows

Lava cools

Weekly Question

How does a volcano eruption change Earth?

Readers can ask questions about an interesting topic because they want to find out more about it. Generate, or ask, questions about volcanoes for informal inquiry.

 **MY TURN** Study the diagram and the photos. Working with your class, write two or three questions you would like to explore about volcanoes.

Syllable Pattern VCCCV

Words with a VCCCV syllable pattern have three consonants between vowels. Two of the consonants could be blends (like **nd, cl, st**), two letters whose sounds are blended together. Two of the consonants could be digraphs (like **ch, th, sh, ph**), two letters that spell one sound. A word with the syllable pattern VCCCV would not be divided between either a blend or a digraph. If you come to a VCCCV pattern word, divide it into syllables. Then you should be able to read the word. See how these VCCCV pattern words are divided into syllables:

explain ex / plain   **dolphin** dol / phin

sandwich sand/wich   **athlete** ath / lete

MY TURN Decode, or read, the words with the syllable pattern VCCCV. Each of these words either has a blend or a digraph, so make sure that when you read the words, you do not split those letter combinations.

hamster	panther	handsome	mushroom

TURN and TALK Reread the words in the chart with a partner. Draw a line between the syllables. Then read the words again, blending the syllables together.

Syllable Pattern VCCCV

Divide a VCCCV word between the single consonant and the blend or digraph formed by the other two consonants. Then read each syllable.

MY TURN Underline the word with the VCCCV syllable pattern. Draw a line between the syllables. Read the word. Then write a sentence using it.

1. students   children

_____

2. pumpkin   supper

_____

3. hundred   thousand

_____

4. mister   monster

_____

My Words to Know

MY TURN Read the words in the box. Complete the sentences using the words.

measure	remember	early

1. Ms. Ramos often comes to school _____ .

2. _____ to tie your shoes!

3. Please use a ruler to _____ the poster.

TURN and TALK Read the sentences aloud with a partner. Then make up your own sentences. Use each word. Exchange sentences with your partner and read each other's sentences.

I remember new words better when I read them and write them several times.

Lizard's Move

Early one morning, Lizard felt the earth shake. Suddenly, he saw the mountain begin to explode! "Oh my! I must get out!" he exclaimed.

He jumped into the water in an instant and swam as fast as he could. Then he turned and watched his homeland change.

"I simply can't live there now," said Lizard. "I'll have to move."

1. What does Lizard do when the mountain begins to explode?

_____

2. Why must Lizard find a new home?

_____

3. Draw a line to show where syllables break in these words. Then find and underline the words in the story.

explode   instant   simply

I can read poetry about the Earth.

Poetry

A poem is a piece of writing that uses vivid words to appeal to the senses. The words express feelings and ideas, often in a rhythmic way. Usually, the words are arranged in lines, and the lines are arranged in stanzas. Sometimes, however, a poem:

- is arranged to make a shape.
- becomes part of a picture.
- has different styles of lettering.

A poem's shape, placement, and lettering can add meaning and fun.

TURN and TALK How are poems different from informational text? Do you think poems are written to explain facts? Why or why not?

Many poems rhyme, but not all poems.

Volcano Wakes Up!

Preview Vocabulary

Look for these words as you read *Volcano Wakes Up!*

lava	construction	cinders	crater	detour

First Read

Read to understand the poems.

Look at the structures of the poems.

Ask yourself questions about how the words and structures are connected.

Talk about what you found interesting.

Meet the Author

Lisa Westberg Peters loves science, especially earth science. In fact, she looks at and touches rocks and landforms wherever she goes. Lisa Westberg Peters lives in Minneapolis, Minnesota, within walking distance of the Mississippi River and three public libraries.

VOLCANO WAKES UP!

BY
LISA WESTBERG PETERS

ILLUSTRATED BY
STEVE JENKINS

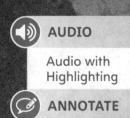

AUDIO

Audio with Highlighting

ANNOTATE

Make Connections

Highlight words that make you think of people in a family you might know.

VOLCANO

I'm the baby.

I'm much smaller than my

big sister volcanoes. I'm a little sleepy

now, but when I wake up, *watch out!* I throw

5 nasty tantrums. It always works—I get the most attention!

Explain Patterns and Structures

Underline words and phrases in the poem that are repeated.

FERNS

We ferns love cool,

we ferns love

gray,

we ferns love

5   the mornings when

Fire-maker

sleeps

late. Let's

celebrate! Let's

10   uncurl

our

fiddleheads,

let's strrrrrretch out

our fronds,

15   let's

hang misty

streamers and throw

raindrops around.

Hey,

20   everyone,

come to the caldera.

Let's party!

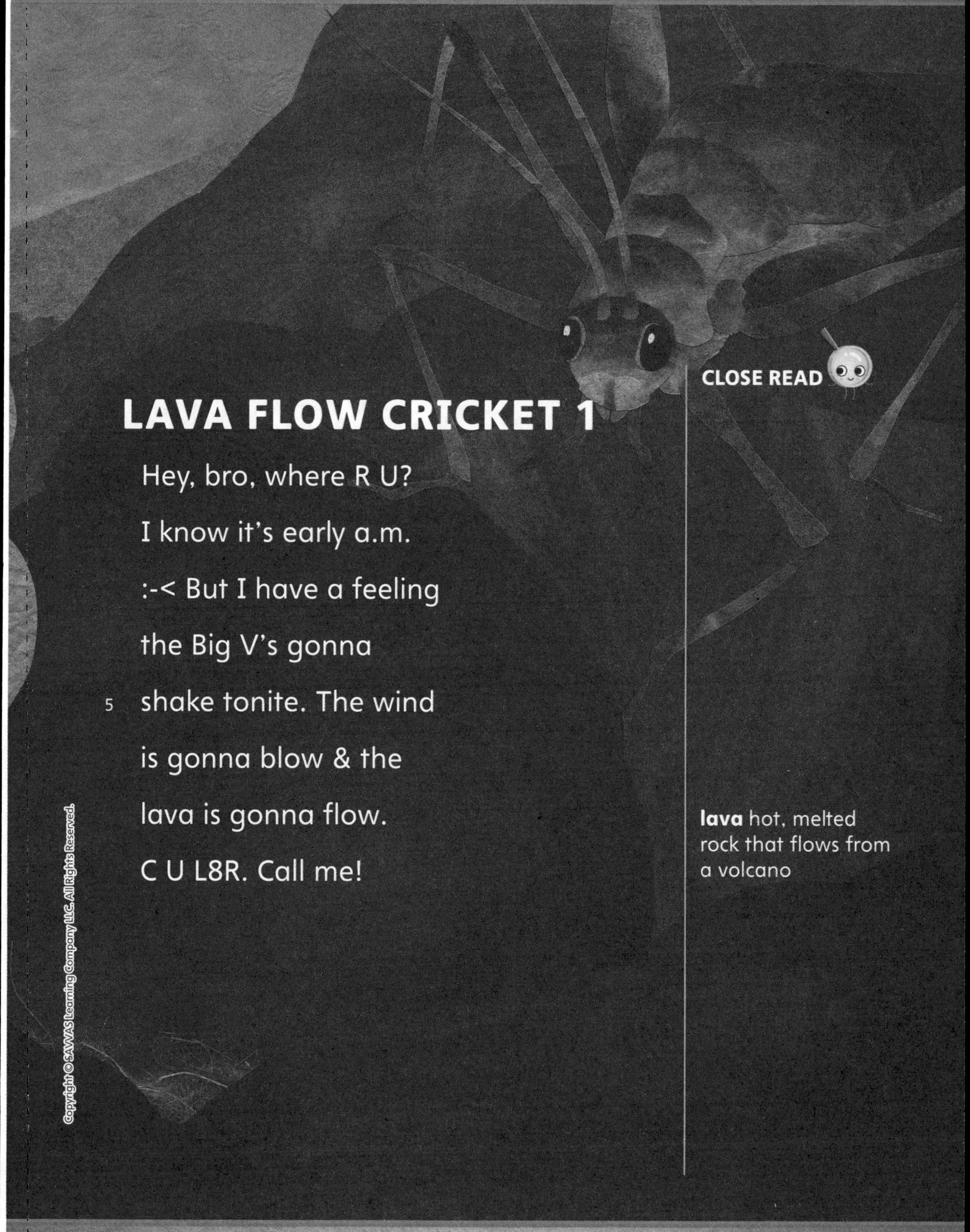

LAVA FLOW CRICKET 1

CLOSE READ

Hey, bro, where R U?

I know it's early a.m.

:-< But I have a feeling

the Big V's gonna

5 shake tonite. The wind

is gonna blow & the

lava is gonna flow.

C U L8R. Call me!

lava hot, melted rock that flows from a volcano

Make Connections

Highlight the groups of words that you have seen on signs or heard people say.

SMALL BLACK ROAD

ON THIS
ACTIVE
VOLCANO
I PROCEED WITH
5 CAUTION

I
BUCKLE UP
FOR SAFETY
BUT I DON'T EXPECT TO
HAVE A
NICE DAY

FOR
EARTH CRACKS
I DIP,
FOR
STEEP CLIFFS
I TURN

10

Explain Patterns and Structures

Underline the letter in each line of the poem that helps spell the time of day the poem takes place.

SUN TO MOON

Moon, my friend! You look so pale.

Or is it just my glare? You should

Rest and dream for now, but why

Not meet me later over bread?

5 **I**'ll ask the earth, my baker friend, at

Noon to bake you something warm.

Good morning, Moon! I'll see you tonight.

VOLCANO

Hey! It's a little

quiet around here.

It's time to kick up a lot of

dust and ash, time to shake the ground

5   and make a big stink. *Watch this, everybody!*

Explain Patterns and Structures

This poem is tall and thin and shaped like a fern. Underline a line that is part of the stem of the fern and one that is a part of the fronds, or leaves.

FERNS

Fire-maker's awake!
She's about to
make
this caldera
5 a lake of fire and
lava. Ah, the
party
must be over.
Put away all the
10 streamers.
Say
good-bye,
honeycreepers.
But wait . . . it's
15 not
hot yet. It's
not even warm
yet. What a
lucky
20 delay on this
beautiful day. Hey,
everybody, let's
party!

LAVA FLOW CRICKET 2

Hey, bro, I M way back

in the cave. I was

ZZZZZZ hard, but that

nsty smll woke me up.

5   P U! :-o The Big V

must be cranking up.

Where R U? Bye4now.

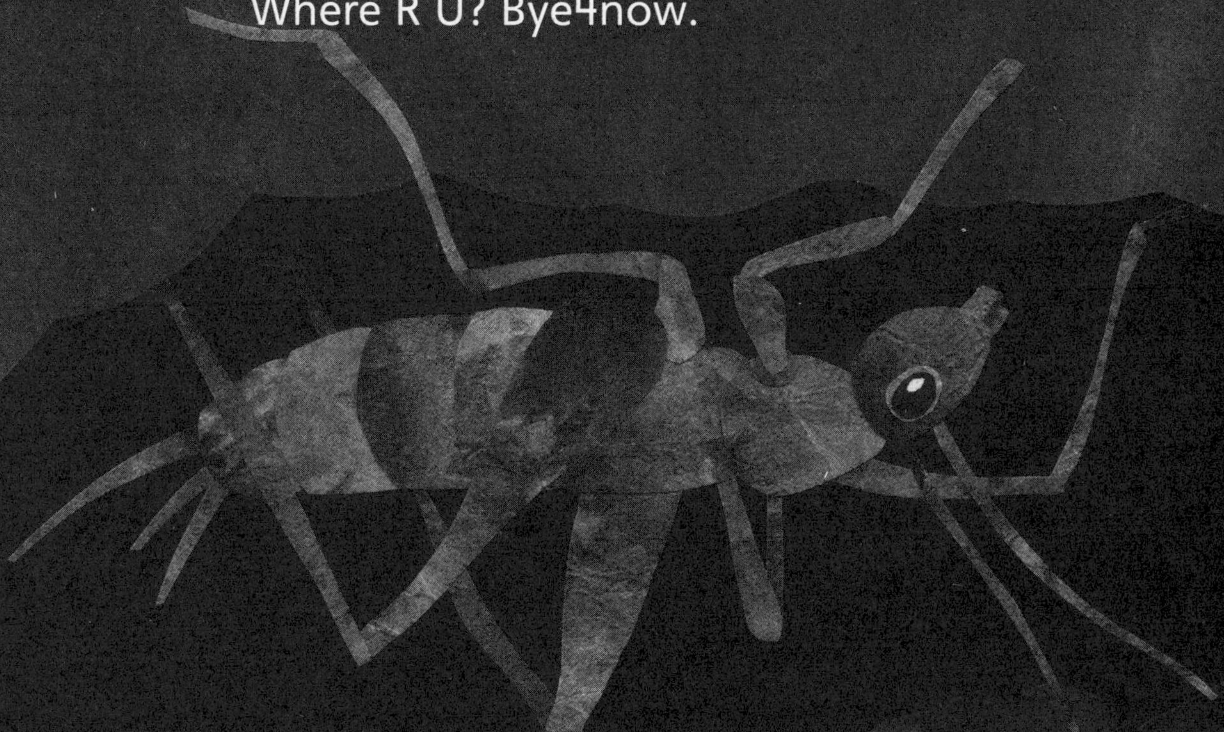

SMALL BLACK ROAD

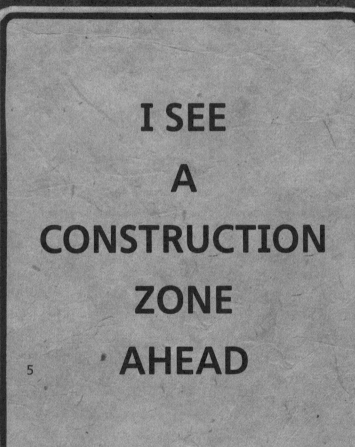

I SEE
A
CONSTRUCTION
ZONE
AHEAD

5

DARN!
THIS
ACTIVE
VOLCANO
IS
ALWAYS
UNDER
CONSTRUCTION

10

construction the act of building something

SUN

My baker friend has just begun!

I know because it's noon. I look straight

Down and see the steam escape her

Door. By twilight, she'll be finished

5   **A**nd Moon and I will share a feast.

Yes, the bread will be delicious.

VOLCANO

Look at me!

I can fling cinders

and ash into the sky. I can

huff and chuff and pour rivers of

5   lava down my side. *Rain, you can't douse my*

fire. Wind, you can't blow it out. Fog, you can't hide it.

cinders pieces of rock and wood that are partly burned

609

FERNS

Eeeeee-yikes!

That was

close!

A cinder

5 so big and so hot,

it glowed!

We're

all going

to fry to a crisp

10 and die! No . . .

wait.

Fire-maker

flows, but she's

passing us

15 by.

We might

not burn, at least

not tonight.

Hey,

20 everybody,

come to the crater.

Let's party!

crater a hole at the top of a volcano

LAVA FLOW CRICKET 1

Hey, bro, I M at the

AllUCanEat, AllNt,

HotLavaBBQ! The

food is xlnt—loads

5   of bugs toastd &

roastd by the heat!

:-) There U R. Look

up. Sweet, no?

Make Connections
Highlight words in the text that are missing letters. Use what you know to figure out what the words mean.

SMALL BLACK ROAD

Make Connections Highlight words in the text that you have seen on signs.

OH NO! THIS RED HOT PAVING OPERATION

IS GIVING ME A SOFT SHOULDER AND MELTING MY FRESH PAINT

detour go a different way when a road is blocked; a different route

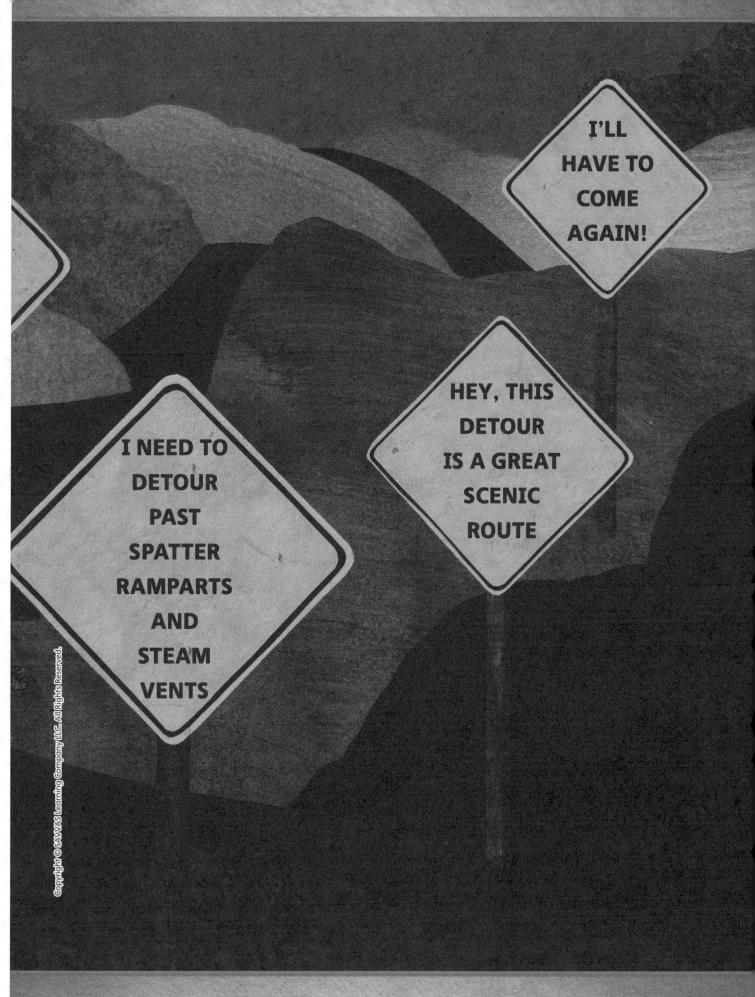

MOON TO SUN

Tonight, my sunny friend,

We haven't too much time.

I crack the oven door and …

Look! The bread is done.

5   It's hot and holds the oven's

Glow. Let's have a bite! I

Hope you dream tonight and

Thanks, my friend. I'm full.

Explain Patterns and Structures

Underline the words that are in the shape of a flow of lava.

VOLCANO

Moon, are you

already here? I should

go to bed, but I'm wide awake

and I'm bigger! I have new layers of

5   lava and cinders. *Sea, are you awake too?*

What should we do? I know! I'll send you a ribbon

of red lava,

a gift!

Moon,

10   *watch*

this!

lava lava lava lava lava

615

Develop Vocabulary

MY TURN Use a dictionary to look up the words.
Write each meaning in your own words. Then pronounce the
words with a partner and compare the meanings you wrote.

Word	Meaning
lava	
construction	
cinders	
crater	
detour	

Check for Understanding

MY TURN Look back at the texts to answer the questions. Write the answers.

1. How can you tell these texts are poetry?

_____

_____

_____

2. Why do you think the poet arranged the lines of the poem "Volcano" in a triangle?

_____

_____

_____

3. Which poem do you like best? Why?

_____

_____

_____

_____

_____

Explain Patterns and Structures

Poems often have special patterns or structures.

Rhythm is the pattern of sounds in a poem. The rhythm of a poem can sound like music. One way a poet creates rhythm is with **repetition**, or by repeating words.

Rhyme is a pattern of words that have the same ending sounds. Poems can have **visual patterns**, too.

MY TURN Go to the Close Read notes. Follow the directions to underline the text. Use what you underlined to explain the patterns and structures of the poems.

Poem	What I Underlined	How It Helped Me Read the Poem
"FERNS" 1		
"Sun to Moon"		
"FERNS" 2		

Make Connections

You make all kinds of connections when you read.
Some of the connections you can make include

- connections to personal experiences.

- connections to other texts you have read.

- connections to society.

MY TURN Go back to the Close Read notes.
Follow the directions to highlight the text. Use what
you highlighted and other details from the poems to
complete the chart.

When I read ...,	it reminded me ...
the text symbols in the "Lava Flow Cricket" poems,	
words like "UNDER CONSTRUCTION," "LOOK BOTH WAYS," and "DETOUR" in "Small Black Road,"	

Reflect and Share

Write to Sources

This week you read poems and facts about volcanoes. On a separate sheet of paper, write a poem using facts you learned in "Earth Erupts" and at least one character from *Volcano Wakes Up!*

Write Poetry

A poem creates a picture with words. Not all poems rhyme. A poem can be written in lines that make a shape, like a volcano.

- Use words that have a rhythm when read aloud.
- Use words that help readers see a clear picture in their mind.

Write a poem that uses facts about volcanoes. You might tell what happens to Lava Flow Cricket 1 or how Volcano feels after an eruption. Have fun!

Weekly Question

How does a volcano eruption change Earth?

I can use language to make connections between reading and writing informational texts.

My Learning Goal

Academic Vocabulary

Word parts can help you figure out the meaning of a new word. The words **rebalance** and **unbalance** have two parts, a prefix and a base word:

re-   +   balance   =   rebalance
un-   +   balance   =   unbalance
prefix   +   base word   =   new word

Adding the prefix **re-** to balance, means to balance again. Adding the prefix **un-** to balance, means to make it not balanced.

MY TURN Add the prefix **re-** or **un-** to each base word to build a new word. Then use the new word in a sentence.

Prefix	Base Word	New Word	Sentence
re-	read		
re-	play		
un-	tie		

Look in a dictionary to find other words with the prefixes **re-** and **un-**, and identify the base words.

Read Like a Writer, Write for a Reader

Poets arrange words in creative ways. They use the sounds of words to create beats. They repeat sounds or repeat words to get a feeling or idea across. Sometimes they even arrange the words in the shape of the topic of the poem.

Poem's Patterns and Structures	What They Create
the Volcano poem	The words are arranged in the shape of a volcano.
"nasty tantrums"	The short **a** and the sound of **t** are repeated. They create a harsh sound, like a tantrum.
"I'm the baby," "I'm much smaller," "I'm a little sleepy," "I wake up," "I throw," "I get"	The word **I** is repeated. This tells me that the volcano thinks a lot of itself!
"It always works—I get the most attention!"	These words and word parts are stressed, creating a beat.

MY TURN Write a short poem about something natural in our world. Use repetition and explain its meaning in your poem.

Spell Words with Syllable Pattern VCCCV

🗑️ **MY TURN** Write the Spelling Word that best matches each clue. Then write the My Words to Know words.

1. large, fast bird _____

2. gripe, whine _____

3. make better _____

4. make-believe, scary _____

5. draw attention away _____

6. used for sidewalks _____

7. cents in a dollar _____

8. describe, tell _____

9. orange vegetable _____

10. location _____

11. don't forget _____

12. use a ruler _____

Spelling Words

distract
address
concrete
ostrich
complain
pumpkin
hundred
explain
monster
improve

My Words to Know

measure
remember

Compound Subjects and Predicates

A sentence with more than one subject has a **compound subject**: <u>Eduardo</u> and <u>Jess</u> are great friends.

A sentence with more than one verb has a **compound predicate**: The friends <u>play</u> soccer and <u>ride</u> bikes.

Use the **coordinating conjunctions and** and **or** to form compound subjects and compound predicates.

<u>Fruit</u> makes a good snack. <u>Popcorn</u> makes a good snack.

<u>Fruit</u> or <u>popcorn</u> makes a good snack.

The kids <u>swim</u> in the pool. The kids <u>splash</u> in the pool.

The kids <u>swim</u> and <u>splash</u> in the pool.

MY TURN Edit this draft. Combine sentences to form compound subjects and predicates. Cross out words and write the correct coordinating conjunctions above.

Haley wanted to do something fun. Isabel wanted to do something fun. They could play a game. They could see a funny movie. They chose the funny movie. They laughed at the funny parts. They clapped at the funny parts.

I can use elements of informational text to write a procedural text.

Adverbs That Convey Time and Place

An **adverb** can convey, or tell about, the time or place something happens. Authors edit their writing to make sure they have used adverbs correctly.

> soon   inside
> The play will begin. I can hardly wait. Let's go!

MY TURN Edit the sentences. Use adverbs that tell time and place. Write your adverbs above the lines.

> I wake up on school days. I get dressed, and I eat
>
> my breakfast. I check that all my books are in my
>
> backpack. I go and walk to the bus stop. I'm the
>
> first one.

MY TURN Edit your how-to text to check that you have used adverbs to convey time and place.

Revise Drafts by Adding or Deleting Words

Authors revise their writing to improve it.

- They may add words, phrases, or sentences to give more information or make their writing more interesting.

- They may delete, or take away, words, phrases, or sentences that are not needed or do not make sense.

an amazing   spewing lava
On a trip to Hawaii, I saw a volcano. The day we
visited the volcano I wore my blue jacket. It was the
best day of the trip!

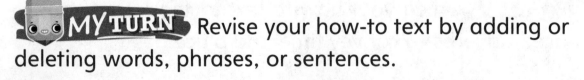 Revise the draft. Add or delete words, phrases, or sentences to make it clearer and more interesting.

The new park is nice. It has a playground with a

climbing wall. There are bike trails, too. I got a new

bike for my birthday.

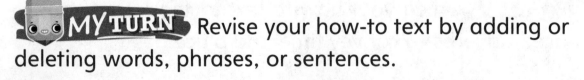 Revise your how-to text by adding or deleting words, phrases, or sentences.

Revise Drafts by Rearranging Words

Authors may rearrange, or change the order, of words, phrases, or sentences to make their writing clearer or more interesting. For example:

My mother told me to clean my room. It was after dinner.

After dinner, my

‸My mother told me to clean my room. ~~It was after dinner.~~

MY TURN Revise the draft. Rearrange words, phrases, or sentences to make it clearer or more interesting.

Trees are covered with beautiful red, yellow, and orange leaves. It is great to be outdoors in autumn. The air is crisp and cool.

MY TURN Revise your how-to text by rearranging words, phrases, or sentences.

Famous Rocks

Gutzon Borglum, a sculptor, wanted to honor four presidents by carving their images. He chose Mount Rushmore in South Dakota. Mount Rushmore is granite, a very hard rock. Dynamite was used to blast parts of the granite away. It took Borglum 14 years to complete the sculpture.

George Washington

Thomas Jefferson

Theodore Roosevelt

Each of the eyes on Mount Rushmore is about 11 feet wide.

Each mouth is about 18 feet wide.

The granite of the mountain formed below the surface of Earth over many, many years. It got pushed up by forces within Earth.

Abraham Lincoln

Weekly Question

What can rocks reveal about how Earth changes?

For informal inquiry, readers generate, or ask, questions after reading a text because they want to learn more about the topic.

Quick Write What questions do you have about rocks after reading the Weekly Opener? Write down your ideas. As a class, come up with a list of questions. Look for the answers as you read about rocks this week.

Abbreviations

An abbreviation is a short form of a word. If it is part of a proper noun, the abbreviation begins with a capital letter. Most abbreviations end with a period.

St. = Street, as in Main St.   **in.** = inch or inches

Ave. = Avenue, as in Park Ave.   **ft.** = foot or feet

Dr. = Doctor, as in Dr. Baez   **U.S.** = United States

These titles are written like abbreviations:

Mr. (say mister) = a man   Mr. Hill

Ms. (say miz) = a woman   Ms. Hill

Mrs. (say missus) = a married woman   Mrs. Hill

MY TURN Compare the abbreviations for the days of the week to the spelled-out names. Read, or decode, them.

Sun. = Sunday   **Thurs.** = Thursday

Mon. = Monday   **Fri.** = Friday

Tues. = Tuesday   **Sat.** = Saturday

Wed. = Wednesday

TURN and TALK What abbreviations do you know?

Abbreviations

An abbreviation is a short form of a word. It is usually followed by a period. It may be capitalized as part of a proper noun.

MY TURN Read the abbreviations. Rewrite the names, dates, and places, writing out the abbreviated words.

St.	Ave.	in.	ft.	Dr.	U.S.
Sun.	Mon.	Tues.	Wed.	Thurs.	Fri.	Sat.

1. Dr. Roberts _____

2. Fri., Sat., and Sun. _____

3. 3 ft. 8 in. _____

4. Tues., June 14 _____

5. 145 Oak Ave. _____

6. U.S. Navy _____

Write the name of your teacher using Mr., Ms., or Mrs.

_____

My Words to Know

MY TURN Read the words in the box. Write one of the words to complete each sentence. Read the sentences.

listen	covered	several

1. "_____ to this story," said the teacher.

2. There are _____ kinds of apples to choose from.

3. Be sure the table is _____ so it doesn't get dirty.

Now write your own sentence for each word.

_____

_____

_____

TURN and TALK Read your sentences aloud with a partner.

Welcome, Max

Grace got a card in the mail.

Welcome Party for Max!
Please come to 543 Forest St.
on Sat., May 3, at 3:00.

"I want to find a gift for Max!" said Grace. She looked around and saw her box of rocks. She chose several stones with green lines or shiny spots. Grace put them in a box and covered it. She couldn't wait for the party!

1. What is happening on Sat., May 3?

_____

2. Why does Grace choose stones?

_____

3. Find and <u>underline</u> two abbreviations in the story. Write the words they stand for on the lines.

_____   _____

Spotlight on Genre

Informational Text

Informational text includes **main ideas**, or **central ideas**, and supporting evidence, or **details**.

- A **main idea,** or **central idea**, is the most important idea about the topic.

- **Details** are bits of information that explain or support the main idea.

Informational text has text features and graphic features that help you know what is important.

Be a Fluent Reader It takes practice to read fluently. Read aloud with a partner. Have your partner help with hard words. Take turns reading the same page over and over until you both can read it with no mistakes.

When you can read with no mistakes, you are reading with accuracy.

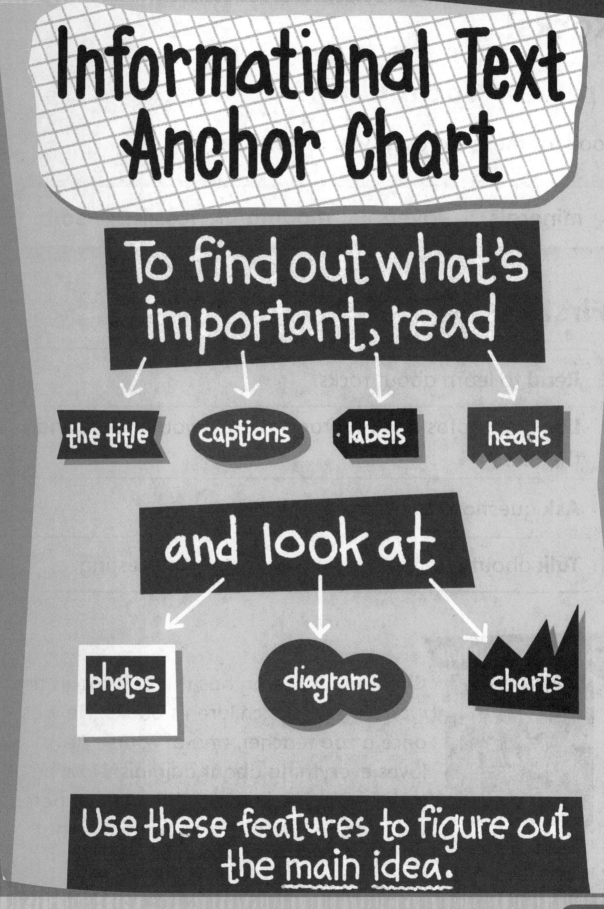

Informational Text Anchor Chart

To find out what's important, read

the title · captions · labels · heads

and look at

photos · diagrams · charts

Use these features to figure out the main idea.

Rocks!

Preview Vocabulary

Look for these words as you read *Rocks!*

minerals	layers	magma	fossils	soil

First Read

Read to learn about rocks.

Look at photos and diagrams to help you understand the text.

Ask questions to clarify information.

Talk about a section of text you found interesting.

Meet the Author

Christopher Cheng has the best job in the world. He writes children's books. He was once a zoo teacher, and of course he loves everything about animals. Now he travels a lot, so he doesn't have any pets. He says the best thing about him is that he can make a brilliant mud pie!

Rocks!

by Christopher Cheng

AUDIO

Audio with Highlighting

ANNOTATE

Identify Main Idea

Underline sentences that help state the main idea of the first paragraph.

1   You are standing on a rock. Right now. Maybe you are not standing right on top of a rock, but if you dig down far enough, you will hit rock. That's because Earth is made of rock. Rock is the building block that makes up our planet. Rock lies under every bit of land. There is rock on the bottom of every ocean. Rock is everywhere!

What Is a Rock?

2   Rock is a hard material made of minerals. Minerals are solid, nonliving matter found in nature. To form a rock, it takes one or more minerals. Heat and pressure form the minerals into the hard things we call rocks. Pressure is a force, similar to pressing down on something. Rocks can be as small as a grain of sand or taller than a skyscraper. They can be as dark as night or as light as milk. Mountains, the seabed, and beach stones are all rock.

minerals solid materials, usually dug from Earth, such as coal and gold

3   There are rocks in space too. Some rocks called meteorites crash into Earth from outer space.

Space rocks!

igneous

sedimentary

metamorphic

CLOSE READ

layers thin or thick parts of something that are over or under one another

4   Geologists are scientists who study rocks. Geologists usually sort rocks into three different kinds. Each kind of rock is formed, or made, in a slightly different way.

- Igneous rocks form when hot, liquid rock cools.

- Sedimentary rocks form when layers of minerals pile up over a long period.

- Metamorphic rocks form when pressure and heat change the make-up of a mineral.

The Rock Cycle

5 Rocks are always changing. These changes are called the Rock Cycle. The changes happen in different ways. They usually take thousands of years to happen. Parts of igneous rocks can become sedimentary rocks. Sedimentary rocks can change to metamorphic rocks. Metamorphic rocks can become sedimentary rock or even igneous rocks.

CLOSE READ

Make Inferences

Sometimes the main idea is not stated, but you can use evidence in the text to figure it out. Highlight the sentences that can help you figure out the main idea of this section.

The Rock Cycle

igneous rocks

sedimentary rocks

metamorphic rocks

Vocabulary in Context

You can sometimes figure out the meaning of a word by reading the words nearby. Identify the word in the second sentence that is a homograph. <u>Underline</u> the words in the sentence that tell the meaning of the homograph. What other meaning of the homograph do you know?

magma hot, melted rock under the surface of Earth

Igneous Rocks

6 Igneous rocks are made from hot, liquid rock. The top layer of Earth is called the crust. Beneath the crust is liquid rock, called magma. Magma is melted rock. Magma often comes through the crust from cracks or holes called volcanoes. When magma comes to Earth's surface, it's called lava. Lava cools very quickly when it meets the air. This creates igneous rocks. Magma can cool slowly in the crust. This can create igneous rocks too.

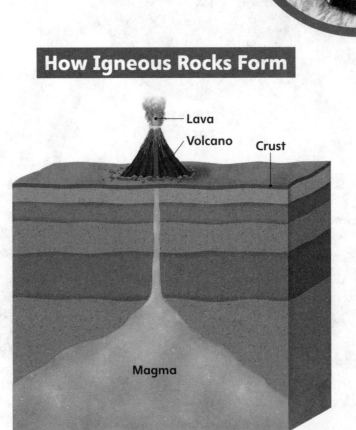

How Igneous Rocks Form

Lava

Volcano

Crust

Magma

642

Sedimentary Rocks

7   Sedimentary rocks are made from tiny pieces of other rocks. Wind and water can break up big rocks into very tiny pieces. These small pieces are called sediment. Sand is similar to sediment. Sediment might roll down hills, be blown by the wind, or pushed by water. Over thousands of years, the sediment forms layers. The layers press down on each other. They become a solid, new kind of rock— sedimentary rock.

How Sedimentary Rocks Form

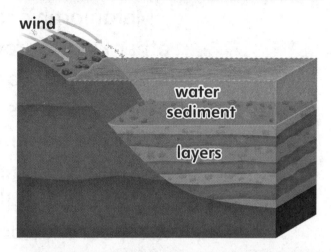

wind

water
sediment

layers

Metamorphic Rocks

8   Metamorphic rocks are also made from other kinds of rock. Over long periods of time, rocks in Earth press down on each other. This pressure creates heat. There is also heat from magma deep inside Earth. The heat changes these rocks. It's like the heat is cooking the rock. These rocks don't melt, but they do change into a new type of rock—metamorphic rocks.

How Metamorphic Rocks Form

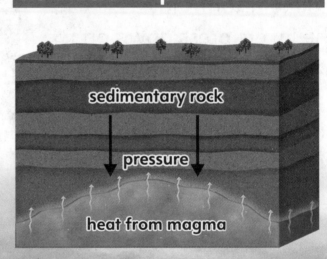

644

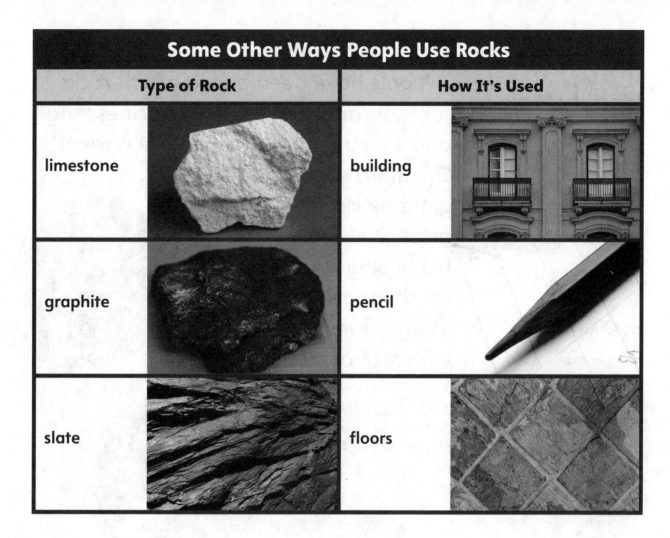

Some Other Ways People Use Rocks			
Type of Rock		**How It's Used**	
limestone		building	
graphite		pencil	
slate		floors	

Rocks and People

9   Rock and stone are used in many ways. We use small rocks such as diamonds for jewelry. Artists cut stones such as marble to make art. Many kitchens in America have rock countertops. Glass is made from melting sand, and sand is rock. Even metal comes from rocks. If you look around wherever you are right now, you'll probably see something made from rock.

CLOSE READ

Make Inferences

Highlight the sentences that can help you decide what the main idea of this section is.

Identify Main Idea

<u>Underline</u> the sentence that tells the main idea of this section.

building

Building with Rocks

10   People have been building with rocks for thousands of years. Many cities long ago were made from rock. The ancient Egyptians made pyramids with giant blocks of limestone. In most cities today, rock is in buildings and sidewalks. Crushed rock is in roads. Many bridges are built with rock or stone.

bridge

A team of artists carved the giant sculptures of Mount Rushmore in rock.

Egyptian pyramid

moray eel

Many birds build nests on rocks.

Animals and Rocks

11   People aren't the only creatures who use rocks. Animals use rocks too. Some animals swallow small rocks to help them digest food. These swallowed rocks are called gastroliths. Ostriches are birds. They have no teeth. They need help grinding food in their stomachs. So they swallow gastroliths—small rocks and sand.

12   Some animals use rocks for their homes. Some eels and octopuses live in cracks in undersea rocks.

ostrich

gastroliths

Make Inferences

Highlight the sentences that can help you figure out the main idea of this section.

fossils parts or prints of a plant or animal that lived a long time ago

Rocks and Fossils

13 Rocks help scientists learn about animals from the past. Fossils are what is left of animals and plants that lived long ago. Long ago, some animals were buried in layers of mud or sand. Over time, these layers become solid rock. The animals' bodies break down. The bodies leave shapes in the rock. These shapes show what animals from long ago looked like.

1 An animal dies.

2 Mud and sand cover the animal.

3 The mud and sand become rock.

Soil

14   Rock is important because it provides people and animals with food. Soil is made up of small pieces of rock. Soil is the loose upper layer of the surface of Earth. The rock mixes with air, water, and humus to make soil. Humus is tiny pieces of dead plants and animals. The plants that people and animals eat grow in soil.

CLOSE READ

soil the loose top layer of Earth; dirt

Vocabulary in Context

<u>Underline</u> the words in the text that help you understand the meaning of **nutrients**.

15 Soil provides water and nutrients to plants. Nutrients in soil help plants grow. Different kinds of soil have different amounts of water and nutrients. Clay soil is thick and heavy. Clay soil can hold a lot of water. It can also dry out and become hard as a brick. Desert soil is loose and sandy. Clay and sandy soils are not very good for growing plants. Loam is a very rich kind of soil. It holds some water but not too much. Loam also contains a lot of nutrients. The best farmland has loamy soil.

Soil Homes

Soil provides homes to many living things. Earthworms live in soil. So do animals such as prairie dogs.

clay soil   sandy soil   loam

16   Rock. It's much more important to us than you probably thought. It gives us places to live. It helps us create and build. It gives us the soil to grow our food. It is home to animals. It makes up our entire planet!

Identify Main Idea

The topic of a text is what the whole text is about. Underline the topic of this text. Then underline the words that tell the main idea about the topic of this text.

Fluency

Practice reading every word correctly. Read aloud the last two paragraphs several times with a partner.

Develop Vocabulary

MY TURN Write a sentence to tell how each of the following vocabulary words is related to rock.

Word	What does it have to do with rock?
minerals	
layers	
magma	
fossils	
soil	

Check for Understanding

MY TURN Look back at the text to answer the questions. Write the answers.

1. How can you tell this is informational text?

2. Why did the author include headings like "What Is a Rock?" and "The Rock Cycle"?

3. What is one way Earth would be different if there were no rocks?

Identify Main Idea

One characteristic of informational text is that it has a **main idea**, or **central idea**. Every text has a topic. You can state the topic in a word or two. The main idea is the most important idea about the topic. A paragraph or a section of text can also have a main idea. The author supports each main idea with evidence.

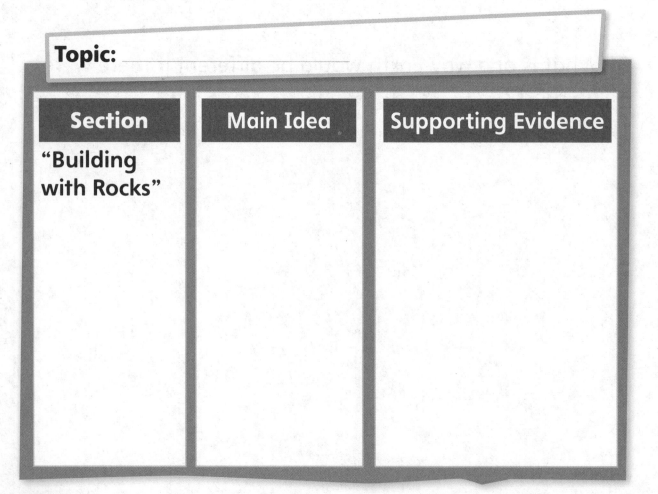

MY TURN Go to *Rocks!* to complete the Close Read notes. Working with your class, use what you underline to complete the chart.

Topic: _____

Section	Main Idea	Supporting Evidence
"Building with Rocks"		

Make Inferences

When an author doesn't state the main idea of a text or a section directly, you make inferences to figure it out. To make inferences, use evidence and what you already know to support your understanding of a text.

MY TURN Go back to the Close Read notes. Follow the directions to highlight the text. Use what you highlighted to make inferences about the main idea of each section.

Section	My Inference About the Main Idea
"The Rock Cycle"	
"Rocks and People"	
"Rocks and Fossils"	

Reflect and Share

Talk About It

Discuss what you have learned about rocks. Talk about how the rocks you see every day are related to the information in the texts.

Take Turns

Taking turns is an important part of a discussion.

- Make your point and then let someone else talk.
- Let another speaker finish before it is your turn to speak.

Sometimes you might get excited and interrupt another speaker. If that happens, say you are sorry and let them finish. You might say:

I'm sorry. I didn't mean to interrupt. Please finish what you were saying.

Weekly Question

What can rocks reveal about how Earth changes?

I can use language to make connections between reading and writing informational texts.

Academic Vocabulary

Choose a word you learned this week and write it in the center of the word web. Then complete the word web with words that have something to do with the word you chose.

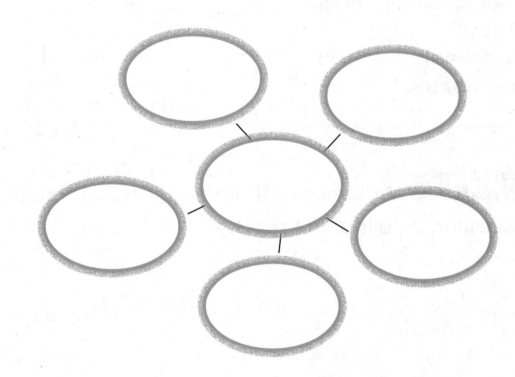

TURN and TALK Tell your partner about your word web. Explain why you chose the words you did. Then use a few of the words from your web to respond to the Essential Question: **How does Earth change?**

Read Like a Writer, Write for a Reader

Authors include details to help readers understand a topic better. Details give specific and relevant, or closely connected, information about the topic.

Details	What the Details Tell Me
"Rock is a hard material made of minerals. . . ." "Mountains, the seabed, and beach stones are all rock."	These details give me information that is relevant to learning what rock is.
"Animals use rocks too. Some animals swallow small rocks to help them digest food. . . ." "Some animals use rocks for their homes."	These details tell me specific ways animals use rocks.

MY TURN Write two or three sentences with specific and interesting details about rocks.

_____

_____

_____

Spell Abbreviations

An abbreviation is a short form of a word. It usually ends with a period. If the abbreviation is part of a proper noun, it begins with a capital letter.

MY TURN Write each Spelling Word next to its match. Then write the My Words to Know words.

1. Doctor Jones _____

2. Oak Street _____

3. United States _____

4. Mount Rushmore _____

5. title used with a man's name _____

6. inch _____

7. Elm Avenue _____

8. foot _____

9. titles used with a woman's name

   _____ _____

10. hear _____

11. hidden _____

Spelling Words
Mrs.
Mr.
St.
in.
Ave.
Dr.
Ms.
Mt.
ft.
U.S.

My Words to Know
listen
covered

Spell Words Correctly

Readers will understand your writing better if you spell words correctly. Here are some tips for spelling words:

- Think of the sounds in each word as you write it.

- Think of words you know that have the same sound. For example, if you don't know how to spell **couch**, think of words you know with the same vowel sound: **loud, count,** and **round**.

- Some common words are hard to spell. You have to memorize words such as **beautiful** and **friends**.

- The spell check on your computer will tell you if a word is misspelled. It will also suggest ways to spell the word correctly.

MY TURN Edit this draft to fix mistakes in spelling.

Water causes many difrent changes to Earth. A river

can wear away the siol and rocks. It can even create a

beutiful canyon like the Grand Canyon. Waves can

braek down rock and turn it into sand. A flood can

destroy roads and huoses.

I can use elements of informational text to write a procedural text.

My Learning Goal

Edit for Pronouns

Subject Pronouns	are subjects of sentences	I, you, he, she, it, we, they
Object Pronouns	are used as objects	me, you, him, her, it, us, them
Possessive Pronouns	show ownership	my, mine, your, yours, his, her, hers, its, our, ours, their, theirs
Reflexive Pronouns	refer back to the subject	myself, yourself, himself, herself, itself, ourselves, yourselves, themselves

MY TURN Edit this draft. First, edit for mistakes with subject and object pronouns. Then, edit for mistakes with possessive and reflexive pronouns. Then, edit your how-to text for pronouns.

Mine sister and I went to the mall with our dad. When it was time for we to have lunch, us went to the food court. She and me got pizza. Her had mushrooms, but my was plain. Dad ate a big salad all by hisself.

Edit for Capitalization

Proper nouns, many abbreviations, and the first words of sentences begin with capital letters. Greetings and closings of letters are capitalized too. Authors edit their writing to make sure they have used capital letters correctly.

MY TURN Edit this draft by crossing out mistakes in capitalization and writing the word correctly above.

june 24, 2018

dear grandpa,

We are visiting Washington, D.C. On saturday we

went to a really great museum. I got to touch a rock from

the moon. We will be home in july. See you soon!

love,

mateo

MY TURN Edit your how-to text to make sure you capitalized correctly.

Publish and Celebrate

Now it is time to celebrate what you have written and let others enjoy your writing! Here are some things to keep in mind when you share your work with an audience:

- Introduce yourself before you begin.

- Look up from your reading to make eye contact with your audience.

- Speak clearly and slowly (but not too slowly!).

- Speak loudly enough so everyone can hear you.

- Vary the pitch and speed of your voice.

- Be enthusiastic.

- If there are visuals, hold them up so that all your listeners can see them.

- After giving oral instructions, complete your presentation by having students follow your instructions.

Read your text ahead of time. Practice until you can read it smoothly.

UNIT THEME

Our Incredible Earth

WEEK
3

Where Do They Go in Rain or Snow?

You would likely find a chipmunk under the snow in a field.

TURN and TALK

True or False?

With your partner, read each statement. Revisit the text to determine if the statement is TRUE or FALSE. If it is true, write *True*. If it is false, rewrite the statement to make it true. Use this information to help you answer the Essential Question.

★ **BOOK** CLUB

WEEK
2

How Water Shapes the Earth
How Earthquakes Shape Earth

Afterquakes are small earthquakes that happen after an earthquake.

★ **BOOK** CLUB

WEEK
1

Introducing Landforms

Mountains are the biggest landforms on Earth.

BOOK CLUB

Volcano Wakes Up!

In the text, Volcano gets bigger after it erupts.

WEEK
4

BOOK CLUB

WEEK
5

Rocks!

The three kinds of rocks are sedimentary, minerals, and expecting.

Essential Question

My TURN

In your notebook, answer the Essential Question: How does Earth change?

BOOK CLUB

Project

WEEK
6

Now it is time to apply what you learned about Earth's changes in your **Week 6 PROJECT: This is so exciting!**

Final Stable Syllables consonant-le, -tion, -sion

Final stable syllables are at the ends of words. The letters in these syllables usually spell the same sounds. Say the names of these pictures:

10 – 7 = 3

purple   subtraction   television

The final stable syllable you hear at the end of **purple** is spelled with a consonant plus the letters **-le.** The final stable syllables you hear at the end of **subtraction** and **television** can be spelled **-tion** and **-sion.**

MY TURN Read, or decode, the words below.

consonant-le	-tion	-sion
riddle	action	version
table	mention	mission

TURN and TALK Reread the words in the chart with a partner. Underline each final stable syllable.

Final Stable Syllables consonant-le, -tion, -sion

The final stable syllable you hear at the end of **title** is spelled with a consonant and the letters **-le**. The final stable syllables you hear at the end of **addition** and **television** can be spelled **-tion** or **-sion**.

MY TURN Read the words below. Write each word's syllables on the lines next to it.

1. circle _____ _____

2. motion _____ _____

3. mansion _____ _____

4. maple _____ _____

5. nation _____ _____

6. giggle _____ _____

7. title _____ _____

8. vision _____ _____

9. addition _____ _____

My Words to Know

MY TURN Read the words in the box. Then complete the sentences using the words.

toward	against	numeral

1. Ron leaned his bike _____ the wall.

2. Write the _____ 5 on the line.

3. Kate moved slowly _____ the bunny.

Choose the word that is described by each clue below.

4. not for something, but _____ it

5. not away from something, but _____ it

6. not a letter, but a _____

TURN and TALK Read the sentences aloud with a partner. Then take turns making up your own clues for the words and having your partner guess the correct word.

Spell Words with consonant-le, -tion, -sion

Final stable syllables **consonant-le**, **-tion**, and **-sion** come at the ends of words.

MY TURN Sort and spell the Spelling Words by their final stable syllables. Then write My Words to Know.

-tion

_____

_____

_____

_____

consonant-le

_____

_____

_____

_____

-sion

_____

_____

My Words to Know

_____

_____

Spelling Words

action

turtle

addition

motion

vision

fraction

purple

sparkle

tension

angle

My Words to Know

toward

against

669

This is SO EXCiTiNG!

Activity

You have been hired to create a TV infomercial. An infomercial is a commercial that gives information in a persuasive way. Your infomercial should persuade viewers to agree with your opinion about the most exciting way that Earth changes.

Let's Read!

This week you will read three articles. Today's article will give you important background information about the history of advertising.

1 The History of Advertising

2 Player One

3 Turn it Off!

Generate Questions

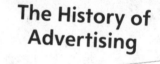 **COLLABORATE** With a partner, decide on the topic for your infomercial. Which Earth change do you think is most exciting? Record questions to guide your research to learn more about your chosen topic.

Use Academic Words

COLLABORATE Look at the photo of a volcano erupting. Talk with your partner about what makes this Earth change exciting. Use your newly acquired academic vocabulary. Try to use these words in your infomercial too.

Academic Vocabulary

destroy	reaction	resources
environment	balance	

Earth Change Research Plan

Look back at your other research plans. A research plan includes generating questions, conducting research, writing, revising and editing, and presenting. With adult help, develop and follow a research plan.

Day 1 _____

Day 2 _____

Day 3 _____

Day 4 _____

Day 5 _____

Is That a Fact?

Like a persuasive text, an ad tries to persuade you to do something. An ad may have both facts and opinions. It is important to identify the facts and recognize opinions. When you read, watch, or listen to an ad, pay attention to:

- what the author or speaker wants you to think or do.
- facts and opinions the author or speaker gives to support the argument and persuade you.

COLLABORATE With a partner, read "Player One." Then fill in the graphic organizer.

The author is trying to persuade the reader to

Facts	Opinions

Use Media to Research

Media include TV shows, Web videos, and DVDs. You can use media to research. Multimodal media include sound and action. As you watch, take these steps:

1. Determine the main idea and the key details.

2. Take notes. Remember to paraphrase, or write the ideas in your own words.

   • Pause the video if you can.

   • Note the time so you can find the information again.

   • Note the URL and the title of the video.

   • Note information that answers your questions.

Start/
Pause
Button

URL

Time marker

COLLABORATE Find media about your topic. Watch the video and take notes. Find and write the URL and the title of the video.

Infomercial Script

Infomercials contain persuasive words to get the reader, viewer, or listener to do something.

Opinion

Fact

Persuasive Words

Conclusion

Many things change Earth, but no changes are as exciting as those from an erupting volcano! Everyone should watch a video of a volcanic eruption. I don't recommend watching it in person, though! At first glance, it looks like the eruption ruins everything. But just wait. The ash puts nutrients in the soil that will help new plants grow. Another awesome effect is that a volcano allows Earth to cool itself. In addition, a volcano can create an island and a gorgeous scene. You must learn more about volcanoes! They are the most exciting way to change Earth.

Cite Your Sources

When you use information from sources, you need to cite, or name, them. It shows readers you did research to understand the facts.

For an online video:

1. Name of video's creator (last name, first name)
2. Title of the video (in quotations)
3. Title of the Web site (in italics)
4. Date published
5. URL

> Example: Mathis, Blake. "The Effects of a Volcano." *The Volcano Guy*. February 2018, www.url.here.

COLLABORATE With a partner, cite your media source.

Media source:

_____

_____

Make a Video or Record Your Infomercial

COLLABORATE Using your infomercial script to make a video gives you the chance to add images and sound to your message. Recording your infomercial allows you to add sounds. Plan your video or recording.

☐ Name of speaker

☐ How the speaker will sound (happy, excited, etc.)

☐ Target length of recording

☐ Background music (not required)

☐ Sound effects

☐ Visuals

Revise

COLLABORATE Before you make your video or record your infomercial, revise your script. First, look for places where you might add, delete, or move words around to make your ideas clearer. Be sure to make your argument as well as give facts and opinions to support it. Reread your script and look for places to add Academic Vocabulary and content vocabulary to make your argument stronger.

destroy	balance	resources
environment	reaction	

Edit

COLLABORATE Now edit your script.

Check to be sure you:

☐ used prepositions and prepositional phrases correctly

☐ formed contractions correctly

☐ combined ideas to make compound subjects and predicates correctly

Share

COLLABORATE If you made a video, have a viewing party with your classmates. If you recorded your infomercial, have a listening party. Otherwise, read your script with your partner to the class as if you were on TV. Keep these speaking and listening rules in mind.

- Speak clearly at an appropriate pace, but remember your purpose. You may speak more excitedly and slightly faster to help persuade your audience to agree with your claim.

- Listen actively to other presenters. Listen for facts and opinions. Then ask questions to clear up ideas.

Reflect

MY TURN Complete the sentences.

The best part of my infomercial is

_____

_____

If I make another infomercial, I will

_____

_____

Reflect on Your Goals

Look back at your unit goals. Use a different color to rate yourself again.

MY TURN Complete the sentences.

Reflect on Your Reading

I was most surprised by _____

because _____

_____

_____

Reflect on Your Writing

The writing that was most challenging was

_____ because _____

_____

_____

_____

_____

_____

A book review gives opinions about a book you have read.

I can write a book review.

Book Review

An **opinion** tells what you think about something. In a book review, the author tells readers about a book and states an opinion about the book. The author gives supporting reasons that help readers know if the book is one they might like to read.

Opinion Writing

♥ Topic and Opinion	I think everyone will enjoy <u>Amelia</u> <u>Bedelia</u>.
☆ Reason	Boys and girls will love this book because Amelia is so funny. She will make everyone laugh.
☆ Reason	This book is also great because it teaches a lesson about following directions.
⋈ Conclusion	These are the reasons why I think you will love reading <u>Amelia</u> <u>Bedelia</u>.

Brainstorm Ideas

An author of a book review chooses what book to write about and decides if other people should read the book. Then an author thinks about why the book is a favorite and what parts of the book are examples of that reason.

MY TURN Think of a book you have enjoyed. Write the title. Write two reasons why you think other people will like it too. What parts of the book are examples of each reason? Write what you could tell readers.

Book Title:	
Readers will enjoy this book because: Tell readers about:	Readers will enjoy this book because: Tell readers about:

Plan Your Book Review

Authors need to plan their book reviews to be certain everything important is included.

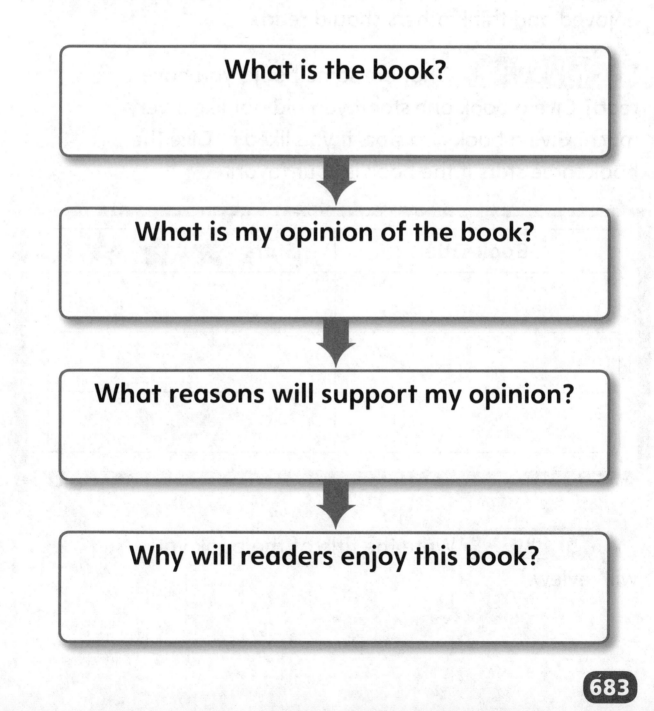

MY TURN Develop ideas for your book review. List ideas you might want to include.

What is the book?

What is my opinion of the book?

What reasons will support my opinion?

Why will readers enjoy this book?

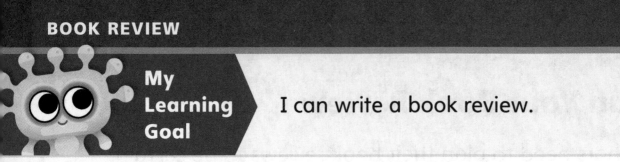

My Learning Goal

I can write a book review.

Choose a Book

Book review authors often choose a book they feel strongly about. They usually choose books they enjoyed and think others should read.

MY TURN What are some books you have read? Give a book one star if you did not like it very much. Give a book two stars if you liked it. Give the book three stars if the book is your favorite.

Book Title	Stars ★ ★ ★

MY TURN Write the title of the book you will review.

_____

_____

State an Opinion

An opinion tells how the author thinks or feels. The opinion in a book review tells if the author liked or did not like the book. The opinion should be stated clearly.

MY TURN Circle Yes or No to tell if each sentence clearly states an opinion.

1. I read <u>Nate the Great</u>.　Yes　No

2. <u>Snowy Owl Invasion</u> was a wonderful book!　Yes　No

3. I think you will love <u>Rodent Rascals</u>.　Yes　No

MY TURN Write a strong opinion statement about your book for your book review.

_____

_____

_____

_____

_____

_____

Supply Reasons

Reasons help readers understand the opinion of a book review author. The reasons may include some examples that will make readers want to read the book.

 MY TURN Read the text. Underline the reasons that support the opinion.

I read <u>Jumanji</u>. I think you would love to read this book if you like fun adventures. One reason is because the children in the book find a game and the excitement begins right away. It is also fun when the wild animals come to life and start running around. Will the children make it out of the game alive? You will need to read the book to find out.

MY TURN Add reasons that support your opinion to your book review.

My
Learning
Goal

I can write a book review.

Introduce a Book and Opinion

The beginning of a book review should let the reader know the title of the book and a detail about the book. The introduction needs to tell if the reviewer enjoyed the book or not.

| Title | I read <u>Flossie and the Fox</u>. It is about a smart girl. |
| Opinion | I think this is one of my favorite books. |

MY TURN Read the text. Circle the title. Draw a star by the sentence that tells the opinion.

I just read an animal book titled <u>Freeda the Cheetah</u>. I think every person in my class will love this book.

MY TURN Revise the introduction to your book review to include a detail about the book and your opinion.

Organize Reasons

Book review authors organize the reasons in a specific way. The writer might put the strongest reason first to get the reader's attention.

MY TURN Put a star by the reason you think is stronger.

The book has nice pictures.
The book is good.
The main character is so funny that you will laugh out loud.

MY TURN List the reasons you will include in your book review. Put a star by the strongest reason. Then number the reasons in the order you will use them in your book review.

Provide a Conclusion

The ending of a book review is called the **conclusion.**
The conclusion should retell the writer's opinion in a
new way. Also, the conclusion should suggest why
others should read the book.

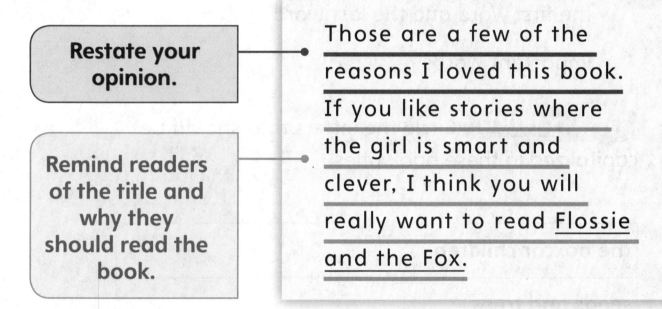

Restate your opinion.

Remind readers of the title and why they should read the book.

Those are a few of the reasons I loved this book. If you like stories where the girl is smart and clever, I think you will really want to read <u>Flossie and the Fox.</u>

MY TURN Answer these questions and revise
the conclusion to your book review.

1. What is your opinion of the book?

_____

_____

2. Why do you think other people will enjoy the book?

_____

_____

My Learning Goal > I can write a book review.

Capitalize Book Titles

In a book title, you should capitalize:

- the first word and the last word

- important words

MY TURN Circle the letters that should be capitalized in these book titles.

the boxcar children
seeds and trees
billy the bug
the last puppy

MY TURN Edit your book review to make sure you have capitalized the book title correctly.

Simple and Compound Sentences

A **compound sentence** is made of two simple sentences that are joined by a comma and the word *or*, *so*, *and*, or *but*.

Simple Sentences

I liked this book. I hope you enjoy it too.

Compound Sentence

I liked this book, and I hope you enjoy it too.

MY TURN Write S next to the sentence if it is a simple sentence. Write C next to the sentence if it is a compound sentence.

_____ The girl in the story is brave.

_____ The fox runs away, but he does not go far.

_____ Flossie can give up, or she can try to trick the fox.

_____ The fox thought he was very clever.

MY TURN Revise your book review to include at least one compound sentence.

Conjunctions

Conjunctions are words that join parts of sentences. *And* and *because* are examples of conjunctions. When writing a book review, you can use conjunctions to connect the opinion and reasons.

> I think you will enjoy this book **because** it is full of surprises.

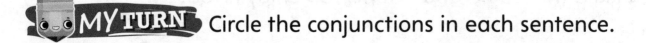 Circle the conjunctions in each sentence.

This book is interesting and includes photos of all the coins I like to collect.
I learned about interesting jungle animals and about wild animals near where we live.
One reason I think this book is funny is because the hero keeps getting lost.

MY TURN Revise your book review to include conjunctions that connect your opinion and reasons.

I can write a book review.

My
Learning
Goal

Edit for Capitalization of Book Titles

Book titles follow special rules for capitalization. Always capitalize the first and last word in a book title. Capitalize all the important words.

MY TURN Write the titles of three of your favorite books. Circle the capital letters.

_____

_____

_____

_____

_____

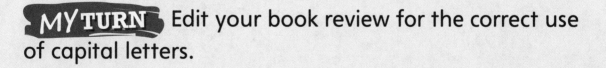 **Edit your book review for the correct use of capital letters.

Edit for Conjunctions

A conjunction is a word that joins together words and parts of sentences. *And* and *because* are conjunctions.

MY TURN Write the conjunction that makes sense in each sentence.

One reason I like this book is _____ it is about snakes.

The book has photos _____ charts to help you learn more.

The snake photos are great _____ they have labels.

MY TURN Edit your book review for conjunctions.

Assessment

Congratulations! You have learned how to write a book review.

MY TURN Read the list. Put a check next to what you can do.

☐ I can introduce the book I am writing about.

☐ I can clearly state my opinion.

☐ I can supply reasons that support my opinion.

☐ I can write a strong conclusion.

☐ I can correctly capitalize a book title.

☐ I can use both simple and compound sentences in my writing.

☐ I can use conjunctions to connect the opinion and reasons.

How to Use a Glossary

A **glossary** can help you find the meaning and pronunciation of words. Words in a glossary are listed alphabetically, from A to Z. **Guide words** at the top of each page show the first and last words on the page. A print or online **dictionary** is like a glossary, but it has more words. To use an online dictionary, type the word in the search box. You will get the definition. Sometimes you can hear how to say the word.

> **The pronunciation guide shows you how to say the word.**

Cc

crater (KRAY tuhr) A **crater** is a hole at the top of a volcano. NOUN

> **All words that begin with c will be after Cc.**

> **This sentence tells you what the word means.**

MY TURN Find the word **exhausted** in the glossary. On a piece of paper, write its meaning. Write a sentence using the word. Decide how to say it. Then find the meaning of a word that is not in this glossary. Use a dictionary.

Aa

accept (ak SEPT) If you **accept** something that is offered to you, you take it. VERB

admiration (ad muh RAY shuhn) **Admiration** is a feeling of great respect and approval. NOUN

alarmed (uh LARMD) Someone who is **alarmed** feels fearful of danger. VERB

allowed (uh LOWD) If you were **allowed** to do something, you were told you could do it. VERB

amount (uh MOWNT) The **amount** of something is how much there is or how many there are. NOUN

arches (ARCH iz) **Arches** are curved structures that often form the tops of doors, windows, and gateways. NOUN

architect (AR kuh tect) An **architect** is a person who designs buildings. NOUN

Bb

balance (BAL uhnss) If something is in **balance**, it is in a steady condition. NOUN

belief (bi LEEF) A **belief** is something thought to be true or real. NOUN

blossoms (BLOSS uhmz) **Blossoms** are the flowers of a plant that produces fruit. NOUN

Cc

canyons (KAN yuhnz) **Canyons** are narrow valleys with high, steep sides, often with a stream at the bottom. NOUN

challenge (CHAL uhnj) A **challenge** is something difficult that requires extra work. NOUN

cinders (SIN derz) **Cinders** are pieces of rock and wood that are partly burned. NOUN

coast (KOHST) The **coast** is the land along the sea. NOUN

communication · disasters

communication (kuh myoo nuh KAY shuhn) **Communication** is the sharing of information. NOUN

connect (kuh NEKT) If you **connect** something to something else, you join the things together. VERB

construction (kuhn STRUHK shuhn) **Construction** is the act of building something. NOUN

contentment (kuhn TENT muhnt) **Contentment** is a feeling of happiness. NOUN

crater (KRAY tuhr) A **crater** is a hole at the top of a volcano. NOUN

creations (kree AY shuhnz) **Creations** are things that are made or produced. NOUN

crumble (KRUHM buhl) To **crumble** is to break apart into small pieces over time. VERB

culture (KUL chuhr) A **culture** is a group of people with the same language and traditions. NOUN

cure (KYUR) To **cure** is to get rid of sickness. VERB

Dd

damage (DAM ij) **Damage** is harm or injury. NOUN

den (DEN) A **den** is a wild animal's home or resting place. NOUN

desert (DEZ ert) A **desert** is a dry, sandy area of land without water and trees. NOUN

destroy (di STROI) To **destroy** something is to hurt it very badly. VERB

determined (di TER muhnd) Someone who is **determined** shows strong purpose and is unwilling to quit. ADJECTIVE

detour (DEE tur) To **detour** is to go a different way when a road is blocked. VERB
A **detour** is another way of getting to a place. NOUN

disappointments (diss uh POINT muhnts) **Disappointments** are feelings of not getting what you wanted. NOUN

disasters (duh ZAS terz) **Disasters** are events that cause great damage, loss, or suffering. NOUN

discuss (dis KUS) To **discuss** something is to talk about it with other people. VERB

drooped (DROOPT) If something **drooped**, it hung down. VERB

Ee

environment (en VY ruhn muhnt) The **environment** is everything around us that helps us live, especially air, water, and soil. NOUN

equal (EE kwuhl) If two things are **equal**, they are the same in size, number, or amount. ADJECTIVE

exhausted (eg ZAW stid) To be **exhausted** is to be very tired. ADJECTIVE

expensive (ek SPEN siv) When something is **expensive**, it costs a lot of money. ADJECTIVE

Ff

faded (FAYD id) Something that has **faded** has lost its freshness or color. VERB

flows (FLOHZ) If something **flows**, it moves along smoothly. VERB

forgave (fer GAYV) **Forgave** means stopped being angry with someone for something the person did. VERB

fossils (FOS uhlz) **Fossils** are parts or prints of a plant or animal that lived a long time ago. NOUN

Gg

garbage (GAR bij) **Garbage** is scraps of things thrown away. NOUN

Hh

hopes (HOHPS) **Hopes** are things wanted in the future. NOUN

Ii

improve (im PROOV) If you **improve** something, you make it better. VERB

ingredients (in GREE dee uhnts) **Ingredients** are foods you use to make a dish. NOUN

inhaled · organizing

inhaled (in HAYLD) **Inhaled** means breathed in. VERB

Ll

lava (LAH vuh) **Lava** is hot, melted rock that flows from a volcano. NOUN

layers (LAY erz) **Layers** are thin or thick parts of something that are over or under one another. NOUN

Mm

magma (MAG muh) **Magma** is hot, melted rock under the surface of the earth. NOUN

maintain (mayn TAYN) To **maintain** something is to take care of it. VERB

mechanic (muh KAN ik) A **mechanic** is a person whose job is fixing machines. NOUN

medicines (MED uh suhnz) **Medicines** are things used to make a sick person well. NOUN

messenger (MES n jer) A **messenger** is a person who carries news or a message to someone else. NOUN

minerals (MIN uhr uhlz) **Minerals** are solid materials, usually dug from the earth, such as coal and gold. NOUN

moccasins (MOK uh suhnz) **Moccasins** are soft leather shoes. NOUN

monuments (MON yuh muhnts) **Monuments** are buildings, statues, and places that honor a person or an event. NOUN

mural (MYUR uhl) A **mural** is a large picture painted directly on a wall. NOUN

Nn

natural (NACH er uhl) Something that is **natural** is produced by nature, not people. ADJECTIVE

Oo

observes (uhb ZERVZ) Someone who **observes** watches carefully. VERB

organizing (OR guh nyz ing) **Organizing** is planning so things run smoothly. VERB

Pp

participate (par TIS uh payt)
To **participate** is to take part
or join. VERB

plain (PLAYN) If something is
plain, it is simple and does not
have a lot of extra things on it.
ADJECTIVE

plains (PLAYNZ) **Plains** are flat
areas of land. NOUN

plastic (PLASS tik) **Plastic** is a
light, strong material that can
be made into things. NOUN

plots (PLOTS) **Plots** are small
pieces of land used for a
purpose. NOUN

products (PROD uhkts)
Products are things people use
or eat. NOUN

purpose (PER puhss) A
purpose is a reason for
something that someone wants
to do. NOUN

Rr

rage (RAYJ) **Rage** is a feeling
of strong anger. NOUN

reaction (ree AK shuhn)
A **reaction** is an action in
response to something. NOUN

refused (ri FYUZD) If you
refused, you did not do
something. VERB

resources (REE sors is)
Resources are things that meet
a need. NOUN

respect (ri SPEKT) When you
respect something or someone,
you feel or show honor to
them. VERB

responsible (ri SPON suh
buhl) If you are **responsible** for
something, you are expected to
take care of it. ADJECTIVE

ruin (ROO uhn) To **ruin**
something is to break or spoil it
completely. VERB

Ss

sauce (SAWSS) A **sauce** is a
liquid served with food to make
the food taste better. NOUN

scents (SENTS) **Scents** are
strong smells, good or bad.
NOUN

shelter • volunteers

shelter (SHEL ter) A **shelter** is a home for a short time. NOUN

skill (SKIL) A **skill** is something a person does well. NOUN

slippery (SLIP er ee) Something that is **slippery** is likely to cause slipping or sliding. ADJECTIVE

society (suh SY uh tee) A **society** is a group of people living together. NOUN

soil (SOIL) **Soil** is the loose top layer of the Earth. Soil is dirt. NOUN

spicy (SPY see) If something is **spicy**, it has a strong, sharp flavor. ADJECTIVE

stranded (STRAND id) If you are **stranded**, you are not able to leave because there is no way to get anywhere else. *VERB*

surface (SER fiss) A **surface** is the top or outside part of something. NOUN

survive (suhr VYV) To **survive** is to continue to live. VERB

Tt

traditions (truh DISH uhnz) **Traditions** are beliefs, stories, and ways of living passed down from parents to children. NOUN

Uu

underground (UHN der grownd) **Underground** describes something that is beneath the ground. ADJECTIVE

useless (YOOSS luhss) If something is **useless**, it is not helpful or good for anything. ADJECTIVE

Vv

volcano (vol KAY noh) A **volcano** is an opening in the Earth's crust through which steam, ashes, and lava are sometimes forced out. NOUN

volunteers (vol uhn TIRZ) **Volunteers** are people who do jobs without getting paid. NOUN

Text

Chronicle Books LLC
Interstellar Cinderella, 2015 by Deborah Underwood; illustrated by Meg Hunt. Used with permission of Chronicle Books LLC, San Francisco.

Crabtree Publishing Company
Introducing Landforms by Bobbie Kalman, 2008. Used with permission from Crabtree Publishing Company.

HarperCollins Publishers
"The Hen and the Apple Tree," Copyright ©1980 by Arnold Lobel. Used by permission of HarperCollins Publishers. This selection may not be re-illustrated without written permission of HarperCollins. "The Frogs at the Rainbow's End," Copyright ©1960 by Arnold Lobel. Used by permission of HarperCollins Publishers. This selection may not be re-illustrated without written permission of HarperCollins. "The Mouse at the Seashore," Copyright ©1980 by Arnold Lobel. Used by permission of HarperCollins Publishers. This selection may not be re-illustrated without written permission of HarperCollins.

Henry Holt & Company
Who Says Woman Can't Be Doctors? The Story of Elizabeth Blackwell by Tanya Lee Stone. Reprinted by Henry Holt Books for Young Readers. Caution: Users are warned that this work is protected under copyright laws and downloading is strictly prohibited. The right to reproduce or transfer the work via any medium must be secured with Macmillan Publishing Group, LLC d/b/a Henry Holt & Company. *Volcano Wakes Up!* By Lisa Westberg Peters. Reprinted by permission from Henry Holt Books for Young Readers. Caution: Users are warned that this work is protected under copyright laws and downloading is strictly prohibited. The right to reproduce or transfer the work via any medium must be secured with Macmillan Publishing Group, LLC d/b/a Henry Holt & Company.

Houghton Mifflin Harcourt Publishing Company
Legend of the Lady Slipper, retold by Lise Lunge-Larsen and Margi Preus, illustrated by Andrea Arroyo. Text copyright © 1999 by Lise Lunge-Larsen and Margi Preuse. Illustrations copyright ©1999 by Andrea Arroyo. Reprinted by permission of Houghton Mifflin Harcourt Publishing Company. All rights reserved. *The Garden of Happiness* by Erika Tamar, illustrated by Barbara Lambase. Text copyright ©1996 by Erika Tamar. Illustrations copyright ©1996 by Barbara Lambase. Reprinted by permission of Houghton Mifflin Harcourt Publishing Company. All rights reserved.

Lerner Publishing Group, Inc.
My Food, Your Food by Lisa Bullard, illustrated by Christine M. Schneider. Text copyright © 2015 by Lerner Publishing Group, Inc. Illustration copyright © 2015 by Lerner Publishing Group, Inc. Reprinted with the permission of Millbrook Press, a division of Lerner Publishing Group, Inc. All rights reserved. No part of this excerpt may be used or reproduced in any manner whatsoever without the prior written permission of Lerner Publishing Group, Inc. *One Plastic Bag: Isatou Ceesay and the Recycling Women of the Gambia* by Miranda Paul, illustrated by Elizabeth Zunon. Text copyright © 2015 by Miranda Paul. Illustration copyright © 2015 by Elizabeth Zunon. Reprinted with the permission of Millbrook Press, a division of Lerner Publishing Group, Inc.

All rights reserved. No part of this excerpt may be used or reproduced in any manner whatsoever without the prior written permission of Lerner Publishing Group, Inc.

Peachtree Publishers, Ltd.
Peachtree Readers Theater Script for "Under The Snow" prepared by Melissa Stewart. Copyright © 2016 by Peachtree Publishers. Published by arrangement with Peachtree Publishers. Peachtree Readers Theater Script for "When Rain Falls" prepared by Melissa Stewart. Copyright © 2016 by Peachtree Publishers. Published by arrangement with Peachtree Publishers.

Weigl Publishers Inc.
How Earthquakes Shape the Earth by Aaron Carr, pp. 4-5, 14-19. Reproduced by permission from AVZ by Weigl, How Earthquakes Shape the Earth (New York, NY: AVZ by Weigl 2015). *How Water Shapes the Earth* by Jared Siemens, pp. 4-5, 14-19. Reproduced by permission from AVZ by Weigl, How Water Shapes the Earth (New York, NY: AVZ by Weigl 2015).

Photographs

Photo locators denoted as follows Top (T), Center (C), Bottom (B), Left (L), Right (R), Background (Bkgd)

7 Hero Images/Getty Images; **8** (TL) Taiga/Shutterstock, (TCL) Image Source/Getty Images; **9** Russ Bishop/Alamy Stock Photo; **10** (BR) Monkey Business Images/Shutterstock, (Bkgd) Inge Johnsson/Alamy Stock Photo; **15** Patryk Kosmider/Shutterstock; **19** (BC) Rsooll/Shutterstock, (BL) Steve Byland/Shutterstock, (BR) AlohaHawaii/Shutterstock, (TC) Sergiy Kuzmin/Shutterstock, (TL) Venus Angel/Shutterstock, (TR) Rook76/Shutterstock; **26** Naddya/Shutterstock; **30** Naddya/Shutterstock; **34** Naddya/Shutterstock; **47** Valentina Razumova/Shutterstock; **50** (BL) MiVa/Shutterstock, (T) Ken Gillespie/All Canada Photos/Alamy Stock Photo; **51** (B) Terrance Klassen/Alamy Stock Photo, (T) Sam Dao/Alamy Stock Photo; **58** (T) Used with permission from Lise Lunge-Larsen, (B) Shirleen Hieb; **102** John Vias; **103** Stilllifephotographer/The Image Bank/Getty Images; **138** B & T Media Group Inc./Shutterstock; **139** Robotrecorder/Shutterstock; **140** (CL) ATU Studio/Shutterstock, (CR) ESB Professional/Shutterstock, (TL) Lindasj22/Shutterstock, (TR) Ivan Ponomarev/Shutterstock; **150** Ellen McKnight/Alamy Stock Photo; **151** (BR) Igorsm8/Shutterstock, (CL) Design Pics Inc/Alamy Stock Photo; **154** Ta Khum/Shutterstock; **156** Lee Rentz/Alamy Stock Photo; **172** (B) Karissaa/Shutterstock, (Bkgd) Leyasw/Shutterstock, (T) Timolina/Shutterstock; **173** (B) Highviews/Shutterstock, (T) Tlapy007/Shutterstock; **174** Ricardo Reitmeyer/Shutterstock; **180** Used with permission from Lerner Publishing Group; **215** Fatihhoca/iStock/Getty Images; **216** (C) Rvlsoft/Shutterstock, (L) Andrey Lobachev/Shutterstock, (R) 123RF; **222** Fatihhoca/iStock/Getty Images; **230** (Bkgd) Rawpixel/Shutterstock, (BL) Michaeljung/Shutterstock; **231** Hero Images/Getty Images; **235** (TL) Monkey Business Images/Shutterstock, (TR) India Picture/Shutterstock, (BL) sonya etchison/Shutterstock, (BR) Rawpixel/Shutterstock; **236** (Bkgd) Severija/Shutterstock, (BR) Fotosearch/Getty Images, (CL) NASA, (CR) Bettmann/Getty Images; **237** Photo File/MLB Photos/Getty Images; **244** Used with permission from Macmillan Publishers Ltd.; **278** (CL) Nikreates/Alamy Stock Photo, (TR) Victor Zong/Shutterstock; **279** (B) Olena Tur/Shutterstock, (T) Philip Scalia/Alamy Stock Photo; **286** Used with permission from Macmillan Publishers Ltd.; **320**